Software Verification and Analysis

Janusz Laski • William Stanley

Software Verification and Analysis

An Integrated, Hands-On Approach

 Springer

Janusz Laski
SofTools, Inc.
Rochester Hills, Michigan
USA

William Stanley
SofTools, Inc.
Rochester Hills, Michigan
USA

ISBN: 978-1-84996-829-4   e-ISBN: 978-1-84882-240-5
DOI 10.1007/978-1-84882-240-5
Springer Dordrecht Heidelberg London New York

British Library Cataloguing in Publication Data
A catalogue record for this book is available from the British Library

Printed on acid-free paper

Springer is part of Springer Science + Business Media (www.springer.com)

To my Children
Magdalena and Zem

Preface

"The situation is good, but not hopeless"
(Polish folk wisdom)

The text is devoted to the Software Analysis and Testing (SAT) methods and supporting tools for assessing and, if possible, improving software quality, specifically its correctness. The term *quality assurance* is avoided for it is this author's firm belief that in the current state of the art that goal is unattainable, a plethora of "guaranteed" solutions to the problem notwithstanding. Therefore, the rather awkward phrase "improving correctness" is to be understood as an effort to minimize the number of residual programming faults ("bugs") and their impact on the software's behavior, that is, to make the faults *tolerable*. It is clear that such a minimalist approach is a result of frustration. Indeed, having spent years developing software and teaching (preaching?) *"How to do it right,"* I still do not know how to go about it with any degree of certainty! It appears then I probably should stop right now, for who with a modicum of common sense would reach for a text that does *not* offer salvation but (as will be seen) hard work and misery? If I intend to continue, it is only that I suspect there are many professionals out there who have similar doubts. And they are the intended audience of this project.

The philosophical underpinning of the text is the importance of sound engineering practices in software development. One may recall that engineering is often defined as *"Science at Work."* Paraphrasing this, one could define Software Engineering as *Mathematics at Work*. It is thus surprising that while in engineering proper mathematical modeling is a standard practice, it is not so in software engineering. Most concepts used there are undefined, ambiguous, or imprecise; clearly, the discipline has a long way to go. Simply put, if we cannot define a mathematical model for the problem at hand, we really do not know what we are talking about. A caveat is in place, though: A *mathematical formalism in and of itself is not a panacea*; the proper role of mathematics in engineering is to provide foundations for the art of *modeling the reality*. A sound model helps control the inherent chaos underlying an engineering project, provides a well-defined fallback position in the case of (inevitable!) failure, and offers a predicting power of future product behavior.

Presently, SAT tools are rarely used in software development. This is due to two factors. First, available tools typically support clerical, rather than semantic, activities. However, at least 80% of software development effort concerns semantic problems. Second, a typical tool supports only one specific activity; so to address the entire development cycle the user would have to use a variety of tools, likely based on different paradigms and targeting different languages. At the current state of the art, semantic-based SAT techniques can be roughly grouped into the following three categories:

1. *Program proving.* Demonstrating the correctness of the program by proving its consistency with its specification
2. *Static analysis.* The detection of real or potential problems by analyzing the source code without its execution (the *proscriptive* analysis) and/or providing explanations about program behavior (the *descriptive* analysis)
3. *Dynamic analysis.* Structural (white-box) testing; Dynamic dependencies (e.g., dynamic slicing); debugging

The following are the main tenets of the approach taken in the book:

1. There is no silver bullet to guarantee software correctness and, consequently, *all* available techniques for fault detection and correction should be used.
2. Suitable software tools *must* support SAT techniques. *A best technique without a tool support may do more harm than good by introducing another level of complexity.* Therefore, *wherever possible*, the reader should test concepts discussed in the book using an appropriate tool. Clearly, although I firmly believe in Boltzmann's dictum that *"Nothing is more practical than a good theory,"* I also believe that *"Nothing can better elucidate a theory than putting it to practice."* In reality, however, not everything can be supported by the tools and the implementation of some concepts will have to be left to the reader.

Structure of the Text

Conceptually the book consists of three parts: The Semantic Analysis (Chaps. 1–4), Static Analysis (Chaps. 5–7), and Dynamic Analysis (Chaps. 8 and 9). The opening chapter "Introduction" provides an overview of the problems discussed in the book and of the potential and scope of program modeling, verification, static and dynamic analysis. Here are just two lessons learned there. First, even for a simple problem, a narrative specification tends to be *ambiguous* and *imprecise*; this fact not only negatively affects the program design but also makes the testing ill defined. Second, and somewhat counter-intuitively, the very notion of *programming fault* (bug) is not unique but depends on the assumed *design* of the program.

Chapter 1 illustrates *formal modeling* in software development, using the VDM-SL notation and the supporting CSK Toolbox. The development starts with the synthesis of the high-level specification which is not only a blueprint for an implementation but also an indispensable *test "oracle"* for test evaluation. On the one hand, it is demonstrated that a formal, disciplined approach does increase the level of confidence in the product. On the other hand, however, it is shown that faults are still possible and their detection might even be harder than those in traditionally developed software, thus making the case for the SAT methods even stronger.

Chapters 2 and 3 are devoted to formal program verification. *Path analysis* for programs without cycles is covered in Chap. 2; the orthogonal to it *assertion method* for arbitrary programs, including the ones with loops, is covered in Chap. 3. In each case the formal presentation is richly illustrated by the use of Praxis' SPARK's verification support. The discussion demonstrates two important issues (1) the main intellectual challenge in program verification is the synthesis of assertions, a process which does not lend itself easily to automation and (2) tool support is essential in carrying the proof. In Chap. 4 various informal or semi-formal techniques for the synthesis of a specification-based Black-Box test (BB-test) are discussed. It is emphasized that test synthesis should go hand-in-hand with the synthesis of the specification itself, rather than being addressed at the end of the development process. Also, *random testing* is discussed: It is argued that without an automatic test evaluation ("test oracle") random testing is not practical.

Chapter 5 introduces intermediate program representations, most importantly the program *control flowgraph*, the backbone of program analysis. It also offers a fair amount of path analysis operations defined in terms of the VDM-SL modeling language. Chapter 6 introduces *data* and *control* program *dependencies*, which model the ways program entities – statements, variables, and control flow – affect each other. The dependencies are then used in Chap. 7 as a tool for static analysis, mostly *proscriptive* (the detection of real or potential *anomalies* in the program), with a modicum of *descriptive*, explanatory analysis. A novel method of *Output–Input Dependency* is offered to model procedure calls to obtain a more accurate identification of the real dependencies between the exported (VAR or OUT) and imported (VAL or VAR). Also, two new classes of program anomalies have been identified: The *signature anomalies*, i.e., the discrepancies between the declared modes of procedure parameters and their actual use, and a *multidata anomaly*, a failure to produce definitions of *all* variables used in a statement.

Structural (White-Box) program testing is discussed in Chap. 8. Several data flow strategies, including three data flow-based strategies, are discussed. Also, the notions of programming *fault* (bug) and *error* are defined formally in terms of the program verification schema introduced in Chaps. 2 and 3. The following are main findings of that chapter. First, in the current state of the art, due to the difficulties of the synthesis of test cases, structural testing in and of itself is out of the question. Consequently, its proper role is to indirectly measure the adequacy of the BB-test. Second, the existing white-box strategies do not, in general, address the most important issues in testing, namely the generation and propagation of errors. Third, program dependencies should be used as the basis of testing strategies that address those issues. Finally, Chap. 9 involves dynamic analysis proper, i.e., one based upon the analysis of the recorded trace of execution. Dynamic data and control dependencies are defined as a counterpart and refinement of the static dependencies. Their application is illustrated by the derivation of *static* and *dynamic slices*, including code with access variables (pointers).

Software Tools

The following three tools are used in the text: VDM-SL (Vienna Development Method – Specification Language) and the corresponding CSK Toolbox; Praxis Critical Systems' SPARK; and SofTools' System for Testing and Debugging STAD. VDM-SL is a formal notation for modeling, development, and analysis of sequential software systems. The language of the VDM is a winning combination of mathematical notation and that of procedural programming languages. A recent ISO standardization of the ASCII version of the notation gave rise to the development of supporting tools. In particular, the CSK's VDM-SL Toolbox allows one to check the consistency of the model (syntax and type checking) and interpret most kinds of models. Technically CSK's VDM-SL Toolbox is not a SAT tool since it does not apply to an existing code. However, if by software one means all artifacts generated during the development process then the Toolbox can certainly be considered a SAT tool.

Praxis' SPARK is a toolset for the analysis and formal verification of programs written in an annotated subset of Ada. It consists of the Examiner, the Simplifier, and the Proof Checker. The Examiner carries out data flow and information flow analysis and also generates verification conditions. The Simplifier attempts to validate the verification conditions. The Proof Checker offers a powerful, interactive proof support.

The basic features of these tools are briefly introduced in the text. However, by no means that is to be construed as an authoritative presentation of the power of these tools. Indeed, their use in the text serves only as an illustration of broader paradigms. It is to be hoped, however, that some readers will succumb to the undeniable attraction of these tools and will start using them for their own projects.

SofTools' System for Testing and Debugging (STAD) is a unique experimental tool for software static analysis, testing, and debugging for a subset of Free Pascal. STAD carries out a fair amount of static analysis at the procedural level and supports five structural testing strategies, both control and data flow based. STAD 4.0, the version used with the text offers a significantly richer scope of static analysis than the previous versions of STAD. However, STAD 3.0 also allows the user to store an execution history (the trace) for further analysis, such as debugging; that feature will be later incorporated into STAD 4.0. The necessity to use so diverged tools to illustrate the main concepts in the text is another testimony to the need for the integration of SAT methods.

The Accompanying Web Site

The current version of STAD can be downloaded from the site

http://www.stadtools.com

The Reader will also find there links to the CSK Toolbox and Praxis SPARK. The site will be continuously updated. In particular, it will contain the most recent versions of STAD, tutorials and case studies and possibly, user blog.

The Audience of the Book

The book does not target a particular audience. Rather, we believe that every professional can benefit from (or be harmed by) the book, as long as he is interested in software quality. Having said that, here is the way how the text can be used by more specific groups of users. Undergraduate students may use the functional features of STAD (*What can be done?*), such as reports on program anomalies and structural test coverage without the underlying theory. The theory (*How is it done?*) should be, however, a significant part of senior undergraduate and graduate level. Software practitioners can use the text to review and test the software analysis and testing methods offered in the book. Finally, researchers, can be possibly inspired positively (*How can it be improved?*) by the ideas in the book and come up with their own. Each group can test their ideas using the quite extensive set of static analysis files produced by STAD.

Acknowledgments

My most heartfelt gratitude goes to Bill Stanley who has revived the original version of STAD 1.0 written in and for (subset of) Turbo Pascal, significantly extended it and eventually ported it to the STAD 4.0 adding also many of the new ideas presented in the book. He also helped format the text, an activity that in and of itself should guarantee sainthood. Also, I want to thank Electronic Data Systems Corporation for a generous Software Verification and Testing Laboratory at Oakland University (OU), which allowed us to significantly expand the scope of our expertise. Finally, my thanks go my students at the OU who suffered the unenviable fate of captured audience during testing of the earlier draft of the text.

Rochester Hills, MI   Janusz Laski

Contents

Introduction: What Do We Want To Know About the Program?

Abstract In this chapter, we provide an overview of various verification activities and illustrate the approaches that are studied in detail later in the text. We emphasize that there is no single method that guarantees correctness and that one has to use all possible techniques to achieve that goal. The techniques include writing a good specification, reasoning about the program, be it informal or formal, testing, debugging, and static analysis.

1 What is the Program Doing: Specification

Consider the Pascal function Monotone in Fig. 1 and assume that you are asked the question "Is the function correct?" Certainly you cannot answer the question without knowing what the program is *supposed* to be doing. An even simpler question: "Is the concrete result produced by the program for a concrete input correct?" cannot be answered without that knowledge. One way to identify the behavior of the program is to analyze the code. However, there are two problems with that approach. First, reading someone else's code is a frustrating and an unreliable task. Even comments, which are supposed to clarify the design, can be found misleading and confusing; most likely only the program's author can understand their meaning. Second, even if we do succeed in the attempt to understand "what's going on," we still cannot decide about the program's correctness because by reading the code we can only identify the actual program behavior, rather than the *intended* one. Indeed, those two are rarely, if ever, identical – otherwise we would not need that rather unsavory process of *debugging*!

Clearly, one needs a separate statement about the intended program's behavior. Usually such a statement is referred to as the *specification* of the program, intended to provide a *model* of the problem. Typically it is a narrative, possibly supplied with charts, figures, and one or more examples of the inputs and expected outputs. In the case of large systems, the narrative might take the form of a sizeable book that undergoes a series of modifications until some "final" version is agreed upon.

To illustrate the issue, consider the following narrative specification of the function:

J. Laski and W. Stanley, *Software Verification and Analysis*,
DOI: 10.1007/978-1-84882-240-5_1, © Springer Verlag London Limited 2009

```
Function monotone(
         A : Int_Array; { array[1..20] of integer }
         n : integer )   { size of the defined lower }
           : integer ;   { portion of A }
VAR
  i , {index for current limseq }
  j , {index for predecessors of current limseq }
  maxj,     {length of current longest predecessor subsequence}
  pmax,            { end of current limseq in A[1..i-1] }
  curr,            { = A[i] }
  maxl : integer;   { length of limseq ending at pmax }
  length: Int_Array; { length[k] is the length of}
                      { limseq at k }
      begin   { monotone }
{ 1}    { <STAD> Initialization of parameter A }
{ 2}    { <STAD> Initialization of parameter n }
{ 3}    length[ 1 ] := 1 ;
{ 4}    pmax := 1 ;
{ 5}    maxl := 1 ;
{ 6}    i := 2 ;
{ 7}    while i <= n do
           begin
{ 8}         curr := A[ i ] ;
{ 9}         if curr < A[ pmax ] then
                begin
{10}              max j:= 1 ;
{11}              j := 1 ;
{12}              while j <=( i - 1 ) do
                     begin
{13}                   if A[ j ] < curr then
                          begin
{14}                        if maxj < length[ j ] then
{15}                           maxj := length[ j ] ;
                            end ;
{16}                   j := j + 1 ;
                     end ;
{17}              length[ i ] := maxj + 1 ;
{18}              if length[ i ] > maxl then
                     begin
{19}                   maxl := maxl + 1 ;
{20}                   pmax := i ;
                     end ;
                end
             ELSE    { if curr < A[ pmax ] }
                begin
{ 21}             maxl := maxl + 1 ;
{ 22}             length[ i ] := maxl ;
{ 23}             pmax := i ;
                end ;
```

(continued)

```
{ 25}    monotone := maxl ;
{ 26}      { <STAD> EXIT USE OF monotone  (FUNCTION RESULT) }
{ 27} end ;  { monotone }
```

Fig. 1 STAD 4.0 listing of Function Monotone, adapted from [2], P. 174–18. *Numbers* in the first column label *instructions*, ie., the smallest *executable* parts of program's statement, which constitute the set of *nodes* in the *flowgraph* of the subprogram. Instructions 1,2, and 26 are introduced by STAD to simulate the initialization of the value parameters *A* and *n*, respectively, and the exit use of the function result

SPECIFICATION[1]: *Given is an array A[1...n] of integers. The function returns the length of a longest strictly increasing monotone sequence in A (limseq, in short).*

At first glance the above narrative looks clear enough. But, is it really the case? What is meant by a "strictly increasing monotone sequence?" Apparently the originator of the problem must have assumed that the reader (or the programmer who has to write the program) is familiar with that concept. What is to be done when the programmer fails that expectation? The best case scenario is to consult a textbook in which the concept of monotonicity might be defined as "changing always in the same direction or staying the same." That would suggest that *strict* monotonicity must stand for "a continuous change in the same direction." Too often, unfortunately, the programmer will *believe* that the problem is clear and will act upon that belief, producing an incorrect program.

Nevertheless, trying to be optimistic, *assume* that the concept of strict monotonicity has been clarified. Now, what is the "sequence *in A*" that is monotonic in that sense? Are we talking about the *elements* in the array, or the *indices* to those elements? For example, for $N = 10$ and $A=[1, 2, 9, 4, 7, 3, 11, 8, 14, 6]$ in the former case one would expect $maxl = 6$, because of the sequence 1, 2, 4, 7, 8, 14 or 1, 2, 4, 7, 11, 14 of values in *A*. In the latter case, $maxl = 6$ would be due to the sequence 1, 2, 4, 5, 8, 9 or 1, 2, 4, 5, 7, 9 of the corresponding indices. Either sequence is strictly monotonic but that is due to the fact that the elements in the array are distinct. Otherwise, when *A* can hold multiple occurrences of values, the value sequence might not be strictly monotonic.

This example illustrates the notorious drawback of narrative specifications: Natural language narratives are notoriously *ambiguous* and *imprecise*,[2] although deceptively readable. In contrast, *formal specifications* that use the language of mathematics are unambiguous, but notoriously unreadable. Although there is little doubt that the effort put into writing formal specification is well spent, mastering the technique might be prohibitive for many practitioners of the programming craft. That is discussed in Chap. 1 in some detail. For the rest of the text a compromise approach is taken: more or less rigid structure of the specification will be used, while the contents are allowed to be less formal. In what follows, we analyze the information that a "reasonable" specification should contain.

---

[1] The problem has applications in the study of random sequences and file comparison.

[2] Following Nissanke [NISS99], a sentence is ambiguous if it can have more than one meaning. In contrast, an imprecise (or vague) sentence has only one meaning but it is not clear when it is true or false.

The specification should provide a high-level *model* of the problem and thus function as an interface between the program, its implementation, and its environment. This corresponds to the "Black-Box" view of the program, describing *WHAT* the program is doing, rather than *HOW* is it doing it. Assuming that the program is really a subprogram, i.e., a function or a procedure (Ada, Pascal) or function (C++), it is reasonable to require that the specification provide the following items of data:

- *IN parameters*, i.e., those whose initial values *may* potentially be used in a computation. The identifiers and types of the variables should be specified.
- *OUT parameters*, i.e., those which are important outside the program on its termination; observe that they may overlap with the *IN* parameters becoming thus *IN OUT* (or *VAR*) parameters. In the case of functions, the returned result value should be specified.
- *External* or *global* variables that the subprogram can read or modify, considered as part of the *state* (*persistent memory*). Like parameters, state variables can be IN, OUT, or IN OUT. The input and output of the program is identified by taking the state and the parameters together. The *input* consists of IN or IN OUT parameters and state and the *output* consists of IN OUT and OUT parameters and state.
- A *restriction on input values* that identifies those values for which the programming problem is *defined*, i.e., there is a solution to it. Such a restriction on the set of all inputs to the program is referred to as the *precondition* of the program. Any input that meets the precondition is *valid*.
- The *desired relationships between the input and the output*. One way to specify an output object is to provide an expression or, in general, an algorithm, whose arguments are valid input objects and which returns the final value of the output. This is the case of *operational* (or *direct* or *operational*) specification. Another way is to provide a restriction on the output values generated for valid inputs, i.e., ones that meet the precondition. Such a restriction is referred to as the *postcondition* of the program; it determines the intended properties of the output. An output is *valid* when it meets the properties established by the postcondition, *assuming that the corresponding input is valid*. This is the case of a *declarative* (or *indirect* or *declarative*) specification. Observe that both methods can be used to specify the same problem, as illustrated informally below for the function Monotone from Fig. 1.

SPECIFICATION FUNCTION Monotone;

IN PARAMETERS	n: integer, A: array$[1\ldots20]$ of integer;
OUT PARAMETERS	None
RESULT	integer;
STATE VARIABLES	none;
PRE(condition)	$1 \le n \le 20$;

INDIRECT SPECIFICATION

POST(condition)	RESULT holds the length of the longest strictly monotonically increasing sequence in the subarray $A[1\ldots n]$;

DIRECT SPECIFICATION

begin

    Compute the set *S* of all monotonically increasing
    sequences in the subarray A[1 … *n*];
    Find the longest length of the sequences in S;

end;

Observe that although the direct specification does provide a method for a solution to the problem, it is still viewed as the *What*, rather than the *How*, model of the problem. This is because the algorithm used is typically easy to understand (as it should be) but not necessarily efficient. The actual implementation might use a different approach. These issues are discussed later in Chap. 1 in some detail.

2 How to Make Sure That the Program is Doing it Right: Verification

The specification of the program tells us *What* has to be done; in contrast, a program shows a particular way *How* it can be done. The program is an implementation of a solution to the problem; obviously there is usually more than one way of solving a programming problem but also more than one way to implement a particular solution. Now, we want the *What* part, i.e., the specification, to be consistent with the How part, the program. If this is the case, we say that the program is *correct* for the specification or is *consistent* with it. Thus, the *concept of program correctness is relative, rather than absolute.* There is always some specification for any program for which the program is correct. This is the specification which states what the program is actually doing, whether this is what we really want or not.

However, if *P* is correct for *S*, it does not necessarily mean that *P* and *S* are equivalent. First, *P* can actually accept more inputs than prescribed by the precondition. For example, a search procedure whose precondition restricts the inputs to sorted arrays may actually be implemented for arbitrary arrays. Second, *P* can produce results that are more restricted than those required by the postcondition. For example, a search procedure may return any position of the element searched for to be returned, while the actual implementation may return the smallest such a position. These issues will be discussed in some detail in Chap. 1.

The objective of *verification* is to establish whether the program is correct or not. (In contrast, the goal of *validation* is usually understood as establishing whether the specification really captures the user's need.) To demonstrate the program's correctness we have to establish two facts. First, we want to make sure that the program terminates for any valid input data. Indeed, if the program does not terminate, its output is irrelevant; in fact, there is no real output. Second, we want to make sure that for any valid input the program produces a valid output on termination.

Obviously, we have to clarify the meaning of the term "termination." We say that the program *terminates* for input X if a designated exit point in the program is reached during the execution. For instance, the function in Fig. 1 terminates if instruction 25 is reached. If, however, one is interested in a code segment embedded in the program, then the "exit" in question is the statement that immediately follows the segment.

Problem 1 *Try to verify function Monotone in* Fig. 1, *using any method you deem relevant. What is your decision: Is the function correct or not?*

The outcome of the verification can be either (1) Positive (yes, the program is correct) or (2) Negative (no, it is not correct) or (3) Inconclusive ("don't know" or "perhaps"). The first outcome can only be achieved through a successful proof of correctness. The second outcome is due either to a successful proof of incorrectness or to a successful testing, when a bug is detected. The third outcome is typical for inconclusive proof attempts, for unsuccessful testing when no bug is detected and for informal methods of program analysis such as "walks-through."

In any event, program verification is based on the assumption that the specification is valid, i.e., that it faithfully captures the requirements. In general, the only way to establish the validity of the specification is by its analysis and testing against the user's requirements. Let us consider testing for, if successful, it detects flaws *both* in the implementation and the specification. According to the specification of the Monotone function, for $n = 10$ and $A = [1, 2, 9, 4, 7, 3, 11, 8, 14, 6]$ the valid result is 6 and this is exactly what the implementation returns. However, for the input $n = 3$, $A = [2, 2, 2]$, the expected valid result is 1, while the implementation produces 3. Consequently, the function is incorrect for the specification: the implementation mishandles arrays with multiple entries. Nevertheless, the problem originator might want to exclude such arrays by strengthening the precondition by the following restriction:

"All elements in the array A between 1 and n are distinct."

Now, since the input $[2, 2, 2]$ violates the above requirement, the function's output for it is undefined. This is because the specification allows any behavior for invalid input, including nontermination. Therefore, one no longer can claim that for $A = [2, 2, 2]$ the function returns an incorrect result 3. (A yet another example of that phenomenon is offered when the value of n is 0: the function then returns a meaningless value 1).

Choosing then the more restricted specification of the problem and assuming that the function has passed a collection of tests (i.e., a test suite), is now the code correct for the specification? Formal verification is the only verification method which, if successful, guarantees correctness of the program. It is based upon the knowledge of the adopted method of solution for the problem at hand. To illustrate the approach, let us abstract the main loop 7–24 in function Monotone in Fig. 1 as **while** $i \le n$ **do** B, where B stands for the entire loop body 8–24. Now, to reason about that loop one needs to know the intended behavior of B. We know that on termination, when the value of variable i becomes $n + 1$, the variable max1 should hold a correct final result. This observation gives rise to the following question: What should be the properties of the variables in the program to let us draw the conclusion that, indeed, the loop does what it is supposed to do? One way of answering that question is to specify the *relationships* between the values of the program variables (rather than the concrete values themselves!), whenever instruction 7, the beginning of the main loop, is reached during execution. If we know that a certain property always holds at the entry into the loop, then we know that it also holds on termination. Suppose then that the relationships in question are expressed by the following statement, also known as an assertion at instruction 7:

Assertion A7 (at 7): *Assume that the (i − 1)th iteration of the main loop is about to begin. For the current value of variable i, the array length is defined only for entries from 1 through i−1 as follows: For any position k between 1 and i−1 inclusive, length[k] is the* length *of a longest increasing monotone sequence ending at k. Call such a sequence Limseq(k). The end of the longest Limseq(k) found so far, for k between 1 and i−1, is pointed to by the variable* pmax. *Thus,* maxl=length [pmax], *every time instruction 7 is reached.*

Observe that the above assertion is expected to hold for every iteration including the last time instruction 7 is reached, when $i = n + 1$. It is clear then that the assertion, together with the termination condition, allows one to conclude that on exit the value of maxl holds the length of the longest sequence in A between 1 and n.

Unfortunately we cannot rest at this point. Indeed, the above reasoning was based on the *assumption* that assertion A7 is true every time instruction 7 is reached. However, to establish the validity of that assumption, one has to demonstrate two facts. First, one has to show that A7 is true the very *first* time instruction 7 is reached. Second, one has to show that if the loop body B is executed, on its termination A7 is *again* true. The first fact can easily be established by analyzing the initialization sequence 3–6. The second fact, however, is much more challenging since one has to verify the loop body B on its own! To do that one needs some specification of B; Where does it come from? Fortunately there is a simple answer to that question. Clearly, on entry to the loop body the assertion A7 and $i \leq n$, the loop entry condition, must both be satisfied; therefore, their conjunction can be treated as the precondition of B. Now, if A7 is to be true every time statement 7 is reached then A7 must be true after every iteration of B, being effectively the postcondition of B. It is important to remember that although different values of variables are involved each time, the relationships between those values are the same.

The verification of B will involve some assertions internal to B; for example, to verify the inner loop 12–16 one needs an assertion at 12. The process stops until the level of individual instructions is reached. When the language and laws of logic (predicate calculus) are used in reasoning, the latter becomes formal verification. If successful, *formal verification* constitutes a correctness proof, a technique discussed later in Chap. 2 and 3. Meanwhile, an ad hoc but very valuable technique can be used to get some practical evidence about the correctness of the loop body.

Problem 2 *Write a Boolean function* Test_A7 *that returns true only when the assertion A7 at instruction 7 is true. Insert calls to* Test_A7 *right before* *instruction 7 and after instruction 24 (why?). Call* Monotone *for some test data (a driver program will be needed); does the function ever return false?*

Apparently, the difficulty of writing function Test_A7 matches that of writing the original code and it is not easy to get it right the very first time. Nevertheless, assuming optimistically that Test_A7 is itself correct one may get a few *false* results returned by Test_A7 when running Monotone. This happens, for example, when you choose the test $n = 2$, $A = [5, 1]$ that leads to an incorrect final value of max1=2, rather than the expected value of 1. Thus, the function is obviously incorrect.

In Chaps. 2 and 3 we will show the power and limitations of formal verification. On the one hand, formal verification is an invaluable framework of thought, around which all verification activities should revolve. On the other hand, its limitations justify the *need* for testing. Let us then see what the main problems are in that area and how can we address them.

3 Trying to Show That the Program is Incorrect: Testing

Historically, there has been a lot of misunderstanding about the role of testing in software development. The practitioners of the craft (that is to say, *everybody* involved in the development of software) tended to view testing as a means to establish correctness, *when all tests pass*. They viewed program proving, informally illustrated in the preceding Sect. 2, as an esoteric exercise in futility. In contrast, computer scientists (that is, people involved in the development of *theories* in the area of computing), tended to treat testing as an ad hoc, unreliable method of necessity, rather than that of choice. Fortunately, in recent years the chasm between these two camps have been narrowed, if not yet entirely bridged. Here are the facts needed to understand the situation; let us start with testing first.

On the one hand, the confidence in testing as *the* way of ascertaining program correctness is misplaced. The truth is that the *main* objective of testing is the opposite to that of proving: It is to show *incorrectness*, rather than correctness, of the program. Clearly, when a test "fails," it *succeeds* in revealing an error. In contrast, when a test "passes" it simply *fails* to detect an error, if one only believes in the old adage, "There is always one more bug"! On the other hand, when a considerable number of tests *fails* to detect the bug our confidence in the program increases, even if the correctness cannot be guaranteed. This is equivalent to the proposition that "There are no grounds to reject the hypothesis that the program is correct". This might not seem too encouraging, if taken literally. However, things are not as bad as they seem. Clearly, software development is always guided by the underlying reasoning, however, informal the latter may be. Thus, the absence of errors during "judicious" testing (whatever that widely used term means), *together* with reasoning about the design, *may* provide some justification for high confidence in the final product, though never in its correctness. That is, there always are, as they should be, doubts. Consequently, even the most ardent opponents of a more formal approach to software verification tend to modify their position to embrace techniques that, at least in *principle*, offer a guarantee of success.

Now, returning to the realm of the theory, the good news is that if the proof succeeds, then the program is for sure correct. The bad news, however, is that if the proof fails, one cannot claim that the program is incorrect, unless one successfully proves *incorrectness*, an exercise undertaken rarely, if ever. Clearly, as illustrated later in Chaps. 2 and 3, if the proof fails, the program can still be correct. To make things worse, even if the proof does succeed, the specification of the problem may change, a rather typical situation, forcing one to redo the entire proof from scratch.

As a remedy to those difficulties, a method of *top-down* refinement has been advanced to guarantee the correctness by *construction*. In it, one starts with a high-level specification and carries out a sequence of successive data and/or control refinements until the final code level is reached. It is hoped that if the "distance" between subsequent refinements is small, one should be able to maintain the correctness along the sequence of refinements, just rendering testing obsolete in *principle*. Indeed, this is a powerful method and, if practiced carefully, renders programs that are "almost" correct. The qualifier "almost" is due to Murphy's Law reigning supreme: Errors are simply unavoidable. Consequently, testing is unavoidable. Ironically, however, we are prepared to formulate yet another law: The better the development method, the fewer the number of residual errors and the more difficult is to detect them! That is because the errors are rather subtle and tend to escape "typical" testing. We illustrate the power and limitations of top-down refinement in Chap. 1.

Now, back to testing. Please forget for a moment that the program is incorrect for it does fail on the (successful!) test data $A = [5, 4]$.

Problem 3 *Synthesize your own test for the program in* Fig. 1. *Justify your selection.*

In all likelihood, you have your test "guessed," by simply following your intuition, rather than some well-defined method. That should not be surprising as it is not clear how to formulate such a method. Truth be known, there exists a plethora of testing methods and, claims to the contrary notwithstanding, that fact itself suggests that there is no "perfect" method as yet.

A particular method for the synthesis of test data is referred to as a *testing strategy*, or a *test selection criterion*. A testing strategy should lead to a set of test data that (1) has a high potential of detecting faults, (2) is of a relatively small, economically acceptable size, and (3) leads to high confidence in the software when all tests pass. Unfortunately, there is yet no theory to express these requirements in a meaningful way. Quite naturally then, even a well-defined strategy, i.e., one that specifies exactly what should be tested, is usually justified intuitively, drawing on programming practice and some assumptions about possible sources of errors.

There are essentially two basic sources for the generation of tests. The first is the specification of the program; the corresponding strategies are collectively referred to as *Black-Box testing*. The second is the code of the program; the corresponding strategies are known as *structural* or *white-box testing*. A black-box (BB) test, derived solely on the basis of the specification of the problem at hand, is applicable

t1 = (5, [5, 4 ,3, 2, 1])	(all sequences have length equal to one)
t2 = (5, [1, 2, 3, 4, 5])	(strictly increasing lengths of sequences)
t3 = (9, [1, 3, 5, 7, 9, 6, 4, 2, 0])	(increasing segment followed by a decreasing one)

Fig. 2 A black-box test for the Monotone program; each test is a pair $(n, A[1...n])$

to any *implementation* of it. Figure 2 shows a BB-test for the program in Fig. 1, with comments indicating the properties of the input deemed relevant for the success of testing. The test is certainly incomplete, although we use that term informally, conveying the intuitive notion of "not enough."

The test in Fig. 2 illustrates the fact that Black-Box testing is not well defined, since it is not clear what properties of the problem specification should be tested. Thus, a BB-test does not lend itself easily to automation and test synthesis has to be done manually. Intuition, common sense, and an old-fashioned talent (usually relegated to the status of "knack" for testing), play decisive role in BB-testing. Clearly, BB-testing is an art, rather than a science. This is not to demean the importance of BB-testing: Its ambiguity notwithstanding, BB-testing is quite often the most powerful method for error detection.

In contrast to Black-Box testing, at least partial automation of structural testing appears a more realistic goal. Most popular structural strategies are formulated as *code coverage* criteria. A coverage criterion requires that certain parts of the code or combinations thereof, be exercised (activated). We will use the generic term Required Elements (REs) to refer to those parts. Traditionally, the REs are defined in terms of the flow of control of the program. For example, one can require that every instruction in the program be activated at least once (Instruction Coverage), or that every branch of every test instruction be taken at least once (Branch Coverage). A relatively recent approach to coverage testing is the use of data flow patterns in the program to synthesize tests, discussed later in the text.

The percentages in Fig. 3 represent the *cumulative* coverage of Instruction and Branch Coverage for the Monotone function executed for tests t1 and t2 from Fig. 2. For example, test t1 activates 66.67% of all branches in the program and this figure goes up to 75% after test t2 is executed. The report also shows those REs that have not been covered by the overall BB-test. Now, the user should synthesize test data that lead to execution of the missing REs. At this point, the relevant questions are: Why have instructions 14 and 15 not been executed? Why have the branches (13 14), (14 16) and (14 15) not been taken?

Problem 4 *Find input data, i.e., the values of n and A[1...n] that cause execution of the missing instructions and branches reported in* Fig. 3.

You may have found the above task quite frustrating; perhaps you have even given up. Indeed, the problem posed in Problem 4 is difficult and cannot be automated in general. Nevertheless, it is enough to notice that if test t3 is run in addition to t1 and t2, 100% of instruction and branch coverage is obtained. Thus, the test in Fig. 3

```
Test       Percentage of              Percentage of
           Instruction Coverage       Branch Coverage
        ----------------------------------------------------------=
t1            87.7%                      66.67%
t2            92.3%                      75.00%
        ----------------------------------------------------------
Not executed:
Instructions: 14, 15
Branches:     (13 14), (14 16), (14 15)
```

Fig. 3 Instruction and branch coverage history for the sample program in Fig. 1 for tests t1 and t2 from Fig. 2

meets the requirements specified by these coverage criteria. We see, however, how weak they are: It is hard to imagine a respectable tester accepting that test for the "release" of the program! Stronger, more demanding, coverage criteria are needed and are discussed later in the text.

Problem 4 illustrates the difficulties in a direct application of a code coverage strategy. Does this mean that structural testing is useless? Most emphatically not. However, claims to the contrary notwithstanding, it cannot be used in and of its own. Instead, if used as a *side effect* of a BB-test, structural testing provides an indirect *measure of the thoroughness* of the former! In other words, a coverage criterion tells us *when to stop testing*, when BB-testing is *not* successful, i.e., when it fails to detect an error. As a by-product, one also gets a numerical measure of the thoroughness (adequacy) of code coverage which, in turn, can be used as a measure of the reliability of the program.

Moreover, there is ample anecdotal evidence that many programming errors are not necessarily found during testing proper but during the synthesis of test data! Apparently, the coverage report turns the programmer's attention toward situations in the program that otherwise would have been overlooked. This observation emphasizes the importance of *static program analysis* as a reasoning-supporting tool (Sect. 5).

Another version of structural testing is Fault-Based testing, in which tests are developed to detect various classes of potential faults. Again, the lack of a theoretical model makes this appealing approach difficult to apply. In the specific case of *mutation testing*, "mutants" of the original program are generated and tests sought to distinguish between them and the program being tested.

4   Trying to Locate the Cause of Incorrectness: Debugging

Problem 5   *It has been found that the program in* Fig. 1 *is incorrect. For example, for the input n= 2, A[1...2] = [5, 4], the value of* max1 *is 2, rather than 1. Locate the cause of incorrectness.*

It is perhaps reasonable to expect that, as in the case of testing, you did not follow any specific debugging strategy, but a hit-and-miss one. This is not to say that your approach was totally chaotic. Most likely you "walked through" the program on the input data, trying to find out "what's going on." Perhaps you printed out the intermediate values of some program variables. Whatever the technique used, you were trapped within a "debugging cycle" that consisted of three stages: Analyzing the situation; Formulating a hypothesis about the cause of the error; and Verifying the hypothesis through "fixing" the alleged bug and retesting the "repaired" program on the same offending input. We are lucky when we succeed in exiting that vicious cycle in a reasonable time, before we give up in frustration. There are plenty of reasons for that frustration. It is not unusual to fix the bug in such a way that the corrected program *does* work on the previously offending test, but *does not* work on other tests, for which the original program worked fine. Obviously, we tend to introduce new bugs while trying to fix the original one!

It should be clear that the difficulties in solving Problem 5 are due to the fact that we do not know how the main loop is *expected* to work! This is notwithstanding the fact that we do know the *"What"* part about the loop body, as established by assertion A7 in Sect. 2. Unfortunately, without knowing the *"How"* part, we cannot determine whether the intermediate values of program variables are correct or not.

One can view assertion A7 on entry to the main loop as the specification of the loop, regardless of its actual implementation. That is, *any* correct implementation of the main loop should maintain A7. However, to verify the correctness of the loop it is essential to identify its *design*. Ideally, design decisions should be documented, even if only by means of readable comments. Or, if the debugging is carried out by the author of the program, he probably has in mind some ideas about the loop's inner workings. Otherwise, one has to revert to the totally unwholesome task of reading someone else's code to guess "how is it supposed to work." Suppose then, that whatever the situation, we have arrived at the following statement about the design of the loop body *B*:

Loop Body Design Specification. For position i in the array A, Limseq(i) is defined as the concatenation of c(i) and A[i], where c(i) is a predecessor sequence, "compatible" with A[i]. That is, c(i) is a longest sequence that ends at some k between 1 and i−1, such that the last element of c(i) is strictly smaller than A[i]. The length of Limseq(k) is stored in the array length[k], k = 1...,i−1. After length[i] is computed, maxl holds the maximal value stored in length[1...i], i.e., the length of a longest Limseq(k) that has been found so far in the array A, for some k between 1 and i.

The compatible sequence c(i) for A[i] is either that ending at A[pmax] (if A[i] > A[pmax]) or is located by the inner loop 12–16 (when A[i] > A[pmax]), in which case the length of c(i) is returned in the variable maxj.

The design specification tells us *how* assertion A7 is actually established by the loop body. Assume then that on that basis the following diagnosis of the problem has been formulated (we refer to a programming bug as a *fault* and to its run-time manifestations as errors):

Fault F   There is a fault in the expression in instruction 10, which should have been maxj:=0, instead of maxj:=1.

The following is an argument supporting that diagnosis:

The original initialization maxj:=1 *suggests that a compatible Limseq for A[i], of length at least 1, always exists. In fact, this is not true for any A[i] smaller than all preceding entries in A[1...i−1]. In such a case, the body of the inner loop is never executed and* maxj=1 *on termination. The incorrect value of* maxj, *when used in instruction 17, leads to the contamination of length[i], which is set to 2, rather than to 1. Thus, the value assigned to* maxj *in 10 should have been 0*

If this diagnosis is true then the corrected code, with instruction 10 reading maxj := 0, must be correct! Ideally, the new code should be verified formally. Since we are not ready for that endeavor yet, we must make do with testing.[3] It can be checked (in practice) that no errors are detected for the new version of the function. Thus, according to our discussion in Sect. 3, there are no grounds to reject the hypothesis that the bug has indeed been fixed.

It is instructive to note, however, that the above fault in instruction 10 is not unique, since there are at least two other corrections to the code, thus giving rise to two other plausible faults!

Fault F′ Instruction 10: maxj:=1 *is correct, but instructions 14, 15, and 17 are not! There are two correct versions, C1 and C2, of the code depending on the type of the correction to instruction 17:*

C1:

```
14: if maxj<length[j]+1 then 15: maxj:=length[j]+1;
17a: maxj:=maxj-1; {indirect correction of 17: inserting
decrement of maxj in front of 17}
17: length[i]:=maxj+1;
```

C2:

```
14: if maxj<length[j]+1 then 15: maxj:=length[j]+1;
17: length[i]:=maxj; {correction of 17}.
```

The underlying design assumption of fault F′ is that maxj, computed by the loop 12–16, holds the length of a compatible subsequence for $A[i]$ *plus* one. Consequently, in the original code, maxj=1 on entry to statement 12 is correct and the first *data error* caused by F′ is in maxj on entry to statement 17. (Note that under the fault F′ hypothesis, the incorrect test in statement 14: maxj < length[j] causes a *control error* at 15 or at 16.)

Perhaps, these three correct versions do not exhaust all possibilities. However, they vividly illustrate the fact that *the nature of the fault is relative, depending on the underlying design premises!* A particular view of the design corresponds to the decomposition of the program into *action units* at a certain *level of abstraction*. Faults are identified with respect to that level. For example, the fault in 10 occurs at the instruction level. However, when the instruction level is also assumed in the

---

[3] Retesting the program after modifications to it is referred to as *regression testing*.

case of F′, then we deal with three faults, rather than one. Clearly, three instructions have to be modified to correct F′ (an insertion of an instruction can be considered a modification of the instruction that follows it)! To abstract these into a single fault, instructions 12–16 (for C1) or 12–17 (C2) have to be considered together as one faulty unit.

Unfortunately, the main ideas about the design typically reside in the programmer's mind, quite often as fuzzy images of "how things are done." Consequently, if the design is not documented then it is not possible to tell which fault is present and debugging becomes ill-defined. This fact shows the importance of even such an imperfect form of documentation as "general" comments. The situation dramatically improves when the comments represent assertions about the program.

Assume now, somewhat optimistically, that the design premises are indeed known. Is there a more systematic method to locate the fault, other than the hit-and-miss "strategy"? The sad truth is that debugging is the least researched and, consequently, least understood area in software engineering, despite the fact that it is most likely one of the most time-consuming and costly activities. Having said this, one can be cautiously optimistic in stating that there are methods which, if supported by suitable tools, seem to be potentially useful in debugging. The methods are based on the fact that the very essence of debugging is the formulation and testing of a *Fault Hypothesis*, an assumption that a specific component of the program is incorrect. The hypothesis can be tested either analytically (e.g., by employing a proof technique) or dynamically by checking the correctness of the data produced by the suspected component on the failing execution. The formulation of the fault hypothesis is a creative step which can be, nonetheless, supported by a suitable tool. Such a tool can help identify those program statements that have contributed to the final values of the incorrect output variables on an execution causing the program's failure. For example, for the input $n = 2$, $A = [3, 2]$, function Monotone from Fig. 1 returns 2, rather than 1. The following are the statements in the function that have been executed *and* have an impact on the final value of the returned result:

$$4\text{–}10,\ 17\text{–}19,\ 24,\ 25.$$

The above set of statements is the *Dynamic Slice* of the program for *that* particular test data (2, [3, 2]). Usually a dynamic slice is much smaller than the entire program, allowing the programmer to narrow the search area in order to formulate the fault hypothesis. In this example, the slice does contain the offending statement 10, whose incorrectness corresponds to fault *F*. However, as far as fault F′ is concerned, the slice contains only statement 17, without statements 14 and 15. This strongly suggests that fault *F*, being much simpler, is a preferred model of incorrectness,[4] assuming of course, that design assertions suggesting otherwise are not available. Observe that the above illustrates the essence of the integrated approach: dynamic analysis serves here as an extension of static analysis. Debugging can also be

---

[4] This is an example of Occam's razor in software engineering.

assisted by formal reasoning about the program and by its static analysis, which answers questions about the program without executing it.

5 What One Can Tell About The Program Without Executing It: Static Analysis

Although the title of this section seems self-explanatory, it still has to be qualified. We are interested in the properties of the program that can be identified automatically by specialized software, rather than by humans.[5] Is that bad or good? On the one hand, whatever is done by automatic tools can potentially be done by humans, too. However, tools are capable of things that people cannot do in a reasonable amount of time and without the inevitable blunders. On the other hand, people can think while machines cannot; thus, the proper role of static analysis tools is to *support human reasoning*, rather than to replace it; the latter goal is better left to the Creator.

We illustrate the usefulness of static analysis on two problems which, of course, do not exhaust the list of all its possible applications. It is to be hoped, however, that they do illustrate the power of the technique. Let us start then with the following rehash of the problem already met in Sect. 3:

Problem 6 *Find input data which ensures the branch (14, 15) for the code in* Fig. 1 *is executed.*

What kind of help can we possibly get to solve the problem? Well, after some analysis you will surely realize that the first step here is the identification of a sequence of instructions that lead from the start of the program until 15 is reached. Such a sequence will be referred to as a *path*. The second step is the identification of the values of input parameters that actually cause that path to be traversed during execution.

Manual inspection of the code tells us that the path 1–7, from the start 1 to 7, is always taken for any valid data. So, the problem is how to get from 7 to 15. Now, if we start at 15 and move backward toward 7, recording all instructions on the way we will get a path from 7 to 15. For example, the sequence 7, 8, 9, 10, 11, 12, 13, 14, 15 of instructions is such a path. This is simple enough. However, for a really complex program things could be much more complicated. Moreover, there are usually many paths between two instructions in the program. For example, one can reach 15 from 7 by first traversing path 7, 8, 9, 24, 7, back to 7 and then continuing through 15 on the previously found path. The obvious question is, "How does one identify such a collection of paths?"

---

[5] Sometimes formal verification is also considered to be part of static analysis, since it does not involve execution. However, since it does involve human input (assertions, proofs) it is not considered part of static analysis proper in this text.

The above question falls into the realm of *control flow* analysis of programs. Control flow analysis provides answers to many important questions about the structure of the potential executions. To name only a few: the shortest paths between points of interest, the identification of instructions that control the selection for execution of other instructions, and the identification of ill-formed flow of control.

Now, returning to Problem 6, suppose that we have selected the path 7, 8, 9, 10, 11, 12, 13, 14, 15 and want to find data that causes its execution. Can static analysis offer a solution to that problem, too? The answer to that question is negative. This problem is, in general, unsolvable by automatic tools and ultimately calls for human reasoning.[6] Nevertheless, static analysis can offer significant help in that case, too. For example, it can tell us which variables at 7 are potentially responsible for the execution of the path. These are: i, n, A, pmax, length.

There is more help possible, however: One can also identify the logical (Boolean) expression for the condition that these variables have to meet for that path to be executed. In our case, the condition at 7 that guarantees execution of the path is

```
(i≤n)  AND  (A[i]<A[pmax])  AND  (1≤i-1)
AND  (A[1]<A[i])  AND  (1<length[1]).
```

That expression can be generated automatically. Now, you can use the expression to find concrete values of the variables involved that make it evaluate to true; this task is left to the reader as an exercise.

Problem 7 *Modification of existing code happens more frequently than writing new code. It is important then to know how a modification propagates throughout the program. Suppose that instruction*

20: pmax:=i

has been changed to read

pmax:=j

Which variables besides pmax will be affected by that change?

To solve the problem, one has to clarify the meaning of the statement "variable V1 affects variable V2." The following interpretation of that concept will be adopted: V1 affects V2 if, on some computation, a change of value of V1 *may* lead to a change of value of V2. Thus, our problem becomes the following: Which variables in the program can have values other than the original ones (before the modification of 20) due to a new value of pmax at 24, i.e., after 20 is executed?

Assume that your understanding of the problem is consistent with the one above. Then you probably tried to identify those variables that are assigned expressions in

---

[6] Problems of that kind are called *undecidable*. That means, that there are no algorithms for their solution but it does not rule out human ability to solve them anyway.

which pmax occurs. Since there is no such assignment, you may have concluded that no variable is affected by the modification of 2. If that is the case, you are correct, albeit for an entirely wrong reason! Clearly, pmax is used in test 9 and thus can influence the flow of control in the program. As a result, all variables but i, A, n, and curr are potentially affected by the new value of pmax.

The identification of those affected variables is a tedious process. Fortunately, static analysis offers a helping hand here: It does it efficiently, although erring on the conservative side, using Dependency Analysis as a vehicle. For now, we have to deal with the apparent contradiction in our discussion: First, we agreed that no variable is affected by the modification of 20 and then claimed that all but four are affected! Well, both answers are correct depending on who is making the corresponding claim. Here is the solution to the mystery.

An analysis will show a nonempty set of variables which are affected by the modification. However, that set usually represents a potential worst case. This fact is illustrated by the following observation: When instruction 20 is entered, the variables i and j have the *same* value, due to the termination of the inner loop 12–16. Thus, the modification of instruction 20 will have, in reality, no effect on the program. However, that conclusion is due to semantic analysis that is the realm of human reasoning and cannot be derived automatically in general.

Our discussion has shown the importance of static analysis as a goal in and of itself. However, there is more to it. In fact, some static analysis is a prerequisite for any verification activity. For example, consider the following question: "Assuming that the fault in the program is due to an incorrect statement, which are the statements that may be faulty?" The dependency analysis between program entities leads to the identification of such a set of statements, known as a Static Slice of the program, which can be used for reasoning, testing, and debugging.

Also, by using static analysis to answer particular questions about the program, one can build one's knowledge about the program in an incremental way. This seems to go well with human approach to problem solving.

6   The Scope of the SAT Methods

Ideally, we should be able to write a correct program in the first place. In general, that is an unattainable goal. There are development methods that do increase the level of confidence in the delivered program, making it "almost" correct. Such a method, based on the Vienna Development Method paradigm, is illustrated in Chap. 1. It is to be hoped that the reader will be convinced of the power of that rigorous approach. Ironically, the law of unintended consequences reasserts itself here. The quality of the produced code tends to be high, with relatively few "hidden" and usually rather subtle bugs. Unfortunately, their detection tends to be more difficult than in the case of poorly designed software, where errors just pop up at almost every run. Consequently, it is fair to state that software analysis and testing will always be with us.

Questions about the program arise at every phase of its development, including high-level modeling (cf. Chap. 1). However, regardless of the phase, they fall into two broad categories: *Quality Assessment* and *Explanatory Analysis*. In either category static and dynamic analysis can be employed and either can be carried out at the *Procedural Level* (individual subprograms) or at the *System Level* (the entire program).

The objective of Quality Assessment is passing judgment on the existing code. However, the very notion of software quality is multifaceted. Program correctness, efficiency, readability, modifiability, reliability, and other related concepts all contribute to the quality of the product. Unfortunately, of those only the efficiency, correctness, and to some degree the reliability are well defined; the other concepts are subjective and are better treated as part of the art of programming, rather than of its science. In this text, we concentrate solely on the problem of correctness. In that context, the process is based on a healthy assumption that, regardless of the development methodology, *"There is always one more bug."* The problem lies in finding it.

When static analysis is used for Quality Assessment, its outcome is of proscriptive nature. The goal here is to identify real or potential problems with the code, known as control or data flow anomalies. Here are some examples: A statement that can never be executed since there is no execution path to it; A statement that has no successor to be executed next; A variable that is referenced before being assigned a value, if at all; A variable that is assigned a value but the variable is not used after that; An invalid sequence of subprogram calls, such as popping from a stack after its initialization to an empty stack.

There exist software development systems that require the user to insert annotations in the code that specify the *intended*, rather than the actual, properties of the code, e.g., the Input–Output data dependency. The system then checks the annotations against both the procedure's signature and the procedure's body. When an anomaly is detected, the developer should either demonstrate that the anomalies are harmless or correct the code and update the documentation (see Chaps. 3 and 4 where Praxis's SPARK handling that issue is outlined).

When dynamic analysis is used for Quality Assessment, its outcome is usually, though not always, also of a proscriptive character. Typically, it deals with the *thoroughness* of test coverage, as illustrated in Sect. 3. If the coverage is insufficient then one has to synthesize new test cases, or show that the uncovered parts of code are not executable, or modify the code.

Now, assume that neither static nor dynamic analysis has detected a problem with the code. Although that may be considered a positive thing by some, it is clearly a failure to detect the bug. Thus, our static and dynamic analysis has been inadequate. We have two choices now. First, we could develop better methods for the detection of programming faults. Second, we could try to answer the following question: "What is the chance that there is still a bug in the program?" In the current state of the art, there is no definite answer to that question. However, research is afoot to couch such an answer in terms of the probability of the existence of certain bugs, as illustrated later in the text.

Explanatory Analysis helps in understanding the program and as such is of a *descriptive* nature. The tools in this category can be broadly divided into Program Browsers and Dependency Analyzers. The former usually provide clerical information, that is, one that can be obtained manually, albeit with some pain. Here are some examples of the information provided by the browsers: The *with* dependencies (Ada) or the *#include* dependencies (C /C++) between the program compilation units; the hierarchy of types and classes. It may be amusing to non-Ada programmers to learn that there are tools out there that compute...the average length of identifiers in the Ada program!

In contrast to the browsers, *Dependency Analyzers* provide information about the impact that program entities – variables, procedures, statements, expressions – have on each other. Toward that goal, they use the Program Call Graph (for interprocedural analysis) and Program Flowgraphs (for intraprocedural analysis). The call graph of the program shows, for each subprogram, subprograms that may potentially be called by the subprogram; the control flowgraph of a subprogram models the flow of control between the subprogram's statements. The information provided by the dependency analyzer is an invaluable help to the programmer in reasoning about the program at every stage of its development. Here are some examples of queries that can be answered on the basis of the derived dependencies in the program under analysis:

Given variable X that is assigned a value in statement S, what are the variables and statements that may be computed using the value of X at S (possibly in another subprogram)? What are the statements that may be selected or deselected for execution depending on the value of X and, those statements having been identified, what are the other variables that may also be affected? Assuming that X is in error, how does that error propagate throughout the program?

Dynamic analysis as an explanatory technique should be treated as a *complement* of static analysis, rather than a technique in and of itself. This is due to the undecidability of static analysis (Sect. 6), a limitation that can be alleviated by the use of execution-based techniques. This brings up the issue of an *integrated* approach to the SAT methods.

One of the main tenets of this text is the use of SAT tools. Unfortunately, with a few notable exceptions, the support offered by commercially available tools is typically of a clerical (e.g., "Capture and Play-Back"), rather than a semantic, nature. Since clerical activities constitute only about 20% of the verification effort [3], the usefulness of those tools is limited. Moreover, the tools usually address isolated aspects of testing or static analysis, making it practically impossible to use several verification methods simultaneously. Consequently, integration of those methods is needed. "Integration" is used here to emphasize (1) the need for the methods to apply to a group of verification activities, rather than to a single activity, (2) the need for the techniques to share a common conceptual framework, and (3) the complementary nature of static and dynamic analysis.

7   Conclusions

It has been shown that there are no *guaranteed* methods to achieve program correctness or the related notions of safety, reliability, integrity, or security. All we can do is to strive to achieve a level of confidence in the software according to the *criticality level* of the application at hand. Toward that goal, Software Analysis and Testing (SAT) techniques can be used individually or in combination to achieve the desired level of criticality. However, the success of that approach depends on several factors. First, the availability of *supporting tools* is essential. It is fair to say that even the best thought-out method, if applied manually, may cause more harm than good. Second, the methods and supporting tools have to be *comprehensive*, applying to a group of verification activities, rather than to a single activity. Third, the methods have to be centered around a *common conceptual framework*.

In the current state of the art, those are rather distant goals. It is true that the power and limitations of some SAT methods have been tested in a laboratory setting. However, a laboratory setting usually involves programs of a rather limited size and complexity. Unfortunately, for real-world size software, the limitations of the SAT methods will most likely get worse, while their power will still have to be field tested. Therefore, further progress hinges on the use of SAT methods in the real world and their continuing improvement. The improvement depends on the continuing research, involving both experimental and theoretical issues. It is impossible to list all research issues, but if one shares our belief that *"There is nothing more practical than a good theory"* (attributed to Boltzmann), what is needed most is the development of a "good" theory of program incorrectness. That involves the origin of program faults and the creation of errors and their propagation.

Finally, the methods described in the text are oriented toward what one may call a "classical" view of programming, without too much attention paid to Object Oriented Programming (OOP). There is one obvious reason for that–relatively little research has been done in the area of OOP and no generally accepted OOP testing and analysis paradigms exist; moreover, there is no general agreement on what the very notion of OOP really means! The lack of a scientific foundation is not only due to the relative novelty of the OOP paradigm, but also due more to the inherent intractability of many of the OOP problems. This is such serious problem that the use of OOP is discouraged in Safety Critical Systems [5]. The prevailing view is that only those programming constructs should be used in high reliability systems that can be proved correct, *even if the proof is dispensed with*. Unfortunately, the main features of the OOP paradigm: type extension (inheritance), polymorphism, and late binding (run–time dispatching) make program proving all but impossible. Note that even some traditional concepts such as recursion are discouraged unless one is able to determine statically (before execution) the depth of the recursion, thus avoiding a run-time stack overflow.

One the brighter side is the conviction of some that one really does not lose too much if OOP is not used, since, to quote Barnes [2]:

"Fancy stuff regarding OOP and Abstract Data Types is all about visibility control; these are important but the ultimate power of the stored program machine is its ability to perform iterative and nested processes." And later in the text, "Programming in some mathematical sense is about subprograms and arrays. Features such as records and OO generally are management gloss giving control of visibility–important but not of essence."

Certainly it remains to be seen whether those views will stand the test of time.

Exercises

Exercise 1 *Consider again the function.* Monotone *in Fig.1. Assume that on some execution the variable* maxj *in statement 10 has been assigned the incorrect value of 1 the very first time; we will refer to this as a primary error at statement 11, the successor of 10. Identify all secondary errors, i.e., the variables and statements affected by the propagation of the primary error.*

Exercise 2 *Establish the conditions for the revealing tests, i.e., one that guarantee the detection of the fault.*

References

1. J. Barnes, High Integrity Software, The SPARK Approach to Safety and Security, Addison-Wesley, Reading, MA, 2003.
2. R.G. Dromey, How to Solve it by Computer, Prentice-Hall, Upper saddle Rive, NJ, 1982.
3. D.R. Graham, Where is CAST Heading? Directions and Trends for Testing Tools, Proceedings of Sixth International Software Quality Week, San Francisco, May 25–28, 1993.
4. N. Nissanke, Introductory Logic and Sets for Computer Scientists, Addison-Wesley, Reading, MA, 1999.
5. G. Romanski, Safety Critical Software Handbook – Aonix, 1997 and Guidance for the use of the Ada Programming Language in High Integrity Systems, Working Draft of ISO/IEC TR 15942, Section 6.6.2.S

Part I
The Semantic Analysis

Chapter 1
Why Not Write Correct Software the First Time?

Abstract Ideally, quality should be built into software by design, rather than being assessed and improved on later. The main quality, without which all other qualities are meaningless, is correctness. One method that purported to guarantee correctness is a top-down program development based on mathematical modeling. We illustrate the method by using the Vienna Definition Method – Specification Language, supported by CSK's Toolbox. Under ideal circumstances, the program and its proof are developed hand-in-hand rendering the final product correct by construction. However, since the Toolbox does not support proof we will use informal correctness arguments which, in most cases, should be sufficient. There are three lessons to be learned in this chapter. First, if carried out with care the process does lead to a better, "almost" correct product. Second, mathematics in and of itself is not the panacea, blunders are inevitable and, therefore, software analysis and testing will always be necessary. Third, the faults that appear in the process tend to be quite subtle and their detection may be more difficult than in the general case. Finally, the VDM-SL is used here only as a tool supporting the top-down development paradigm and, consequently, only features of the notation necessary to achieve that objective are described. The reader is encouraged to get familiar with this ground-breaking methodology.

1.1   Express Yourself Precisely: The Precondition

In the Introduction, we discussed the importance of a good specification that serves not only as a blueprint for the implementation but also as the ultimate test criterion for the final code. We also illustrated the ambiguity and imprecision of natural language. A statement is ambiguous if it can have more than one meaning. An imprecise statement has only one meaning but it is not clear when the statement is true and when it is false, cf. [6]. For example, the following sentence

> "The procedure returns the top of stack"

is ambiguous for it is not clear what is really returned: Is it the top element or a pointer to it? In contrast, the following sentence

J. Laski and W. Stanley, *Software Verification and Analysis*,
DOI: 10.1007/978-1-84882-240-5_2, © Springer Verlag London Limited 2009

"The maximum value in the array is large"

is unambiguous but imprecise (vague) since there is no generally agreed-upon notion of "large." Consequently, while a natural language is an excellent tool to write poetry or the law (only from the lawyers' standpoint, of course), it is not a good tool for scientific or engineering discourse. In contrast, statements expressed in the formal language of logic are clear and unambiguous. Moreover, if supplied with a deductive apparatus, logic offers a possibility of proving the properties of programs.

There are many excellent texts devoted to logic, cf. [6, 3]. In what follows, we only illustrate the use of logic in the development of the monotone function from Introduction. Toward that goal, we use the Vienna Development Method (VDM). The VDM is a formal notation for modeling, development, and analysis of sequential software systems [4]. The main tenet of the method is formal *specification* of the programming problem at hand and its subsequent *refinement* into a series of models, until the code level has been reached. At each refinement one can formulate Proof Obligations (POs), i.e., a set of facts which, if proved, guarantee the correctness of the refinements. However, if the conceptual distance between the models is small the POs are usually discharged.

The language of the VDM is a winning combination of mathematical notation and that of procedural programming languages. A recent ISO standard of the ASCII version of the notation is referred to as the VDM Specification Language (VDM-SL) [1]. The standard motivated the development of supporting tools. In particular, the CSK's VDM-SL Toolbox allows one to check the consistency of the model (syntax and type checking) and interpret certain kinds of models [2].

In what follows features of VDM-SL used in the development are explained at their first occurrences. We start with the formal definition of the precondition in standard logic, then translate it into the VDM-SL notation and, whenever possible, interpret that model under CSK's Toolbox.

Problem 1.1 *As discussed in the introduction, a valid input array A to the Monotone function has to have distinct elements between position 1 and n. Define that property mathematically.*

The essence of that statement is the fact that no two entries in A may be the same. As a first try, one can express this property of A narratively as follows:

"Array A has distinct elements if and only if for every i and j,
A[i]≠A[j], where i, j are between 1 and the size of A, symbolically size(A)."

For a *concrete* array A, the above sentence is either *true* or *false*; sentences of that kind are referred to as *propositions*. However, our intent is to specify the property "A is distinct" for arbitrary arrays. That is, our concept becomes a function, say IsDistinct(A), that takes array A as an argument and returns *true* or *false* depending, respectively, on whether elements in A are distinct or not. Such a function is referred to as a *predicate*. One can define the function precisely using the language of the first-order predicate logic (it is rather likely that most readers are more familiar

with the standard mathematical notation than with its VDM-SL equivalent; that is
the reason we introduce it first):

$$\text{IsDistinct } (A) = \forall i,j : \{1,\ldots, size(A)\} \cdot A[i] \neq A[j].$$

The above definition of IsDistinct takes one argument A (referred to as a free
variable) and returns a Boolean result, i.e., *true* or *false*. The equation symbols "="
stands here for the "defined as." The $\forall$ symbol is the universal ("for all") quantifier,
which introduces two bound variables i and j, which range over the set $1,\ldots, size(A)$
of natural numbers. The dot (bullet) • serves as a separator between the variables
introduced by the quantifier $\forall$ and the formula that is quantified, i.e., $A[i] \neq A[j]$.
The universal quantifier can be viewed as a generalization of the logical operator
(conjunct) AND: For the whole thing to become *true*, the quantified expression $A[i]$
$\neq A[j]$ must be true for every i and j between 1 and $size(A)$; If the expression is *false*
for just one pair (i, j) the whole predicate is *false*.

Now, here is an equivalent definition of *IsDistinct* in terms of the VDM-SL,
introduced by the keyword functions:

```
functions
IsDistinct: array -> bool
IsDistinct(A)       == forall i, j in set{1,…, len A}
                              A(i)<>A(j)
```

In the above, the first line is the *signature* of the predicate: It says that function
IsDistinct takes one argument of type `array` and returns a result of type `bool`, i.e,
Boolean. Now, VDM-SL does not support arrays directly and, therefore, the type
array has to be explicitly defined. This can be done by the following type definition
introduced by the keyword types:

```
types
array = seq of int;
```

In the above, type `array` is defined as a *sequence of integers*. A sequence type
can be viewed as a generalization of the familiar type *string* (of characters) onto
string of (almost) anything. Clearly, a VDM sequence can be of arbitrary length and
can contain arbitrary elements.

The second line of the definition of `IsDistinct` provides the actual definition
of the predicate; in it, the identifier A stands for an arbitrary element of type
`array`. The forall is simply an ASCII notation for the universal quantifier $\forall$ and
the ampersand "&" stands for the bullet " · " that introduces the body of a quantified
formula. The phrase "i, j in set $\{1, \ldots,$ len A$\}$, " states that the bound variables i and
j range over the set of indices of A, i.e., are between 1 and the length of A, returned
by the built-in function len A.

The above is a *direct, operational,* or *explicit* definition of a VDM-SL predicate.
A direct definition provides a method for computing the result for a concrete argument, assuming that the bound variables range over finite sets, rather than over
usually infinite types. Indeed, for direct definitions obeying those restrictions, the
CSK Toolbox allows one to interpret the function for concrete values of its arguments.

To see how it works let us first define a set of VDM-SL constants, introduced by the keyword values:

```
values
a1: array = [1, 2, 9, 4, 7, 3, 11, 8, 14, 6];
a2 = [4, 3, 2, 1];        -- type identifier can be omitted
a3 = [1, 2, 3, 4];
a4 = [2];
a5 = [2, 2, 2, 2];
s1 = {2, 8, 3};           -- set containing the values 2, 3 and
                          -- 8; can be written down in any order
s2 = {};                  -- an empty set
```

In the above, the defined values a1 through a5 illustrate the syntax of the array values, while s1 and s2 illustrate how set values can be defined. Now we can use those values to evaluate the predicate IsDistinct. Below are two examples of the interpretation of IsDistinct:

$$\text{IsDistinct(a5)} = \text{false}$$
$$\text{IsDistinct(a2)} = \text{false}$$

The first result is as expected. However, the second result is incorrect, since array a2 contains distinct elements only.

Problem 1.2   *Identify the course of the problem*

As defined, IsDistinct returns false for *any* array A, since when $i=j$ then $A(i)=A(j)$ and the entire proposition is false! We can fix that problem by requiring $A(i) \neq A(j)$ *only when $i \neq j$*. Here is the corrected definition in VDM-SL:

```
IsDistinct: array -> bool
IsDistinct(A) == forall i, j in set inds A & i<>j => A(i) <> A(j);
```

In the above, => stands for logical *implication*. The use of the implication here should be clear: p => q is false only when p = *true* and q = *false*; otherwise it is true.

   Now all tests of IsDistinct pass. This example illustrates two important facts. First, regardless of the formalism used, we are bound to make errors. Second, with formal approach and a supporting tool it is usually easier to detect *and* correct the error earlier in the development process.

1.2   The Postcondition

Let us turn to a more complicated task of writing down the postcondition of the function monotone from the introduction, whose narrative formulation is repeated here for easy reference:

POSTCONDITION (Monotone): *The result produced by Monotone holds the length of the longest strictly monotonically increasing sequence in the array A.*

The obvious way to write the postcondition appears to be the following. First, define the set of the *lengths* of all longest strictly monotonically increasing sequences that end at each position in array A. Second, define the result returned by Monotone to be the maximum of that set. To address the first issue observe that any sequence ending at position k, $1 \le k \le$ len A, meets one of the following two mutually exclusive conditions: Either there exists a *compatible* subsequence for $A(k)$, i.e, one ending at some j between 1 and $k-1$ and such that $A(j) < A(k)$, or it does not. In the first case, every sequence ending at j can be extended by appending $A(k)$ to it. In the second case, for every j between 1 and $k-1$, $A(j) > A(k)$ (remember that the precondition rules out $A(j) = A(k)$!) and $A(k)$ is the only one-element sequence ending at k.

Now, let *limseq(A, k)* stand for the length of a longest *increasing monotone sequence* ending at k in array A, $k = 1, 2, ..., len A$. Thus, the set of the lengths of all sequences in A can be defined as *{limseq (A, k)| k=1, 2, ..., len A}*. The problem at hand is then the definition of *limseq (A, k)*. One way of doing that is to make use of the fact that *limseq (A, k)* equals 1 plus the largest *limseq (A, j)*, for $j = 1, ..., k - 1$, such that $A(j) < A(k)$. This leads to the following recursive VDM-SL definition of *limseq (A, k)*:

```
limseq: array * nat1 -> nat -- signature of limseq
              -- array * position is a set of pairs (A, k) where
              -- A is of type array and k is of type nat1, i.e.  in set
              -- 1, 2, ...  limseq(A, k) returns the length of a longest
              -- monotonically increasing sequence in A that ends at k
limseq (A, k) ==
  let S = {limseq (A, j | j in set {1, ..., k-1} & A(j) < A(k)}
                              -- S is set of length of
                              -- compatible sequences for A(k)
  in
    if S = {} then 1        -- if no compatible sequence exists A(k)
    else                    -- is appended to a compatible sequence
      MaxSet({l | l in set S}) + 1
  pre distinct(A);
```

In the above, S is defined as the set of the lengths of compatible sequences for $A(k)$, i.e., those that end at some position j between 1 and $k-1$ and for which `A(j)<A(k)`. Observe that the syntax of the definition is similar to the phrase in mathematical texts: "Let S be a set of ....." The scope of visibility of S is the expression that follows the keyword `in`. In the case where there is no compatible sequence for $A(k)$, S is empty and this is the base of the recursion. Note also the inclusion of the precondition `distinct(A)` in the definition of `limseq`. The function `MaxSet`, used in the definition of `limseq`, takes a set of integers as its argument and returns the maximum element in that set. The function is defined recursively as follows:

```
MaxSet: set of int -> int
                        -- returns the maximal element in set S
    MaxSet(S) ==
      if card S = 1
        then let i in set S in i   -- if there is only one
                                   -- element in set S, that
                                   -- element is returned as
                                   -- the maximum
        else let e in set S in
                                   -- select an arbitrary
                                   -- element  e from set S
            let m = MaxSet(S\{e}) in
                                   -- m is maximum of set
                                   -- S without e
                if e<=m then m else e
      pre    S <> {}
      post forall x in set S & x <= RESULT;
                        -- RESULT is a predefined identifier for
                        -- the value returned by a direct function
```

MaxSet has been defined recursively. It takes as its only argument a set of integers and returns an integer. The base case of the recursion is when the argument set *S* contains a single element: in such a case that element is returned. Otherwise, an *arbitrary* element e is selected from *S* by the statement

let e **in set** S **in** ...

and the result is computed as the larger element of e and MaxSet(S\{e}), where S\{e} is the set obtained from *S* by the removal of e.

An interesting feature of the above definition of MaxSet is the combination of operational (expression) and declarative (pre- and postcondition) techniques. Clearly, for MaxSet to be defined, its argument has to be nonempty, as captured by its precondition. Its postcondition seemingly states the obvious: the predefined named RESULT must be greater than or equal to every element in the argument set *S*. Thus, the direct definition of MaxSet and its specification have been combined together so the latter can serve as the presumed "correctness oracle" for the former.

Now, we might feel quite convinced that the definition of limseq is correct and can be used in a simple definition of the problem; that wonderful feeling notwithstanding, we better test limseq under the CSK's Toolbox Interpreter. Here are some results:

```
limseq(a1,  3) = 3
limseq(a1,  1) = 1
limseq(a1,  9) = 6
limseq(a1, 10) = 4
limseq(a2,  4) = 1
limseq(a3,  1) = 1
limseq(a3,  4) = 4
limseq(a4,  1) = 1
limseq(a5,  4) = 1 -- invalid input a5: a5 is not distinct
limseq(a5,  2) = 1 -- invalid input a5
```

So far so good, if not even better than expected, since limseq returns a "correct" result for an invalid input a5. However, CSK's Toolbox allows one to check pre- and postconditions during interpretation. With that feature on, one gets the following error message during the evaluation of limseq(a5, 4):

"Run-Time Error 58: The pre-condition evaluated to false."

Now, after some thought, it becomes clear that there is no need for the precondition at all, since the problem is well- defined for arbitrary arrays. Therefore, we can drop the precondition.[1] Observe that by doing that, we do not violate the initial specification of the program: Indeed, any model of the problem can accept more inputs than required. However, the particular implementation in Fig. 1 of the Introduction would not be considered a valid implementation of the problem unless it is modified to accept an arbitrary array. Assuming then the correctness of limseq we can use it in an indirect definition of monotone, named monotone_ind below:

```
monotone_ind(A: array) Res: nat1
                    -- pre distinct(A), no longer needed
post Res = MaxSet({l| l in set
         {limseq(A, i) | i in set inds A});
```

Unlike the other functions defined so far, the definition of monotone_ind is *indirect, declarative*, or *implicit*. It does not provide a method to derive the result. Rather, it provides a criterion for the correctness of the result, *regardless of the way it has been obtained*. The first line, the signature of the function, states that the function takes one argument of type array and returns a result Res (any name can be used here) of type nat1, i.e, Res can be any natural value greater than 0. Note that the original precondition has been commented out, rather than removed entirely; that is due to this Author's conviction that it is a good practice to leave important evidence of the programmer's inner torment as part of the documentation.

The postcondition of monotone_ind is self-explanatory. However, due to the fact that the function is indirect, it cannot be interpreted. Fortunately, CSK Toolbox automatically provides a predefined predicate post_monotone_ind, which allows one to test the postcondition on two arguments. These arguments are the input array and a result, *regardless of the way it has been obtained*. For instance, Res can be the *expected* result of a test case or Res can be produced by some implementation, not necessarily correct. Therefore, the function post_monotone_ind can be used to check the correctness of Res. The following test cases illustrate that concept.

```
post_monotone_ind(a1, 6) = true
post_monotone_ind(a1, 7) = false
post_monotone_ind(a2, 7) = false
post_monotone_ind(a2, 1) = true
post_monotone_ind(a5, 1) = true
```

---

[1]Dropping" the precondition is rather a misnomer since this is interpreted as pretrue, meaning that every input is valid.

Problem 1.3 *Review the model* monotone_ind *again; is there anything wrong with it? A clue: analyze and test every function used in the model independently, rather than within the context of* monotone_ind.

Admittedly, that problem is somewhat tricky. With some luck you might have synthesized the following test case for the postcondition of MaxSet:

post MaxSet({2, 4, 7}, 10).

This test passes, i.e., the above expression evaluates to true. Now, that surely violates our understanding of the "maximum" of a set. It is easy to see that the error is due to the fact that in the postcondition of MaxSet we failed to require that the result belong to the argument set. The following version of the postcondition of MaxSet fixes the problem.

```
post -- MaxSet
   (RESULT in set S)              -- RESULT must come from set S
                                  -- and must be the maximum in S
      and (forall x in set S & x <= RESULT);
```

A quite important observation is in order. Recall that the very role of an indirect specification is to serve as a correctness oracle for any direct refinement of it, the final implementation included. Therefore, it is of paramount importance that the specification itself be correct. However, the above problem with MaxSet illustrates that it is possible for the specification to be incorrect and the implementation to be correct. It also demonstrates the limitations of formal methods, an issue discussed in Sect. 1.5.

In Sect. 1.4, we discuss several refinements of monotone_ind. However, we first discuss the general principles of top-down, correctness preserving program development.

1.3   The Principles of Top-Down Refinement

There is little doubt that the objective of top-down refinement is noble: To write a correct program the very first time, with testing and debugging duly relegated to the dustbin of history. How is that miracle to be achieved? Well, the first step is to develop a good high level model, that is, the specification of the problem. We dealt with this step in Sect. 1.2. Let S be such a model. Assume for now that the model is indirect, using pre- and postcondition and that it is valid, correctly capturing the requirements. That means that no algorithm for the solution is assumed and the programmer has to invent such an algorithm as a blueprint for the final code.

Now, to get from S to the final code, the *Top-Down Refinement* paradigm advocates the derivation of an (ordered) sequence $S_1, S_2, ..., S_f$ of *models* of S, where $S_1 = S$ and S_f is the final code, that is, the implementation of the problem. For $i = 1, ..., f-1$, model S_{i+1} is a *refinement* of its immediate predecessor model S_i, if the following conditions are met:

1. S_{i+1} is *stronger* than S_i.
2. S_{i+1} is *less abstract* than S_i.
3. It is relatively easy to *validate* S_{i+1} on the basis of *validated* S_i.

Here is the informal definition of those concepts. Condition (1) states that S_{i+1} may allow more inputs than S_i while S_{i+1} may allow fewer outputs than S_i. In other words, S_{i+1} *may* solve the problem for more inputs than required by S_i and may yield results that, while obeying the restrictions of S_i, may restrict the outputs further, that is, do *more* than required. For example, assume that S_i is the following problem: Given a sorted array return the position of its maximum element. A model S_{i+1} that accepts an arbitrary, unsorted array and returns the position of the *first* occurrence of the maximum is clearly stronger than S_i. Condition (2) states that S_{i+1} provides a more detailed description of the problem than S_i does. That means that either S_{i+1} provides a more detailed algorithm for the solution of the problem or it uses less abstract data types, or both. S_f, the last model in the refinement sequence, is an implementation of the problem in the target programming language. Finally, condition (3) means that the "distance" between S_{i+1} and S_i is small enough to allow one to reason about correctness of the refinement. Consequently, the last model in the refinement sequence should be *correct by construction*. If mathematical rigor is to be maintained, a refinement gives rise to *POs*, i.e., facts that have to be proved to claim that S_{i+1} is indeed stronger than S_i. However, if the proximity between the two models is close, an informal reasoning is usually accepted in lieu of the proof.

The following are some consequences of the top-down refinement paradigm. First, S_{i+1} is harder to understand than S_i and therefore harder to prove *on its own*; it is precisely the refinement step that allows the validation of S_{i+1} under the assumption that S_i *has already been validated*. Second, a refinement can involve either operations/functions or data. For example, an operation can be decomposed into a sequence of several simpler operations or an abstract data, e.g, set type, can be represented by an array. Third, subsequent models in the sequence tend to become more and more algorithmic, at some point allowing *interpretation* by a specialized tool.

1.4   The Example Continued

In this section, we illustrate how the general principles of Top-Down Refinement, outlined in Sect. 1.3, can be applied to the problem of the `monotone` function from Sect. 1.2. There, with some pain, we defined `monotone_ind`, as the highest level, indirect model of the problem. Here is the definition repeated for easy reference:

```
monotone_ind(A: array) Res: nat1
-- pre distinct(A)
post Res = MaxSet({l | l in set {limseq(A, i)| i
                        in set inds A}});
```

Since the objective of top-down refinement is to move to the final code in small, well-defined, and controlled steps, we should aim at a direct definition of the problem. As it happens, the structure of monotone_ind gives rise to the following straightforward *direct* definition monotone_dir of the problem:

```
monotone_dir: array -> nat
    -- returns the length of a longest sequence in array A
    -- argument to MaxSet is never empty since
    -- limseq(A, k)>=1 for k>=1
monotone_dir(A) == MaxSet({limseq(A, k) | k in set inds A });
```

Before we proceed any further, we have to show that monotone_dir is a valid refinement of monotone_ind. Apparently, this proof obligation is easy to discharge since the result produced by the former obviously meets the postcondition of the latter. It always helps, however, to support one's conviction with a few tests. Here are some results:

$$monotone\_dir(a1) = 6$$
$$monotone\_dir(a2) = 1$$
$$monotone\_dir(a3) = 4$$
$$monotone\_dir(a4) = 1$$
$$monotone\_dir(a5) = 1$$

So convinced, our immediate task is to refine monotone_dir. There are two possible ways to go about that. First, one can treat monotone_dir as a blueprint for the solution. Consequently, one would keep refining either control structures or abstract data types (or both) that appear in monotone_dir until the code level has been reached. Second, one could formulate a new model that is more efficient than the one underlying monotone_dir. Observe that although defined directly, monotone_dir is only a specification that does not preempt any implementation. We shall illustrate both approaches.

Assume first that monotone_dir is a blueprint for the implementation. Then the only possible refinement is that of the expression MaxSet({limseq (A, k) | k **in set inds** A}) returned by monotone_dir. An *abstract program*, which first computes the argument to MaxSet and then calls the latter seems to be doing the job. Here is the VDM-SL version of the algorithm, known as an *operation*, rather than a function:

```
monotone_opr: array ==> nat
monotone_opr(A) ==
    ( dcl                       -- declaration of local variable S
        S: set of nat := {};    -- S initialized to empty set
      for all k in set inds A do
        S := S union {limseq (A, k)};
      return MaxSet(S);
    );
```

Here are some clarifications of the above definition. The dcl keyword introduces a declaration of local variables, very much like in standard programming languages. In this case, there is only one local variable S whose type is set of nat, i.e., a set of natural numbers, initialized to an empty set. The for all construct is a counted loop that iterates over the set of indices of A. The union operator is the VDM-SL notation for the set union operation. It is easy to see that the code of monotone_opr resembles a "normal," procedural language except that it accepts Abstract Data Types (ADTs) normally not supported by such a language. Now, for monotone_opr to be a valid refinement of monotone_dir, one would have to demonstrate that the former is correct for the latter. Although this is quite self-explanatory, a few tests are in order. Toward that goal, here is a "test harness" for monotone_opr, which checks correctness of the result produced by monotone_opr against the postcondition of monotone_ind:

```
test_monotone_opr: array -> bool
test_monotone_opr(A) == post_monotone_ind
                       (A, monotone_opr(A));
```

Note that post_monotone_ind takes two arguments: One is the array A and the other is the result returned by monotone_opr(A). Here are a few test results, which support (rather than confirm) our conviction about correctness of monotone_opr:

```
test_monotone_opr(a1) = true
test_monotone_opr(a2) = true
test_monotone_opr(a3) = true
test_monotone_opr(a4) = true
test_monotone_opr(a5) = true.
```

Before we proceed any further, one comment is needed. The operation monotone_opr has been defined as an algorithmic refinement of monotone_ind, which is considered to be easier to understand. However, for some it may as well be the other way round–that is, monotone_opr, expressed in more familiar procedural terms, can serve as the initial model provided that it does not serve as a blueprint for the implementation.

More detailed models of monotone_opr would likely involve refinements of the auxiliary concept of the limseq function and the representation of abstract data types, referred to as *data refinement*. If the model is a blueprint for implementation, then the recursive definition of limseq is very inefficient. Also, the definition might be too hard to understand. Thus, an iterative definition of limseq may be preferable. Such a definition would most likely resemble the inner loop in Fig. 1 of the Introduction.

There are two parts to data refinement. First, one has to represent the ADTs that appear in monotone_opr (sets, sequences) in terms of concrete data types supported by the programming language at hand. Second, abstract operations (such as MaxSet) would have to be expressed in terms of the programming language-supported data representation (arrays, structures, linked lists). Each kind of refinement gives rise to specific POs.

Now, let us briefly illustrate the case where monotone_opr is *not* a blueprint for the design. This means that the developer can use any method for the solution to the problem. In our case, rather than computing the entire set of limseq (A, k), for $k = 1, \ldots,$ len A and then finding the maximum element in that set, one could keep updating the final result when individual lims (A, k) are computed. This is shown in the following operation

```
monotone_opr1: array ==> nat -- a more efficient version
                             -- of monotone_opr
monotone_opr1(A) ==
( dcl                        -- local variable maxl
    maxl: nat := 1;          -- declared and initialized
                             --to 1 holds the final result
  for all k in set inds A do
    if maxl < limseq (A, k) then maxl := limseq (A, k);
  return maxl;
);
```

Observe that the above model is essentially equivalent to the overall design of the function in Fig. 1 of the Introduction. That would become even more obvious if the recursive definition of limseq were replaced by an iterative version. Again, testing monotone_opr1 does not detect errors. Although this does increase our belief that the model is correct, keep in mind that only *a proof can guarantee that*.

It is important to note the difference between proof obligations in each method of refinement. In the first case, when monotone_dir was a blueprint for monotone_opr, one could establish correctness of the latter by establishing correctness of the corresponding parts of the refinement. For example, the set value definition in monotone_dir was replaced by an algorithm that actually computes that set in monotone_opr. Thus, it was established that the two models were *equivalent, regardless of their specifications*. In contrast, it is rather difficult to establish equivalence between monotone_dir and monotone_opr1. Instead, we would have to demonstrate two facts. First, we would have to show that the latter is correct for its *own specification*. Second, we would have to establish that such a specification is not weaker than that of monotone_dir, thus possibly allowing more inputs and fewer outputs.

1.5   Conclusions

If successful, the top-down development process presented in the preceding sections leads to a solution that is *correct by construction*. Let us then identify strong points of the method.

First, the method fosters intellectual discipline, naturally lacking in an informal approach. Second, the use of high-level concepts such as sets, sequences, maps, functions, etc., makes reasoning about the problem, including the concomitant proofs, more reliable. This is due to the fact that an abstract model allows one to express the problem in terms of the domain of discourse and thus use inherent properties of the domain in informal reasoning (for that reason ADTs are also referred to as User Defined Types). Thus, an abstract model is largely independent of the idiosyncrasies of the programming language and therefore, once the notation is mastered, it is easier to comprehend an abstract algorithm than the code in a programming language. Third, bugs can be detected and corrected at early stages of the development process. This helps to identify well-defined rollback points and thus helps to reduce the cost of rework. Fourth, the models generated by the method constitute an unambiguous and precise documentation, an invaluable artifact in the maintenance phase.

Consequently, there is a hope that when the method is practiced with the requisite rigor, it does produce results. One study, for example, shows that high-level proofs appear to be "substantially more efficient at finding faults than the most efficient testing phase"[5].

Unfortunately, in the imperfect world, there are problems with that method, too. First, the mathematical formalism and the discipline needed to follow the method might not be easy for some practitioners of the programming craft to master. Second, current corporate culture favors the delivery of early "working" code at the expense of mathematical modeling. Perhaps the availability of software support like the one offered by CSK's Toolbox will help change that attitude. Third, the method requires that assertions about the intended behavior of the program (e.g, pre- and postconditions or invariants, see Chap.3) be correct. Recall, however, the definition of `MaxSet` in Sect. 1.4. Ironically, the postcondition of `MaxSet`, which should be *the* correctness oracle for the implementation, was found incorrect while the implementation *was* correct. In general, the synthesis of assertions is a challenging task. Fourth, assumptions about the primitives used in the design and/or proof (e.g, library or user-defined procedures) might be false. Finally, the inevitable flaws in human reasoning might lead to flawed conclusions. All things considered the detection of the flaws is more likely to be easier for formal than informal specification. Indeed, we may write silly things using formal notation, bet the silliness will be usually well defined.

Consequently, the process is only partly reliable, leading to programs that are "almost" correct. That is, there might exist residual faults detected only by static analysis or testing. One can safely claim, therefore, that bug detection will always be with us, as an inescapable and legitimate part of the design process. Moreover, the goal of bug detection becomes even more important if a solid development method has been applied. This is because a good development process renders a program with relatively few albeit "subtle" bugs. Consequently, their detection tends to be harder than that of more "obvious" faults introduced by standard methods. This conclusion is also supported by the discussion of the power and limitations of formal program verification in Chaps. 2 and 3.

Exercise Translate the VDM-SL model monotone_opr1 into the programming language of your choice. Identify major steps of that process.

References

1. D.J. Andrews (Ed.), Information Technology – Programming languages, their environments and System Software Interfaces – Vienna Development Method – Specification Language – Part 1: Base language, ISO, Geneva, http://www.iso.ch, December 1996. ISO/IEC 13817-1.
2. J. Fitzgerald and P.G. Larsen, Modelling Systems, Practical Tools and Techniques in Software Development, Cambridge University Press, Cambridge, 1998.

3. J.H. Gallier, Logic for Computer Science, Foundations of Automatic Theorem Proving, Harper & Row, NewYork, NY, 1986.
4. C.B. Jones, Systematic Software Development using VDM, Prentice-Hall, Upper Saddle River, NJ, 1990.
5. S. King, J. Hammond, R. Chapman, A. Pryor, Is proof more cost-effective than testing? *IEEE Transactions on Software Engineering*, 26(8), 675–686, 2000.
6. N. Nissanke, Introductory Logic and Sets for Computer Scientists, Addison-Wesley, Reading, MA, 1999.

Chapter 2
How to Prove a Program Correct: Programs Without Loops

Abstract The correctness of a program is a relative concept, meaning that the program is doing no less than prescribed by its specification. Given a declarative (indirect, implicit) model in the form of the pre- and postcondition, an acyclic program (i.e., one without loops) can be verified by analyzing every path through the program. The objective of the proof is to show that the precondition is strong enough to guarantee that some path will always be traversed for every valid input and the resulting state will satisfy the postcondition on termination. To verify an acyclic program with many paths a finite collection of its *Verification Conditions* (VCs), referred to as the *Verification Schema* for the program, needs to be validated. The schema involves the notion of the *weakest precondition* (wp) of the program postcondition, i.e. , the most relaxed input conditions that guarantee the postcondition satisfied on termination. Also, an orthogonal method to the path analysis, the *assertion* method is presented. The techniques are illustrated by examples that use the SPARK toolset from Praxis Critical Systems Limited.

2.1 Program Correctness

There is little doubt that the very word *proof* strikes terror at the hearts of most students. It is probably more terrifying than the prospect of a root canal. However, as the latter is sometimes unavoidable, so is the former and here is why. In Chap. 1 we illustrated the top-down, step-wise refinement software development paradigm based on the VDM-SL version of mathematical modeling which, if followed rigorously, leads to a program that is correct *by construction*. However, the operative word here is "rigorously." Clearly, the success of the process hinges on our ability to prove the Proof Obligations that underlie the control and/or data refinement stages involved. It is true that in many, perhaps most, cases when the conceptual distance between the stages is relatively small, the proof can be discharged. That is a "scientific" way of saying that things are "obvious." Unfortunately, as we saw in Chap. 1, one can get easily overconfident in one's understanding of the problem and thus commit errors that are quite difficult to detect. To handle cases like that, a proof may be necessary.

J. Laski and W. Stanley, *Software Verification and Analysis*,
DOI: 10.1007/978-1-84882-240-5_3, © Springer-Verlag London Limited 2009

It is not to say that *every* design decision should be proved; rather, it is to say that we should be *prepared* to do so if necessary.

There are two benefits of even *attempting* the proof. First, if successful, the proof guarantees that the program, or part of it, is indeed correct. Second, if failed, the proof may be a very effective tool for error detection, particularly if carried out at the high, design level, cf. [4]. Unfortunately, the VDM-SL Toolbox does not offer any proof support. Therefore, since one of the tenets of this text is that tool support is *a must* in software development, we have to use a tool for a notation other than the VDM-SL. Toward that goal, Praxis' SPARK system is used in the text and is introduced in Sect. 2.4. The first three sections lay down the theoretical background of program proving. That exposition, however, should not be treated as *the* theory of program proving as its only purpose is to introduce the Reader to the basic ideas. The reader interested in the history of program proving is advised to consult the references [1] and [2]; the one interested in SPARK should consult the reference[3]. New developments could be found in the relevant scientific journals.

Consider statement S in the program and the pair (P, Q) of the, respectively, pre- and postcondition of S. Recall that the precondition is a predicate that constrains the values of the input variables of S. In contrast, the postcondition defines the valid *relationships* between the input and the output variables of S. Since a variable can be both input and output, there is a need to distinguish between the initial and final value of the variable in the postcondition. The tilde (~) will be used to denote the initial value while an undecorated variable identifier will stand for the final value of the variable in the postcondition. Observe that in the precondition there is no need for the tilde since $v = v\sim$; the need to use the tilde arises only in the postcondition, *provided* the latter does refer to the initial value of v.

Assuming that all the other elements of the specification of S (input and output variables and their types) are known, the pair (P, Q) will be viewed as an abbreviated specification of S. Let the *state* of a program (usually at some specified point) be a collection of pairs (variable, its value) or, in more elegant terms, a *function* from the set of variables to the union of their types (see Chap. 9). Then, the following symbolic notation

$$\{P\}S\{Q\}$$

will serve as a shorthand for the proposition:

"If P is satisfied by state $s\sim$ on entry to S and *if* S terminates, yielding the final state s, then the initial state $s\sim$ and the final state s satisfy property Q."

As stated above, this is the concept of *partial or conditional correctness* of S, with respect to the specification (P, Q). That means that the postcondition Q is defined only under the assumption that S *terminates*; if S does not terminate, its output is obviously undefined and so is Q.

However, if for a partially correct program, it can also be established that for every state that satisfies precondition P the program indeed terminates, then total correctness of the program has also been effectively established. The notation

$$\langle P \rangle S \langle Q \rangle$$

is used to denote *total (unconditional) correctness* of S for (P, Q). To illustrate the difference between the two concepts of correctness consider the following statement S, for x declared as real:

$$S: x := sqrt(x).$$

The total correctness proposition

$$<true> S <x = \sqrt{x}\text{\textasciitilde}>$$

is false since, for negative x~, $\sqrt{x}$~ is undefined and S does not terminate. In contrast, the partial correctness proposition

$$\{true\}S\{x = \sqrt{x}\text{\textasciitilde}\}$$

is true since *whenever* S does terminate, x~ ≥ 0 and $x = \sqrt{x}$~ holds on termination. The distinction is also of practical importance since quite different techniques are used in each case to show termination and partial correctness.

Problem 2.1   *Consider the following annotated statement S:*

$$\langle x>2 \rangle S: x:=x+3 \langle x>4 \rangle.$$

How would you go about verifying that proposition, i.e,, making sure that if x > 2 is true on entry to the statement, S terminates and x > 4 is true on the exit? (Observe that the postcondition does not involve the initial value of x.)

Your reasoning might have gone along the following lines: Termination seems obvious enough for on most systems (machines/compilers) the above assignment statement always terminates. Now, since x = x~ + 3, one concludes that the condition x~ > 1 has to be satisfied initially, if the final value of x is to be greater than 4. Since x~ > 2 (*by assumption*, owing to the precondition) then x~ > 1 follows. Consequently, the assignment x: = x + 3 is correct for (x > 2, x > 4).

The above reasoning is correct if the arithmetic of integers is assumed. Unfortunately, there is a serious, albeit subtle, flaw in the above reasoning when *finite computer arithmetic* is considered. Clearly, if x > *maxint*-3, where *maxint* is the largest integer available on the installation, the expression x + 3 is *undefined*, although the statement will terminate on most machines. Consequently, the statement S:x: = x + 3 is neither conditionally nor unconditionally correct for the specification (x > 2, x > 4). However, S is both conditionally and unconditionally correct for the specification (x > 2 ∧ x ≤ *maxint*-3, x > 4), where ∧ stands for the logical AND connective. To simplify the discussion, we will assume that all expressions encountered on a computation are defined.

However, the success of our reasoning can be attributed only to the simplicity of the "program." More complex programs require a more disciplined approach. Such an approach is offered in the next paragraph. Even if that approach is not applicable to all practical cases, it does provide a firm mathematical basis for semantic analysis of programs.

2.2 The Weakest Precondition wp(S, Q)

The following two-step approach allows one to handle the correctness problem in a more systematic way. First, ask the following question:

"What is the initial property of the input state to S guarantee that the final state meets postcondition Q?"

Second, assuming that an answer to that question has been found, ask the next question

"Is the precondition P strong enough to imply the above initial property?" If the answer is *"Yes, "* the program is correct; otherwise, it is not.

The required initial property is known as the *weakest precondition* of Q for S, denoted **wp**(S, Q). It is a predicate that specifies restrictions on the inputs under which (1) S terminates and (2) the output produced by S together with the initial state satisfies the postcondition Q. That predicate takes the *initial* state as its argument, i.e., the expression

$$\mathbf{wp}(S, Q)(s)$$

means that if the state s on entry to statement S satisfies **wp**(S, Q), S terminates and the result meets the postcondition Q. It is obvious, for example, that for our "program" $S: x := x + 3$ and the postcondition $Q(x) \Leftrightarrow x > 4$

$$\mathbf{wp}(x := x+3, x>4)(x) \Leftrightarrow x>1 \wedge x \le maxint\text{-}3.$$

Thus, every input value that violates the restriction $x > 1$ (or $x \le maxint\text{-}3$) necessarily leads to an output that does not guarantee $x > 4$. However, x can also have other properties, provided they do not contradict $x > 1$. For instance, x can be required to be even, odd, or prime; none of these properties is needed, however, to establish $x > 4$ at the exit.

If we can derive the weakest precondition, then we can use it in the verification process in a rather straightforward way. All that is needed is to establish whether the precondition is strong enough to guarantee that **wp** is satisfied. In logic, this is expressed as the following *Verification Condition* VC_S for statement S:

$$VC_S \Leftrightarrow \text{for every initial state } x, P(x) \Rightarrow \mathbf{wp}(S, Q)(s).$$

Typically, the symbolic shorthand $\langle P \rangle S \langle Q \rangle$ is used to denote VC_S. Either notation stands for the same proposition, "For every x satisfying $P(x)$, S terminates yielding a state y that meets $Q(x, y)$." Thus, either the proposition is *true* (when the program is correct) or *false* (when incorrect). Returning to our example, since $P(x) \Leftrightarrow x > 2$ and $\mathbf{wp}(S, Q)(x) \Leftrightarrow (x>1 \Rightarrow x \le maxint\text{-}3)$, the verification condition becomes

$$VC_s \Leftrightarrow (x>2 \Rightarrow x>1 \wedge x \le maxint\text{-}3)$$

for every input x (traditionally, the universal quantification over x is dropped). Obviously, the above is not true since there can be $x > 2$ and $x >$ maxint-3. Thus, the program is incorrect for (P, Q).

The qualifier "weakest" reflects the fact that **wp**(S, Q) is the *least restrictive* input condition guaranteeing that S terminates and Q is satisfied on exit from S. Thus, for any predicate P, such that S is correct for (P, Q), there is $P \Rightarrow$ **wp**(S, Q).

Example 2.1   *The following cases illustrate further the concept of the weakest precondition.*

1. **wp**(y: = sqrt(abs(x)), $y \geq 0$)(x) $\Leftrightarrow$ *true*. Clearly, the square root always returns a nonnegative result. Thus, the logical constant *true* means "the postcondition is established by any input data."
2. **wp**(y: = sqrt(x), $y \geq 0$) (x) $\Leftrightarrow x \geq 0$. If defined, the result of sqrt(x) is always nonnegative but its existence is not guaranteed; the condition $x \geq 0$ guarantees that the square root function is always defined.
3. **wp**(y: = sqrt($-$abs(x)), $y > 0$)(x) $\Leftrightarrow$ *false*. The expression sqrt($-$abs(x)) is defined only for $x = 0$, returning $y = 0$ in that case. Thus, the logical constant *false* means that "there is no data for which the segment terminates and returns a strictly positive value in y."
4. **wp**(y: = sqrt($-$abs(x)), $y \geq 0$)(x) $\Leftrightarrow x = 0$

2.3   Finding the wp(S, Q)

The weakest precondition-based verification method presented in Sect. 2.2 is general, in the sense that the verification of *every* annotated statement $\langle P \rangle S \langle Q \rangle$ can be formulated as showing the validity of $P \Rightarrow$ **wp**(S, Q). The problem, however, is how to compute **wp**(S, Q)! So far, we have been using common sense rather than any "algebra" to derive **wp**(S, Q). In what follows, we present a set of simple rules for computing **wp**(S, Q), for a restricted set of programming language constructs.

2.3.1   The Assignment Axiom

Consider the following *annotated* assignment statement to variable v

$$\langle \textbf{wp}(S, Q) \rangle \ S: v: = e \langle Q(v\sim,v) \rangle,$$

where e is an expression and v is a variable that appears free in Q. Recall that in general Q defines the expected relationships between the initial (decorated by $\sim$) and final (undecorated) value of v. Now, if $Q(v\sim, v)$ is satisfied by the final value of v, then the state on entry to S must satisfy $Q(v\sim, e)$, i.e, Q in which *every free occurrence* of v has been replaced by e. Denoting the latter as $Q(v\sim, v/e)$, there must be

$$\mathbf{wp}(v; = e, Q) \Leftrightarrow Q(v \sim, v / e).$$

The above fact is known as the *Assignment Axiom*. The axiom leads to a straightforward way to compute the weakest precondition using the following *Substitution Rule:*

To obtain $\mathbf{wp}(v: = e, Q)$, *replace every free occurrence of v in Q by the expression e.*

Observe that variables other than v that appear in Q (if any) are *not* subject to the substitution. For example, for S: $x: = x + y$ and $Q(y) \Leftrightarrow y > 0$, there is $\mathbf{wp}(S, Q) \Leftrightarrow Q$. That formally confirms the obvious fact that if nothing is done to a variable, its properties do not change.

There is one problem, however. While using the substitution rule, we implicitly assumed that the expression e is defined, i.e., it always returns a value. In fact, this might not always be the case. Therefore, the original assignment axiom has to be qualified by the statement *provided that e is defined.* That qualification is stated explicitly in the following formulation of the assignment axiom

$$\mathbf{wp}(v: = e, Q) \Leftrightarrow e \text{ is defined} \wedge Q(v\sim, v / e).$$

For example,

$$\mathbf{wp}(y: = sqrt(x + 4), y > x)(x, y) \Leftrightarrow sqrt(x + 4) > x \wedge x + 4 \geq 0.$$

For the sake of simplicity, in the above examples the postcondition Q takes a *single final state* as its argument, rather than the pair of initial and final states. For Q of the form $Q(s\sim, s)$, when the relationships between the final (s) *and* the initial ($s\sim$) state are expressed, *only the undecorated final occurrences* of the variables in Q are subject to substitutions. For example, in the statement S: $x: = x + 3$ and postcondition $x > x\sim *y - 1$,

$$\mathbf{wp}(x: = x + 3, x > x \sim *y - 1)(x\sim, y) \Leftrightarrow x + 3 > x\sim *y - 1.$$

However, at this point $x = x\sim$, since the *precondition always refers to the initial values* of the variables; thus the tilde can be dropped and one simply gets $y < 4$.

2.3.2   A Sequence of Assignments: The Composition Rule

The assignment axiom and the substitution rule can be generalized on an arbitrary sequence of assignment statements. Consider first a sequence S of two statements $S1$ and $S2$, i.e., $S = S1;S2$. To derive $\mathbf{wp}(S, Q)$, we first derive $\mathbf{wp}(S2, Q)$, which specifies the least restrictive conditions on entry to $S2$, to establish Q on exit from $S2$. Then, we treat $\mathbf{wp}(S2, Q)$ as the postcondition for $S1$. That means, our problem is solved when we find the least restrictive conditions on entry to $S1$ which guarantee that $\mathbf{wp}(S2, Q)$ is satisfied on exit from $S1$. That procedure is formalized as the following *Composition Rule:*

$$\text{For } S = S1; S2, \mathbf{wp}(S, Q) \Leftrightarrow \mathbf{wp}(S1, \mathbf{wp}(S2, Q)).$$

The composition rule suggests a generalization of the substitution rule for an assignment statement onto an arbitrary sequence of statements. Clearly, one "pushes" Q backward to the beginning of the sequence, each time substituting the expression assigned to a variable into every free occurrence of that variable in the "current" predicate at the top of the currently "visited" instruction. That process is also known as *hoisting* the postcondition.

Example 2.2   Consider the sequence S: x := x + y; y := y−x; x := 2*y + x and some undefined four-place postcondition Q(x~, y~, x,y). For the derivation of wp(S, Q), the actual definition of Q is irrelevant: We simply apply the substitution rule to every occurrence of x and y in the definition of Q along the sequence of statements. Only when we reach the beginning of the first statement do we use the actual definition of Q. This is illustrated in Fig. 2.1.

```
{wp(S, Q)}    S: x := x+y;     y := y-x;     x := 2*y+x {Q(x~, y~,x, y)}

              |                |             |
              |                |             Q(x~, y~, 2*y+x, y)
              |                |
              |                Q(x~, y~, 2*(y-x)+x, y-x)
              |
              Q(x~, y~, 2*(y-(x+y))+ x+y , y- (x+y))
                  ⇔ Q(x~, y~, y-x, -x)
                  ⇔ wp(S, Q).
```

Fig. 2.1 The derivation of wp(S,Q) by hoisting Q

Now, assume the following definition of Q:

$$Q(x\sim, y\sim, x, y) = x > y \wedge y = -x \sim \wedge x = y \sim -x\sim.$$

Substituting, respectively, $y−x$ for x and $−x$ for y, and using the fact that on entry to S, there is x = x~, y = y~, one gets

$$\mathbf{wp}(S, Q)(x, y) \Leftrightarrow y{-}x > -x \wedge -x = -x \wedge y{-}x = y{-}x$$

which simplifies to $y > 0$. Thus, if our transformations were correct, the initial value of x is irrelevant for the postcondition to hold on the exit from S. We illustrate that fact in the Sect. 2.4.

2.4 SPARK Experiments

In this section, we illustrate how the verification activities can be supported by a specialized tool. Specifically, we use the SPARK toolset from Praxis Critical Systems to carry out the verification of some examples and exercises from the previous sections. SPARK is a system for developing and analyzing high quality programs written in an annotated subset of Ada [3][1]. As in the case of VDM-SL used in Chap. 1, the use of SPARK in this Chapter and Chap. 3 is limited only to features needed to illustrate the examples involved and by *no means should be interpreted as an authoritative introduction to the tool.*

SPARK consists of the following three main parts: The Examiner, the Simplifier, and the Proof Checker. The Examiner carries out data flow and information flow analysis and also generates verification conditions. The Simplifier attempts to validate the verification conditions using *transformational proofs*, that is, equivalences in mathematics and logic, e.g., $x*1 = x$ or $(x > 0 \lor true = true)$. When the Simplifier fails to validate the verification conditions, one can use the Proof Checker, an interactive proof system to attempt a formal proof. Each verification condition generated by the Examiner is of the following form:

$$H1, H2, \ldots, Hk$$
$$\rightarrow$$
$$C1, C2, \ldots, Cn$$

where the Hi's are the *hypotheses* assumed to be true and Ci's are *conclusions* that have to be proved on the basis of the hypotheses only.

The following is SPARK code for the "program" of Problem 2.1. The statement $x := x + 3$ is repeated three times for different variables to be able to specify each variable separately, without repeating the code as three different procedures.

```
procedure Ex21(x, y, z: in out Integer) is
              -- Problem 2.1, with various specifications
  --# derives x from x & y from y & z from z;
  --# pre      y > 2 and z > 1;
  --# post     y > 4 and z > 4;
begin
   x := x + 3;
   y := y + 3;
   z := z + 3;
end Ex21;
```

Procedure Ex21 is essentially a standard Ada procedure, annotated as required by the syntax of SPARK. An annotation is introduced by the sequence --# (without the pound character #, the double hyphen introduces an Ada line comment). The first is the derives annotation, which specifies user-defined dependencies between the exported (IN OUT or OUT) and imported (IN OUT or IN) parameters of the procedure. It states that the final value of each parameter is determined by using the initial value of the same parameter. The system compares the user-declared dependencies against the actual code and reports inconsistencies, if any.[2] The second

---

[1]More information on SPARK can be found at the site http://www.sparkada.com.
[2]In Chap. 7 we introduce the Output–Input relation, a novel method for the identification of actual dependencies incurred by procedure calls.

and third annotations are the pre- and post-condition. The SPARK Examiner produces the following verification conditions for Ex21:

```
For path(s) from start to finish:
procedure_Ex21_1.    -- the _1 tag denotes the sequential
                     -- number of the VC for Ex21
  H1:  y > 2 .
  H2:  z > 1 .
  H3:  x >= integer__first .
  H4:  x <= integer__last .
  H5:  y >= integer__first .
  H6:  y <= integer__last .
  H7:  z >= integer__first .
  H8:     <= integer__last .
    ->
  C1:  y + 3 > 4 .
  C2:  z + 3 > 4 .
```

It is easy to recognize the hypotheses H1 and H2 as the constituent conjuncts of the precondition of Ex21. The remaining hypotheses restrict the values of the input variables to those accepted by the installation at hand, e.g., X can be any value between Integer'First and Integer'Last, respectively, the smallest and the largest installation-defined integers in the installation at hand. These restrictions are used to ensure that no run-time out of bounds exception exists in the code. To simplify the discussion, the range assertions will be ignored in the sequel. The conclusions are nothing but the weakest precondition of the postcondition with the use of the assignment axiom quite apparent. We know, of course, that these conclusions can be easily proved. Indeed, if the above verification conditions are processed by the Simplifier one gets the following:

```
For path(s) from start to finish:
procedure_Ex21_1.
  *** true .           /* all conclusions proved */
```

That is, the Simplifier has proved both conclusions C1 and C2, thus establishing (partial!) correctness of procedure Ex21. Consider now the following procedure Ex22:

```
procedure Ex22(x: in out Integer) is
  --# derives x from x ;
  --# pre     x > 0;
  --# post    x > 4;
begin
  x := x + 3;
end Ex22;
```

As expected, SPARK Examiner generates only the following single verification condition:

```
For path(s) from start to finish:
procedure_Ex22_1.
H1:   x > 0 .
   ->
C1:   x + 3 > 4 .
```

Now, the Simplifier transforms the above to the following form:

```
For path(s) from start to finish:
procedure_Ex22_1.
H1:   x > 0 .
   ->
C1:   x > 1 .
```

Now, we *know* that C1 cannot be proved on the basis of H1 so we would not expect the Simplifier to succeed here. Indeed, the Simplifier does fail to prove C1 but it stops short of concluding that Ex22 is in fact incorrect for its specification. It simply modestly states that it is *unable* to prove C1. Finally, we show how the sequence of statements in Example 2.2, with its inputs restricted by a precondition, is handled by SPARK. The following is the SPARK code with suitable annotations:

```
procedure Ex23(x, y: in out Integer) is
                        -- Example 2.2 with a precondition
--# derives x, y from x, y;
--# pre     x>y and y>0;
--# post    (x>y and y = - x~ and x = y~ - x~);
begin
    x := x + y;
    y := y - x;
    x := 2 * y + x;
end Ex23;
```

The Examiner generates the following verification conditions:

```
For path(s) from start to finish:
procedure_Ex23_1.
H1:   x > y .
H2:   y > 0 .
   ->
C1:   2 * (y - (x + y)) + (x + y) > y - (x + y) .
C2:   y - (x + y) = - x .
C3:   2 * (y - (x + y)) + (x + y) = y - x .
```

It is easy to see that the conclusions are simply the result of hoisting the postcondition to the beginning of the procedure. Moreover, recall from Example 2.2 that the conclusions reduce to y > 0. Since y > 0 is also a hypothesis, it should not come as a surprise that the Simplifier finds the conclusions provable. However, some say that form is the essence of art. Here is a supporting argument. If the specification of Ex23 is changed as follows (-> stands for the logical implication in the SPARK annotation language)

```
--# pre x>y;
--# post y~>0 -> (x>y and y = - x~ and x = y~ - x~)
```

then the verification condition generated by the Examiner is the following:

```
H1:  x > y .
   ->
C1:  (y > 0) -> ((2 * (y - (x + y)) + (x + y)
                    > y - (x + y))
     and (y - (x + y) = - x)
     and (2 * (y - (x + y)) + (x + y) = y - x))).
```

Now, the Simplifier is unable to prove C1, despite the fact that H1 -> C1 is indeed true, since it is equivalent to the following formula:

```
H1 and y > 0 -> the consequent of the implication C1.
```

This example illustrates the fact that the user must be creative to effectively use the tool.

2.5   Programs With Many Paths

Consider the following Ada procedure MinMax, which is claimed to compute the minimum and maximum of three reals x, y, and z, and return the results in the variables min and max, respectively:

```
procedure MinMax(x, y, z: in  Integer;
                 min, max: out Integer) is
        begin
<<L1>>    if x < y then
<<L2>>        min := x;
              max := y;
          else
<<L3>>        min := y;
              max := x;
          end if;
<<L4>>    if z < min then
<<L5>>        min:=z;
              goto L8;
          end if;
<<L6>>    if z > max then
<<L7>>        max:=z;
          end if;
<<L8>>    NULL; -- RETURN
        end MinMax;
```

The purpose of using a **goto** statement in MinMax is to illustrate the fact that even an unstructured code can be formally proved correct; to use SPARK, however, we will have to modify the code to remove the **goto** from the code. Also, we will need a formal specification of the problem Here is the specification of MinMax (the pre- and postconditions have been renamed, respectively, P and Q, for short):

$$P(x, y, z) \Leftrightarrow true,\ \text{i.e., every triple of inputs } (x, y, z) \text{ is allowed.}$$

$$Q(x, y, z, min, max) \Leftrightarrow min = \text{Minf}(x, y, z) \wedge max = \text{Maxf}(x, y, z),$$

where functions Minf and Maxf return, respectively, the minimum and maximum of any three integers. For informal reasoning, it is enough to assume that these functions are well understood. However, for a manual proof and necessarily for an automatic proof, they would have to be specified formally, e.g. ,

$$d = \text{Minf}(a, b, c) \Leftrightarrow (d = a \vee d = b \vee d = c) \wedge (d \leq a \wedge d \leq b \wedge d \leq c).$$

We already know that the program is totally correct for (P, Q), i.e., P MinMax Q is true, if and only if the verification condition

$$P \Rightarrow \mathbf{wp}(\text{MinMax}, Q)$$

is valid, i.e., *true* for every initial state. Now, how can one compute **wp**(MinMax, Q) when, unlike in the case of straight-line code, there is not one but many paths in the program? Loosely speaking, a path through a program is a sequence of executable expressions and/or statements, see Chap. 5. There are six paths through the body of MinMax, each denoted by a sequence of labels of the executed statements (the letter L has been dropped for simplicity):

$$w_1 = [1, 2, 4, 5, 8]\ w_2 = [1, 3, 4, 5, 8]\ w_3 = [1, 2, 4, 6, 8]$$

$$w_4 = [1, 3, 4, 6, 8]\ w_5 = [1, 2, 4, 6, 7, 8]\ w_6 = [1, 3, 4, 6, 7, 8].$$

The key to a solution is the observation that the program is correct if the computation along *every executable* path is correct. That leads to the following two conditions:

1. *Termination.* For every valid input, there must exist a path that is traversed for that input. For deterministic program such a path is unique.
2. *Partial correctness.* For every path, *if* traversed, the postcondition must be satisfied on termination. Note that this condition implies that every expression on the path is defined.

To address termination let $\mathbf{tr}(w_i)$ stand for the *Path Traversal* predicate of path w_i. That means that if $\mathbf{tr}(w_i)(s)$ is satisfied at the beginning of w_i for the initial state s, then w_i is traversed. Observe that for deterministic programs only one path can be taken at a time, i.e., $\mathbf{tr}(w_i)(s) \wedge \mathbf{tr}(w_j)(s) = false$, for any state s and $i \neq j$. To address partial correctness let $\mathbf{pwp}(w_i, Q)$ stand for the *Partial Weakest Precondition* of Q under w_i which, if satisfied at the beginning of w_i, guarantees that Q is satisfied at the end of w_i, provided that w_i is traversed in the first place. Thus

$$\mathbf{wp}(w_i, Q) \Leftrightarrow \mathbf{tr}(w_i) \wedge \mathbf{pwp}(w_i, Q)$$

$$\mathbf{wp}(\text{MinMax}, Q) \Leftrightarrow \mathbf{wp}(w_1, Q) \vee \mathbf{wp}(w_2, Q) \vee \dots \vee \mathbf{wp}(w_6, Q)$$
$$\Leftrightarrow \exists i \, \mathbf{wp}(w_i, Q)$$

Thus the program is totally correct for (P, Q) if the following proposition

$$P(x) \Rightarrow \exists i \cdot \mathbf{wp}(w_i, Q)(x)$$

is *true* for every initial state x. The formula suggests separate proofs of termination and conditional correctness. To ensure termination, one has to show that for every valid input there exists a path traversal condition that evaluates to *true*, i.e., to establish the validity of the following formula:

$$\exists i \cdot P(x) \Rightarrow \mathbf{tr}(w_i)(x),$$

which is equivalent to

$$P(x) \Rightarrow \mathbf{tr}(w_1)(x) \vee \mathbf{tr}(w_2)(x) \vee \dots \vee \mathbf{tr}(w_k)(x).$$

To show partial correctness, we have to show that if a path is taken then the computation on the path establishes Q, i.e.,

$$\forall i \cdot P(x) \Rightarrow (\mathbf{tr}(w_i)(x) \Rightarrow \mathbf{pwp}(w_i, Q)(x)).$$

The above is logically equivalent to

$$\forall i \cdot P(x) \wedge \mathbf{tr}(w_i)(x) \Rightarrow \mathbf{pwp}(w_i, Q)(x).$$

The last formula is referred to as the *path verification condition* for path w_i and denoted VC_i. Symbolically,

$$VC_i \Leftrightarrow \{P\} \, w_i \, \{Q\}.$$

A set of verification conditions needed to verify a program will be referred to as the Verification Schema or *Proof Outline*. If termination is included, the schema establishes a formal framework to prove total correctness; otherwise, it is a framework to show partial correctness only (Fig. 2.2).

$\{P\} \, w_1 \, \{Q\}$
$\{P\} \, w_2 \, \{Q\}$

....

$\{P\} \, w_k \, \{Q\}$ -- partial correctness

$P \Rightarrow \mathbf{tr}(w_1) \vee \mathbf{tr}(w_2) \vee \dots \vee \mathbf{tr}(w_k).$ -- termination

----

$\langle P \rangle S \langle Q \rangle$ -- conclusion: total correctness has been established.

Without termination condition only partial correctness $\{P\} \, S \, \{Q\}$ can be established.

Fig. 2.2 The verification schema for an ancyclic program with k paths.

2.6   The Derivation of Partial Weakest Precondition (pwp) and Path Traversal (tr)

To show the validity of the verification conditions, one has to derive the path verification conditions. We illustrate this on the path $w_1 = \langle 1, 2, 4, 5, 8 \rangle$ in procedure MinMax. To find $\mathbf{tr}(w_1)$, observe that **If** instruction 4, the *last* decision instruction on the path, is reached with $z < \min$ satisfied then the rest of the path, i.e., $\langle 5, 8 \rangle$, will always be traversed! Thus, the first condition (from the end of w_1!) to execute w_1 is to establish $z < \min$ when instruction 4 is reached. This ensures the transfer of control from 4 to 5. Consequently, $\mathbf{wp}(\langle 1, 2, 4 \rangle, z < \min)$ has to be satisfied at the beginning of w_1. Thus, $\mathbf{wp}(\langle 1, 2, 4 \rangle, z < \min)$ defines the least restrictive conditions at the beginning of the path that (1) guarantee the traversal of the path $\langle 1, 2, 4 \rangle$ and (2) produce a state at 4 for which $z < \min$ holds. To find $\mathbf{wp}(\langle 1, 2, 4 \rangle, z < \min)$, one can use the substitution rule for sequential composition to "push" $z < \min$ back (hoist) to the top of instruction 2, which results in $z < x$. The latter is the condition that guarantees the traversal of the path $\langle 2, 4, 5, 8 \rangle$.

Now, pushing $z < x$ back to the top of test 1 does not involve any textual substitution. However, to get to 2 from 1, the condition $x < y$ has to be met on entry to test 1. Thus, to get $\mathbf{tr}(w_1)$, $(z < x)$ has to be logically *AND*ed with $x < y$ Consequently,

$$\mathbf{tr}(w_1)(x, y, z) \Leftrightarrow (x < y) \wedge (z < x) \Leftrightarrow z < x < y.$$

The importance of the concept of the path traversal condition is due not only to its use in verification. Equally important is its role in *structural testing* (cf. Chap. 8), where it helps synthesize test data that forces a selected path to be traversed.

The derivation of the partial weakest precondition $\mathbf{pwp}(w_1, Q)$ for path w_1 is a slight modification of the procedure for sequential code. Again, Q is pushed backward from the end of the path towards its beginning. However, this time all decision instructions on the path are ignored since they do not contribute to the change of state on the path.[3] The role of the decision instructions is to select the path and that has been accounted for in the derivation of $\mathbf{tr}(w_1)$. Thus, it is *assumed* that w_1 *has* been traversed. It is easy to verify that for our example,

$$\mathbf{pwp}(w_1, Q)(x, y, z) \Leftrightarrow z = \mathrm{Minf}(x, y, z) \wedge y = \mathrm{Maxf}(x, y, z).$$

Thus one obtains the following verification condition for path w_1:

$$P \wedge \mathbf{tr}(w_1) \Rightarrow \mathbf{pwp}(w_1, Q)$$

$$\Leftrightarrow$$

$$\mathbf{true} \wedge z < x < y \Rightarrow z = \mathrm{Minf}(x, y, z) \wedge y = \mathrm{Maxf}(x, y, z).$$

---

[3] Observe that this is only true when the Boolean expression in a decision instruction does not refer to a function call with side effects.

Note that a verification condition is implicitly universally quantified over all free variables; thus for the above to be *valid* it has to be *true* for all values of x, y and z. It is easy to see that this is really the case. Therefore, one concludes that the computation along path w_1 is correct.

Problem 2.2   *Establish termination of MaxMin and validate the verification conditions VC_2 through VC_6.*

Termination is easy to establish by showing that the traversal condition for all six paths through the code are mutually exclusive and their disjunction is true, thus making sure that for an arbitrary input some path will always be taken. The partial correctness will be shown using SPARK. However, SPARK does not allow the **goto** and thus structured control has to be used, resulting in the procedure MinMax below. Please note that for simplicity the functions Minf and Maxf do not appear in the procedure explicitly but their definitions do appear there in the postcondition of the procedure MinMax below.

```
procedure MinMax(
            x, y, z:  in   Integer;
            min, max: out Integer)   is
--# derives min, max from x, y,z;
--# post (Min=x or Min = y or Min = z)
--#          and (Min <= x and Min <= y and Min <= z)
--#          and (Max  = x or   Max  = y or   Max =   z)
--#          and (Max >= x and Max >= y and Max >= z);
begin
   if x < y then
      min := x;
      max := y;
   else
      min := y;
      max := x;
   end if;
   if z < min then
      min:=z;
   else
      if z > max then
         max:=z;
      end if;
   end if;
end minmax;
```

The following are the verification conditions generated by the SPARK Examiner (the hypotheses corresponding to the variable range restrictions have been omitted):

For path(s) from start to finish:

```
procedure_minmax_1.
H1:   true .
H8:   x < y .
H9:   z < x .
->
C1:   (z = x) or ((z = y) or (z = z)) .
C2:   z <= x .
C3:   z <= y .
C4:   z <= z .
C5:   (y = x) or ((y = y) or (y = z)) .
C6:   y >= x .
C7:   y >= y .
C8:   y >= z .

procedure_minmax_2.
H1:   true .
H8:   not (x < y) .
H9:   z < y .
->
C1:   (z = x) or ((z = y) or (z = z)) .
C2:   z <= x .
C3:   z <= y .
C4:   z <= z .
C5:   (x = x) or ((x = y) or (x = z)) .
C6:   x >= x .
C7:   x >= y .
C8:   x >= z .

procedure_minmax_3.
H1:   true .
H8:   x < y .
H9:   not (z < x) .
H10:  z > y .
->
C1:   (x = x) or ((x = y) or (x = z)) .
C2:   x <= x .
C3:   x <= y .
C4:   x <= z .
C5:   (z = x) or ((z = y) or (z = z)) .
C6:   z >= x .
C7:   z >= y .
C8:   z >= z .
```

```
procedure_minmax_4.
H1:   true .
H8:   not (x < y) .
H9:   not (z < y) .
H10:  z > x .
->
C1:   (y = x) or ((y = y) or (y = z)) .
C2:   y <= x .
C3:   y <= y .
C4:   y <= z .
C5:   (z = x) or ((z = y) or (z = z)) .
C6:   z >= x .
C7:   z >= y .
C8:   z >= z .

procedure_minmax_5.
H1:   true .
H8:   x < y .
H9:   not (z < x) .
H10: not (z > y) .
->
C1:   (x = x) or ((x = y) or (x = z)) .
C2:   x <= x .
C3:   x <= y .
C4:   x <= z .
C5:   (y = x) or ((y = y) or (y = z)) .
C6:   y >= x .
C7:   y >= y .
C8:   y >= z .

procedure_minmax_6.
H1:   true .
H8:   not (x < y) .
H9:   not (z < y) .
H10: not (z > x) .
->
C1:   (y = x) or ((y = y) or (y = z)) .
C2:   y <= x .
C3:   y <= y .
C4:   y <= z .
C5:   (x = x) or ((x = y) or (x = z)) .
C6:   x >= x .
C7:   x >= y .
C8:   x >= z .
```

Observe that hypothesis H1 in each verification condition is simply the precondition, while the other hypotheses determine the traversal condition of the path involved. When submitted to the Simplifier, all the above conclusions are proved.

2.7   The Assertion Method

Path analysis *is* reliable, under the obvious assumption that one does not commit errors in reasoning. Clearly, if all the verification conditions are *true* then the program *is* correct; if one of them is *false*, it is *not*. Unfortunately, due to the difficulties of computing the weakest precondition there are serious limitations of the method, to name only two. First, acyclic programs rarely exist in nature and even if they do, it is usually not necessary to invoke the heavy machinery of program proving to verify them. Thus, the real problem is the verification of programs with loops. Unfortunately, the number of paths through an iterative program is, typically, infinite and, consequently, it is not possible to verify each path separately. Second, for a procedure call one is no longer able to apply the substitution rule to account for the call, since in general one cannot statically identify the actual path taken through the procedure. In the remainder of this chapter, we introduce the assertion method for the verification of programs without loops; the method is then extended onto programs with loops in Chap. 3.

Recall from the Introduction that an assertion *at statement S* in the program is a proposition about the properties of the state *at top* of *S*, i.e., when *S* is about to be executed. Thus, the program precondition is a start assertion, while the postcondition is an exit assertion. However, assertions can be associated with any place in the code the way comments in the program are.

The assertion method is *orthogonal* to path analysis. Rather than analyzing individual paths in the program, assertions are inserted into the code in such a way that between the assertions only *acyclic* or *simple cycles* appear (a simple cycle is a path that begins and ends at the same instruction while all other instructions on the path are distinct, see Chap. 5 for precise definitions). Consequently, path analysis can be applied to the code between assertions. In other words, a pair of assertions serves as the specification of the code between them. As an example, consider again the procedure MinMax from Sect. 2.6. There is one point in the procedure which every path must traverse, namely, statement L4. Assume that there is an assertion A_4 on entry to (top of) statement L4, which specifies the correctness of state whenever L4 is reached, *regardless* of the branch taken on the way from the start. Then the verification task can be split into two parts, resulting in the following verification schema for partial correctness (the letter L in the labels has been dropped for convenience):

$$\{P\}\ W\,(1, 4)\ \{A_4\}$$
$$\{A_4\}\ W\,(4, 8)\ \{Q\}$$
$$\text{-----------------------}$$
$$\{P\}\ S\ \{Q\}$$

In the above, $W(n, m)$ stands for the single entry–single exit code *Verification Segment* that begins at statement Ln and ends at (top of) statement Lm. According to the schema, one can establish partial correctness of the program by showing that (1) If the computation starts at statement 1 with P satisfied and L4 is reached then A_4 is ultimately *true* at L4, and (2) if the computation continues through statement L4 with A_4 satisfied on entry to L4, then Q ultimately holds on termination. Each segment can be verified independently since the intermediate assertions can be used as its pre- or post conditions. For example, assertion A_4 can serve, respectively, as the postcondition of $W(1, 4)$ and precondition of $W(4, 8)$. In verifying a segment, either path analysis or assertion method can be used. However, in the latter case, one needs additional assertions *within* the segment. It is easy to see that the role of the program segment $W(1, 4)$ from the start to L4 is to establish program state that meets the following assertion A_4

$$A_4(x, y, \min, \max) \Leftrightarrow \min = \mathrm{Minf}(x, y) \wedge \max = \mathrm{Maxf}(x, y)$$

where functions Minf and Maxf have been allowed to have a varying arity (number of arguments), as compared to their original formulation in Sect. 2. 5. Now consider the validation of the verification condition of the segment $W(4, 8)$

$$\{A_4\} \ W(4, 8) \ \{Q\}.$$

If no design assertions *within* $W(4, 8)$ are available, a path method has to be used to verify the segment. Thus, each path through $W(4, 8)$ has to be validated. This leads to three more elementary verification conditions, one for each path from instruction 4 to 8. For example, for the path <4, 5, 8>, the traversal condition is $z < \min$, while wp(<4, 5, 8>, Q) is $z = \mathrm{Minf}(x, y, z) \wedge \max = \mathrm{Maxf}(x, y, z)$. Thus, the verification condition for that path becomes

$$\min = \mathrm{Minf}(x, y) \wedge \max = \mathrm{Maxf}(x, y) \wedge (z < \min)$$
$$\Rightarrow z = \mathrm{Minf}(x, y, z) \wedge \max = \mathrm{Maxf}(x, y, z).$$

Obviously, the above proposition is valid.

Problem 2.3   *Validate the remaining elementary verification conditions of segment $W(4, 8)$ and the two conditions for $W(1, 4)$.*

The following procedure `MinMaxAssert` illustrates SPARK solution to the problem. `MinMaxAssert` is essentially equivalent to the `MinMax` procedure from Sect. 2. 5. The only difference between them is that in the former assertion A_4 has been inserted by means of the `--#assert` annotation.

```
procedure MinMaxAssert(
x, y, z:  in  Integer;
min, max: out Integer) is
--# derives min, max from x, y, z;
--# post    (Min=x   or  Min = y or  Min = z)
--#     and (Min<=x and Min <=y and Min<=z)
--#     and (Max=x   or  Max = y or  Max = z)
--#     and (Max>=x and Max>=y  and Max>=z);
begin
   if x < y then
       min := x;
       max := y;
   else
       min := y;
       max := x;
   end if;
```

```
    --# assert (Max=x or Max = y) and (Max>=x and Max>=y)
    --#     and (Min=x or Min = y) and (Min<=x and Min<=y);
    if z < min then
        min:=z;
    else
        if z > max then
            max:=z;
        end if;
    end if;
end MinMax
```

The following verification conditions are generated by the Examiner (as usually, the range hypotheses have been dropped); the references to line 29 indicate the position of the --# assert annotation in the source file.

procedure MinMaxAssert
For path(s) from start to assertion of line 29:

```
procedure_minmaxassert_1.
H1:   true .
H8:   x < y .
   ->
C1:   (y = x) or (y = y) .
C2:   y >= x .
C3:   y >= y .
C4:   (x = x) or (x = y) .
C5:   x <= x .
C6:   x <= y .

procedure_minmaxassert_2.
H1:   true .
H8:   not (x < y) .
   ->
C1:   (x = x) or (x = y) .
C2:   x >= x .
C3:   x >= y .
C4:   (y = x) or (y = y) .
C5:   y <= x .
C6:   y <= y .
```

For path(s) from assertion of line 29 to finish:
```
procedure_minmaxassert_3.
H1:   (max = x) or (max = y) .
H2:   max >= x .
H3:   max >= y .
H4:   (min = x) or (min = y) .
H5:   min <= x .
H6:   min <= y .
H7:   z < min .
   ->
```

```
C1:   (z = x) or ((z = y) or (z = z)) .
C2:   z <= x .
C3:   z <= y .
C4:   z <= z .
C5:   (max = x) or ((max = y) or (max = z)) .
C6:   max >= x .
C7:   max >= y .
C8:   max >= z .

procedure_minmaxassert_4.
H1:   (max = x) or (max = y) .
H2:   max >= x .
H3:   max >= y .
H4:   (min = x) or (min = y) .
H5:   min <= x .
H6:   min <= y .
H7:   not (z < min) .
H8:   z > max .
   ->
C1:   (min = x) or ((min = y) or (min = z)) .
C2:   min <= x .
C3:   min <= y .
C4:   min <= z .
C5:   (z = x) or ((z = y) or (z = z)) .
C6:   z >= x .
C7:   >= y .
C8:   z >= z .
```

When submitted to the Simplifier all but the following two conclusions are proved:

```
procedure_minmaxassert_5.
C1:min = x or (min = y or min = z) .
C2:max = x or (max = y or max = z) .
```

In the above, C1 is a simplified original conclusion C1, while C2 is a simplified and *renamed* original conclusion C5. Even though the Simplifier fails to prove all the conclusions, its efforts cannot be underestimated since the two unproved as yet conclusions can be easily established manually. For instance, conclusion C1 of minmaxassert_5 follows directly from the corresponding hypothesis H4.

Problem 2.4   *Modify the assertion in MinMaxAssert by replacing the first connective OR by an AND to read as follows:*

```
--# assert (Max=x AND Max = y) and (Max>=x and Max>=y)
--# and (Min=x or Min=y) and (Min<=x and Min<=y);
```

When the new verification conditions are submitted to the Simplifier, the first two verification conditions (i.e, minmaxassert_1 and _2) are not discharged, while the last three are. Explain this fact.

Recall that an assertion in the program serves as the postcondition of the first *if* statement in the program and as the precondition of the second *if*. Now, the modified assertion is stronger than the original one and, moreover, it cannot be established by the first *if*. Being stronger, however, the new assertion provides more information for the verification of the second *if*. This example illustrates the importance of the synthesis of the "right" assertion.

2.8 Conclusions

A program without loops has a *finite* number of paths and, therefore, can be verified by analyzing each path separately: if all paths are validated so is the program. It is important to note that it is not necessary for a totally correct program that *every* path through it be traversable. It is only required that for every input meeting the precondition exactly one path is taken. Some paths may never get executed, e.g., any path that needs the predicate $3 < 2$ to evaluate to *true*. Such a path is said to be *nonexecutable* (or *infeasible*), and is a real obstacle in structural program testing, as will be shown later in the text. However, the existence of an infeasible path does not invalidate partial correctness. If path w is infeasible, then $\text{tr}(w) = false$ for every input. Therefore, the path verification condition is valid since $(false \Rightarrow \mathbf{pwp}(w_i, Q))$ is vacuously *true*. This formally confirms the intuitively obvious fact that *if a path cannot be executed at all then the processing on the path is irrelevant and so by default the path is "correct. "*

However, due to the difficulties of computing the weakest precondition, there are severe limitations to the application of path analysis. Also, the sheer number of paths in the program is a powerful obstacle to the use of path analysis. In general, intermediate assertions that specify the properties of the state at certain strategically selected points in the program have to be used. In that scenario, path analysis becomes a supporting technique in the assertion-based verification.

Exercise 2.1 *Using the VDM-SL notation or a programming language of your choice, write a procedure/function which, for a statement S in the program, derives the traversal conditions for a shortest path from the beginning of the program to S.*

Exercise 2.2 *The proving method presented in this Chapter is based on the assumption that the specification of the program is declarative, i.e, it uses the pre- and postcondition. How the method can be modified to handle direct specifications as discussed in Chap. 1?*

References

1. R.C., Backhouse, Program Construction and Verification, , Prentice-Hall Upper Saddle River, NJ, 1986.
2. D. Gries, The Science of Programming, Springer-Berlin, 1982.
3. J. Barnes, High Integrity Software, The SPARK Approach to Safety and Security, Addison-Wesley, Reading, MA, 2003
4. S. King, J. Hammond, R. Chapman, A. Pryor, Is proof more cost effective than testing? *IEEE Transactions on Software Engineering*, 26(8), 675–686, 2000.

Chapter 3
How to Prove a Program Correct: Iterative Programs

Abstract The number of paths in an iterative program, i.e., one with a loop in it, is infinite. Therefore, the assertion method is the only practical verification technique here. Assertions are inserted at "cut-points" in the code to ensure that every nonempty path between two cut points is acyclic (all statements in the path are distinct) or a simple cycle (its start and end points are identical but all other statements are distinct). Such a path, say w, is a *Verification Segment* and the proposition {A} w {B}, where A and B are assertions at the start and end of w, is a *Verification Condition*. To prove a single loop program one needs only three verification conditions. The synthesis of assertions in the program is the most creative step of the verification process. In particular, for a single loop program one needs a *Loop Invariant,* an assertion based on the principles of the mathematical induction. It is shown that in some cases one can synthesize the weakest invariant, referred to as the *Goal Invariant,* from the loop specification. Proof support is illustrated by the use of Praxis' SPARK, including the Simplifier and the Proof Checker.

3.1   When You Cannot Verify All Paths: Programs with Loops

Consider the following Ada type declaration:

type My_array **is array** (Integer **range** <>) **of** Integer;

The declaration introduces an unconstrained array type My_array, i.e., one of arbitrary bounds. The Ada procedure ArraySumFor in Fig. 3.1 computes the sum of array X of the type My_array.

In the procedure ArraySumFor, X'range is an Ada *attribute* standing for the range of indices of a concrete array X, i.e., X'range is the set of integers from X'First to X'Last, or X'First .. X'Last in Ada notation.

Let P and Q stand, respectively, for the pre- and postcondition of ArraySumFor. To synthesize these, it is a good practice *to start with the postcondition and then identify the input conditions under which the postcondition is defined.* Thus, there is

```
procedure ArraySumFor(X: My_array; s: out Integer) is
begin
  s := 0;
  for k in Integer range X'range loop
  s := s + x( k );
  end loop;
end ArraySumFor;
```

Fig. 3.1 An Ada procedure for computing the sum of elements of array X

$$Q(X,s) \Leftrightarrow \sum_{j=X'\text{First}}^{j=X'\text{Last}} X(j).$$

The precondition P requires that only nonempty arrays are allowed and restrict the input accordingly by letting

$$P(X) \Leftrightarrow X'\text{last} \geq X'\text{first}.$$

Note that the above precondition would not be necessary for languages like, say, Pascal which do not allow a declaration of an "empty" array; In Ada, however, the declaration `array(1..0) of ...` is valid. From a purely structural point of view, due to the loop, there is infinite number of paths through the program. However, for a given size of the array, there is only one path that is actually traversed. Assume $X'\text{First} = 1$ and $X'\text{Last} = N$. Then the loop iterates exactly N times; the other paths, with a fewer or larger number of iterations, are nonexecutable (or "infeasible," to use a testing vernacular). Thus, in principle, one could verify the program by "unwinding" the loop, i.e., writing out that path, and applying path analysis introduced in chapter 2.

Problem 3.1 *Let N=3 and B stand for the loop body, i.e., the sequence of statements B= s := s+ X(k); k:= k + 1. Consider the following unwounded version of the body of ArraySumFor:*

```
s := 0;
k := 1;
if k<=N then
    B
    elsif k <= N then
        B
        elsif k <= N then
            B;
end if;
```

Verify the code using the path analysis technique from Chap. 2.

The path traversal condition for the path mentioned above is *true*, meaning that the path is always taken, a formal confirmation that for $N = 3$ the loop iterates exactly three times. The **pwp**(three-iterations, Q) is also *true*, thus completing the proof of total correctness for $N = 3$ (assuming, of course, the absence of an overflow). It is clear, however, that the technique becomes totally impractical for N of some size, e.g., 100. Or, even worse, for an arbitrary N in the range between 1 and N_{max}, it would be necessary to verify N_{max} paths that differ only in the number of times the loop body is iterated! Thus, to verify a loop, one needs a method that allows one to reason about a potentially infinite number of events by analyzing only a *finite number of facts*. The formal basis for such a generalization is the mathematical induction.

3.2   From the Particular to the General: Mathematical Induction

Mathematical induction is a *deduction* technique employed to prove that certain property holds for all elements in an ordered sequence of related elements $e_1, e_2, \ldots$ $e_n, \ldots$. Let P be such a property, usually referred to as the *inductive hypothesis*. Letting $P(n)$ to stand for $P(e_n)$, one wants to prove $P(n)$ for every $n, n \geq 0$. Toward that goal, it is sufficient to establish the following two facts. First, it is necessary to show that $P(1)$ is true. This is called the *base* of the induction. Second, *assuming* that $P(n)$ is true for some $n, n > 1$, it is necessary to show that $P(n+1)$ follows from $P(n)$. This is known as the *inductive step*. If both steps are successfully proved then one infers that $P(n)$ is true for all $n \geq 1$.

Problem 3.2   *Assume that one wants to prove that the sum of the first k odd numbers is k^2, i.e., that the following inductive hypothesis holds:*

$$P(k) \Leftrightarrow k^2 = \sum_{j=1}^{k} (2j-1), \text{ for } k \geq 1.$$

Prove that property by induction.

The induction starts with $k=1$. The base case is $P(1) \Leftrightarrow 1^2 = 1$, which is true. To verify the inductive step, *assume* that $P(k)$ holds and consider the next step, i.e.,

$$P(k+1) \Leftrightarrow (k+1)^2 = \sum_{j=1}^{k+1} (2j-1).$$

Now, since the sum in the above can be rewritten as

$$\sum_{j=1}^{k} (2j-1) + (2(k+1)-1) \text{ and } \sum_{j=1}^{k} (2j-1) = k^2$$

is satisfied by *assumption*, then the sum becomes k^2+2k+1, which is equal to $(k+1)^2$. Thus, $P(k)$ holds for any $k, k > 0$.

The principle of mathematical induction can be formalized as an axiom of the *second-order* logic as follows:

$$\forall p: OnePlacePredicate \bullet \forall n: N \bullet P(n) \Leftrightarrow P(0) \wedge (\forall x : N \bullet P(x) \Rightarrow P(x+1)).$$

In the above, *OnePlacePredicate* is the set of all one-argument predicates on the set of natural numbers. The variable P ranges over that set, i.e., its values are predicates. This illustrates the difference between the *first*- and second- order logic: The former allows the quantification only over sets of constants, the latter also allows quantification over predicates and functions.

3.3 Loop Invariants

How to apply the method of mathematical induction to the verification of programs with loops? Here is the general idea. Consider a **while** α **loop** B; **end loop**. Suppose we are able to show that certain property P holds on every iteration of the loop. Then, *if* the loop terminates, that property can be strengthened by the loop exit condition, i.e., on termination $\neg\alpha \wedge P$ certainly holds. What remains to be done is to check whether $\neg\alpha \wedge P$ is strong enough to guarantee that the postcondition holds too. The property that holds on every iteration is an assertion that specifies the relationships between variables in the program *at a specific point in the loop* ("cut point"). Typically (although not necessarily), the entry to the loop is chosen as the cut point. The property is referred to as a *loop invariant*; this is the inductive hypothesis ([1], [2]). As the term indicates, the property specified by the invariant is not supposed to change, i.e., it is expected to be always satisfied whenever control reaches the cut point. Observe that we say that the property "is not supposed to change," rather than it "does not change!" This is because until we *prove* that the assertion is always satisfied, the assertion remains a *candidate* for the invariant, rather than an actual one.

To apply the technique to the ArraySumFor program from Sect. 3.1, it is convenient to convert the **for** loop in it to its equivalent **while** version, as shown in Fig. 3.2. Suppose we want to synthesize a loop invariant at instruction 3 in Fig. 3.2. One may simulate the program's execution toward that goal and look for some properties that can eventually be generalized. Typically, one tries to answer the question. "What's been done so far?" Eventually, an observation can be made that at the beginning of the kth iteration of the loop, i.e., *before* the **while** statement is executed, the variables s and k are related according to the following assertion $I(X, s, k)$[1]:

$$I(X,s,k) \Leftrightarrow s = \sum_{j=X'First}^{k-1} X(j).$$

---

[1]In Sec. 3.4 we discuss a formal method for the derivation of invariants from the loop specification.

```
procedure ArraySumWh(X: My_array; s: out Integer)
--# derives s from X;
is
    k: Integer;
begin;
    k := X'First;          --1, instruction 1
    s := 0; --2
    -- Invariant I
    while k <= X'Last loop    -- 3
        s := s + x( k );       -- 4
        k := k + 1; --5
    end loop;
    -- 6 (Exit)
end ArraySumWh;
```

Fig. 3.2 A while loop version of ArraySumFor of Fig. 3.1. The *commented out numbers* stand for instruction identifiers, i.e., the smallest executable parts of statements in the program

$VC_0 \Leftrightarrow$	{PRE}	w_1 {I}	w_1=<1,2,3>	*loop initialization, the **base** of induction*
$VC_1 \Leftrightarrow$	{I}	w_2 {I}	w_2=<3,4,5,2>	*iteration, the **inductive step***
$VC_t \Leftrightarrow$	{I}	w_3 {POST}	w_3=<3,6>	***postulated** termination, **exit condition***
{PRE} ArraySumWh {POST}		*partial correctness inferred*		

Fig. 3.3 Verification Schema for the program in Fig. 3.2; invariant *I* is associated with entry to the loop

Now, the above assertion can be used as the inductive hypothesis to verify the program in Fig. 3.2, using the verification schema shown in Fig. 3.3. The verification segments are the three paths w_1, w_2 and w_3 defined in Fig. 3.3.

Fig. 3.3 illustrates the fact that to ensure partial correctness of the program, it is sufficient to establish the validity of the three verification conditions VC_0, VC_i, and VC_t. VC_0 states that if we start the program with the precondition PRE satisfied, then on the very first entry to the loop assertion I (X,s,K) is satisfied. VC_i states that *if*, on some iteration, I (X,s,K) is satisfied on entry to the loop, I (X,s,K) remains satisfied for the new state after one traversal through the body of the loop. Thus, VC_i requires that I (X,s,K) be *maintained* by every single iteration of the loop body. If there is more than one path through the body, every such path should maintain I (X,s,K). In VC_i, the inductive hypothesis *I* is used *assuming* that *I* is, indeed, an invariant. VC_t states that if *I* is true at 3 and if the exit branch is taken, then POST is satisfied. Observe that the principle of mathematical induction is involved only in VC_0 and VC_i, which establish the base step (VC_0) and the inductive step (VC_i), respectively. Only if VC_0 and VC_i are *both* valid then one can conclude that the assertion *I* is indeed an invariant in the program, holding for *every* iteration of the loop.

The choice of the invariant is crucial to the success of the method. This is illustrated by the validation of the three verification conditions VC_0, VC_i, and VC_t from Fig. 3.3. Recall that as far as partial correctness is concerned, the verification condition $VC \Leftrightarrow \{A\}\ w\ \{B\}$ is in logic equivalent to

$$(A \wedge \textbf{tr}(w)) \Rightarrow \textbf{pwp}(w, B),$$

Thus,

$$VC_0 \Leftrightarrow (N \geq 0 \wedge \textit{true}) \Rightarrow I(X, 0, 1).$$

Since

$$I(X,0,1) \Leftrightarrow 0 = \sum_{j=X'\text{first}}^{0} X(j),$$

then $I(X, 0, 1) \Leftrightarrow \textit{true}$ and VC_0 is valid; thus I holds initially. For VC_i there is

$$VC_i \Leftrightarrow I(X, s, k) \wedge \textbf{tr}(w_2) \Rightarrow \textbf{pwp}(w_2,I).$$

Applying the standard path analysis technique from Chap. 2 one gets

$$\textbf{tr}(w_2)(X, N, k) \Leftrightarrow (k \leq N)$$

and

$$\textbf{pwp}(w_2,I)(X,k,s) \Leftrightarrow I(X,s+X(k),k+1) \Leftrightarrow s+X(k) = \sum_{j=X'\text{first}}^{k+1-1} X(j).$$

Since the traversal condition $k \leq N$ guarantees that the operation $X(k)$ is defined (no out of bound errors), $I(X, s+X(k), k+1)$ is also defined and is equivalent to

$$S = \sum_{j=X'\text{first}}^{k-1} X(j),$$

which is I by *assumption*. Consequently, VC_i is valid. Thus, since VC_0 and VC_i are both valid then I is indeed an invariant in the program that can be used in the validation of VC_t.

Problem 3.3   *Validate VC_t, the loop exit verification condition.*

Let N stand for X' Last. Then there is

$$VC_t \Leftrightarrow i \wedge \textbf{tr}(w_3) \Rightarrow \textbf{pwp}(w_3,Q),$$

where

$$\textbf{tr}(w_3) \Leftrightarrow k > N.$$

Now, since there is only an empty statement between instruction 2 and the exit condition, $\textbf{pwp}(w_3, Q)$ is identical to the program's postcondition. Apparently, VC_t

is invalid, since one cannot establish $Q(X, s)$ on the basis of I and $tr(w_3)$! Clearly, it is not true that when

$$s = \sum_{j=X'\text{first}}^{k-1} X(j) \text{ and } k > N \text{ then } s = \sum_{j=x'\text{first}}^{k} x(j)$$

necessarily follows! For example, for $N = 5$, $X(k)$ is undefined for any $k > 5$ and so is the entire formula. Even if the summation were from X'first through some K smaller than X' last with $X(K)$ defined, the desired conclusion could not be proved.

Thus, since VC_t is not valid, the proof has failed. However, since it is "intuitively certain" that the program is correct, something must be wrong with the proof itself!

Problem 3.4   *Identify the reason why* VC_t *fails.*

The invariant I is *too weak* since it, together with the exit condition $k > N$, cannot guarantee that $k = N+1$ holds on termination. Although $k = N+1$ is indeed true on exit, the knowledge captured by the invariant is insufficient to establish that fact formally. There are two ways to achieve that. First, we could change the loop test as follows:

$$\textbf{while } \texttt{k } \texttt{/= } \texttt{X'Last+1 } \textbf{loop} \text{ ...,}$$

which explicitly gives rise to the exit condition $k = N+1$. This solution is somewhat inelegant since it allows $k > X'\text{Last}$, when $X(k)$ is undefined. Second, we could look for an invariant I_1 such that $I_1 \wedge k > N \Rightarrow k = N+1$. One can postulate then $I_1 \Leftrightarrow I \wedge I'$, where I' is the strengthening condition needed to imply $k = N+1$. The weakest I' for which the above is valid appears to be

$$I' \Leftrightarrow k \leq N + 1.$$

Indeed, together with the exit condition $k > N$, I' does imply $k = N+1$. However, the usefulness of this reasoning hinges on the stronger assertion I_1 being an invariant *itself*! Clearly, I_1 should validate the verification conditions VC_0 and VC_i, when I is replaced by I_1. Rather than redoing the validation from scratch, one can use the property that *the conjunction of invariants is also an invariant.*[2] Since it has already been shown that I is an invariant, it remains to be shown, therefore, that I' itself is an invariant; this is left as an exercise for the reader,

In principle, the order of validation of the verification conditions is irrelevant. However, from the pragmatic point of view, it does make sense to handle the exit condition VC_t first. Clearly, if the invariant is too weak, VC_t will fail and one saves on the effort of validation of VC_0 and VC_i, before the invariant is strengthened. This is particularly important if one observes that VC_i is usually more complex than VC_t. VC_0 should be tried second, since it is usually the least complex of all the three. If VC_0 fails, the invariant might be too strong. In such a case, one can try to weaken the invariant to have VC_0 "pass," as long as VC_t still remains valid! VC_i should be tried last.

---

[2] Naturally, this property should be proved formally.

3.4   Where Do Invariants Come From: Goal Invariant

Usually, there exist many invariants in the program. Only some of them, however, are strong enough to carry out the exit verification condition. For example, the following condition as a whole

$$k > 1 \wedge k \leq N + 1$$

and each of its component conjuncts are invariants, but each is too weak to carry out the proof on its own. On the other hand, if the invariant is too strong it may not be possible to establish it initially! Therefore, care has to be taken to formulate an invariant that is "just right." The obvious question here is: Is there a way to synthesize invariants that is more systematic than an informed guess? There is a tentative positive answer to this question, grounded in the concept of *functional correctness* [5], [6]. The key to this method is the specification of the loop on its own, *regardless of its initialization*. To illustrate the approach consider again the postcondition Q of our array summing program:

$$Q(X,s) \Leftrightarrow s = \sum_{j=x'\text{first}}^{X'\text{last}} X(j)$$

Now, consider the loop on its own, *without* the initialization of s and k. Then the final value of s is a function of X and of the initial values $s\sim$ and $k\sim$ of s and k, respectively. This leads to the following *generalized postcondition Q'*:

$$Q'(X,s\sim,k\sim,s,k) \Leftrightarrow s = s\sim + \sum_{j=k\sim}^{X'\text{last}} x(j).$$

Assume now that the loop iterates once or more, and the execution is suspended with the current values of s and k. Then, if the execution is resumed with s and k as the *fresh* values, the final value of s computed for these values must be the same as that computed for $s\sim$ and $k\sim$! This is the idea behind the *goal invariant* $I(X, s\sim, k\sim, s, k)$, defined as follow[7][3]:

$$I(x,s\sim,k\sim,s,k) \Leftrightarrow \sum_{j=k\sim}^{X'\text{last}} X(j)+s\sim = \sum_{j=k}^{X'\text{last}} X(j)+s.$$

Observe that if the loop initialization in Fig. 3.2 is taken into account one gets $k\sim = X'$first, $s\sim = 0$. Moreover, since $k > k\sim$ the above invariant is identical to the one we synthesized earlier informally:

$$I(s\sim,k\sim,s,k) \Leftrightarrow s = \sum_{j=1}^{X'\text{last}} X(j) - \sum_{j=k}^{X'\text{last}} X(j)$$

---

[3]The invariant is referred to as *loop adequate* in [6].

or

$$I(s \sim, k \sim, s, k,) \Leftrightarrow s = \sum_{j=1}^{k-1} X(j).$$

The following two properties of the goal invariant are worth noting [5], [6]. First, the goal invariant has to be satisfied by *any* loop that meets the generalized postcondition. Second, the goal invariant is the *weakest* among all invariants that can be used to verify the loop. Interestingly, the condition $k \leq= N+1$ is not part of the goal invariant and this is so for a good reason. Observe that the final value of k is not specified by the generalized postcondition Q' and, consequently, the programmer can adopt any method to manipulate the variable k *as long as the goal invariant is maintained*. Therefore, the final value of the loop control variable k depends on the actual strategy applied. To put this observation on formal grounds, observe that when the final state, that is, the one on termination, is fed again to the loop, the loop body will not be entered. That means that the final state value computed by the loop is simply a *fixed point* of the function computed by the loop. That is, if $f(\sigma)$ is the function computed by the loop for a state σ, there is $f(\sigma)=\sigma$ on termination. This is the *Termination Assertion* (TA) for the loop [7]. When applied to our array sum problem with the *final* values of s and k one gets:

$$\text{TA} \Leftrightarrow s = \sum_{j=k}^{X'\text{last}} X(j) + s \quad \text{or} \quad \text{TA} \Leftrightarrow s = \sum_{j=k}^{X'\text{last}} X(j) = 0 .$$

The above leads to the following *abstract* version of the loop:

$$\textbf{while not } \sum_{j=k}^{X'\text{last}} X(j) = 0 \textbf{ loop}$$

Maintain Invariant;

end loop;

If the invariant in question is the goal invariant then the above loop does not necessarily terminate: to guarantee termination more needs to be done than simply maintaining that invariant. Now, for a concrete implementation of the above loop

while not Done **loop**

B;

end loop;

the loop body B must maintain the invariant *and* "work" toward termination. If the loop indeed terminates, then the invariant together with the exit condition must imply the termination assertion TA, i.e.,

$$\text{Done} \wedge I \Rightarrow \text{TA}$$

must hold. In the case of our program, using the goal invariant, this becomes the following:

$$s = \sum_{j=x'\text{first}}^{k-1} X(j) \wedge \text{Done} \Leftrightarrow \sum_{j=k}^{X'\text{last}} X(j) = 0.$$

It is interesting to note that in some cases the termination assertion can be satisfied even for a final k smaller than X'Last! For example, if the precondition states that "For the first occurrence of 0 in the array, if any, all remaining entries are also 0," then the exit condition Done becomes $X(k) = 0$. For arbitrary arrays, however, the *weakest* exit condition for which the termination assertion is satisfied is of course $k = $X'last+1. Observe that even a stronger exit condition $k = $ X'Last $+ C$, where C is some nonnegative constant, is possible, as illustrated by the following loop:

```
while not (k=X'Last+20) loop
    s := s+ X(k);
    k := k+1;
    if k = X'Last then
        k :=X'Last+20 ;
    end if;
end loop;
```

3.5   Supporting the Proof: Using the Proof Checker

Consider the following Ada procedure A_sum_wh, which is an implementation of a **while** version of our array sum program:

```
procedure A_sum_Wh
        (X: My_array;
         s: out Integer )
    --# derives s from X;
    --# pre ( true );
    --# post s = Sum(X, X'First, X'Last);
is
    k: Integer;
begin
    k := X'First;
    s := 0;
    loop
        --# assert s = Sum(X, X'First, k-1);
        exit when (k = X'Last + 1);
        s := s + X(k);
        k := k + 1;
    end loop;
end A_sum_Wh;
```

In the above procedure, the weakest exit condition $k = $ X'Last $+ 1$, derived from the termination assertion introduced in Sect. 3.4, is used. The postcondition s=Sum(X, X'First, X'Last) and the invariant s=Sum(X, X'First, k-1) are

expressed in terms of a *proof function* Sum, whose signature is declared as a --#
function in the SPARK annotation language, cf. [3]:

```
--# function Sum(X : My_array;
                 L, U: Integer) return Integer;
```

The Sum function has to be specified so that it returns the sum of elements of
array *X* between L and U. However, at this point only the above signature of Sum
is known. When submitted to the Examiner, the following three verification conditions are generated (the invariant happens to be in line 43 of the source code):

For path(s) from start to assertion of line 43:
```
procedure_asumwh_1.
H1:   true.
H2:   for_all (i___1: Integer, (element(x, [i___1]) >=
             integer__first) and (element(x, [i___1]) <=
             integer__last)).
   ->
C1:   0 = sum(x, x__first, x__first - 1).
```

path(s) from assertion of line 43 to assertion of line 43:
```
procedure_asumwh_2.
H1:   s = sum(x, x__first, k - 1).
H2:   not (k = x__last + 1).
   ->
C1:   s + element(x, [k]) = sum(x, x__first, k + 1 - 1).
```

path(s) from assertion of line 43 to finish:
```
procedure_asumwh_3.
H1:   s = sum(x, x__first, k - 1).
H2:   k = x__last + 1.
   ->
C1:   s = sum(x, x__first, x__last).
```

The first verification condition (procedure_A_sum_Wh_1) is our VC_0. It involves
the initialization segment from the start of the procedure to the cut point of the
invariant (line 43 in the original source code). As expected, its conclusion is the
weakest precondition of the invariant for the initialization sequence, i.e., the invariant
pushed back to the start of the procedure. Observe that VC_0 has two hypotheses.
Hypothesis H1 is simply the precondition of the problem. Hypothesis H2 is Spark-
generated. It ensures that entries of array *X* are all within the implementation-defined
bounds Integer' First and Integer' Last, rephrased by Spark as integer__first
and integer__last, thus making them valid Ada identifiers. H2 involves the
universal quantifier ∀, expressed here as for_all. It is easy to see that
procedure_A_sum_Wh_2 and procedure_A_sum_Wh_3 are, respectively,
the iteration VC_i and termination VC_t verification conditions of our verification
schema. When submitted to the Simplifier, it succeeds in proving the termination
condition only, as shown below:

For path(s) from start to assertion of line 43:
```
procedure_asumwh_1.
H1:   for_all(i___1 : integer, element(x, [i___1]) >=
               integer__first and element(x, [i___1]) <=
               integer__last).

  ->

C1:   0 = sum(x, x__first, x__first - 1).
```

path(s) from assertion of line 43 to assertion of line 43:
```
procedure_A_sum_Wh_2.
H1:   k <> x__last + 1.

   ->

C1:   sum(x, x__first, k - 1) +
      element(x, [k]) = sum(x, x__first, k).
```

path(s) from assertion of line 43 to finish:
```
procedure_A_sum_Wh_3.
*** true .   /* all conclusions proved */
```

Remarkably, the Simplifier proves the termination verification assertion even if it *knows nothing* about the actual definition of the function sum! This is because the Simplifier is smart enough to use H2 to transform H1 into a form that is identical to C1, *regardless* of the definition of Sum. The Simplifier is not smart enough, however, to prove the first two verification conditions. Here is where the (proof) Checker offers its helping hand. Recall from Chap. 2 that the Simplifier uses the transformation proof strategy, that is, it tries to convert the expressions that appear in the verification conditions to an equivalent, yet simpler form. For example, $x*1+0$ may be reduced to x; a Boolean expression $p \wedge true$ may be reduced to p. In contrast, the Checker also uses *deductive proofs*, i.e., ones which allow one to infer some facts from the existing ones. There is a quite rich family of *inference rules* that can be used in proofs. For example, if we know that the implication $A \Rightarrow B$ is true and that its antecedent A is also true then we conclude that B must be true.[4]

Unlike the Simplifier, however, the Checker has to be guided to select the inference rules. Moreover, it needs some knowledge about the proof functions used. In our case there is only one such function, sum. Since the Checker uses Prolog pattern matching technique, the following "natural" specification of sum

$$sum(A, I, J) = \sum_{k=1}^{k=j} X(k)$$

cannot be directly used. Instead, some "rewriting rules" for sum have to be provided to the Checker. For example, the following three rules provide a recursive definition of sum:

```
sum(1): sum(A, I, J) may_be_replaced_by 0 if [I>J].
sum(2): sum(A, I, I) may_be_replaced_by element(A,[I]).
sum(3): sum(A, I, J) may_be_replaced_by sum(A,I,J-1)
                    + element(A,[J]) if [I<J].
```

---

[4] This is the rule of *abduction* or *Modus Ponens*.

In fact, the rule sum(3) may also be allowed for $I = J$. Indeed, in such a case sum (A, I, J-1) = 0 by rule sum(1). The Checker can be directed to use these rules to prove the remaining verification conditions. For example, by selecting the first verification condition procedure_A_sum_Wh_1 and typing the following command

> replace c#1: **sum**(A, B, C) by 0 using **sum**.

the verification condition is proved. In the above command A, B, and C are Prolog variables that are used by the Checker to match the pattern with a rule in the data base for the proof function sum. As it happens, it is the rule sum(1) that matches the pattern. The replacement leads to the condition 0 = 0 which is then easily discharged. Thus, only the iteration verification condition procedure_A_sum_Wh_2 is left to be proved. Apparently, proving it requires more than a casual acquaintance with the Checker. However, consider the following stronger invariant for the loop:

```
--# assert s= Sum(X, X'First, k-1) and
--#            k>=X'First and
--#            k<=X'Last+1;
```

This invariant has to be used anyway if the exit condition k=X'Last+1 is not replaced by k $\leq$ X'Last+1. This is because the traversal condition for the iteration is k <> x__last + 1 and thus allows k>x__last+1, making $X(k)$ undefined! Now, with the new invariant the proof of procedure_A_sum_Wh_2 becomes quite easy. The following is the new iteration verification condition generated by the Examiner:

```
procedure_A_sum_Wh_2.
H1:   s = sum(x, x__first, k - 1).
H2:   k >= x__first.
H3:   k <= x__last + 1.
H4:   not (k = x__last + 1).
   ->
C1:   s + element(x, [k]) = sum(x, x__first, k + 1 - 1).
C2:   k + 1 >= x__first.
C3:   k + 1 <= x__last + 1.
```

The Simplifier transforms the above to the following:

```
procedure_A_sum_Wh_2.
H1:   k >= x__first.
H2:   k < x__last + 1.
   ->
C1:   sum(x, x__first, k - 1) + element(x, [k]) =
          sum(x, x__first, k).
```

Now, to rewrite C1 using the rule sum(3) we have to allow it for $I \leq J$, rather than only for $I < J$. Only then will the rule be directly applied using the hypothesis H1. Otherwise we would have to guide the Checker to establish k>x__first before using sum(3). Then the proof starts with the following Checker command:

> **rep** c#1: **sum**(A, B, C) by D using **sum**(3),

which tells the Checker to replace sum(A, B, C) in conclusion C1 by anything allowed by sum(3). The Checker finds two possible subexpressions in C1 that can be replaced: sum(x, x__first, k - 1) and sum(x, x__first, k). By selecting the latter C1 is immediately proved. Unfortunately, the new invariant being stronger than the goal invariant makes the proof of the *initialization* more difficult, as predicted earlier in the text.

The above admittedly very simple example suggests that the ideal of "automatic" proof is rather hard to achieve. It seems that to use a Checker in an effective way the prover has to have some general ideas about how the proof is to proceed. The success of the proof depends on the prover's ability to derive consistent set of rewriting rules (as, for example, for the sum function) and design an effective proof strategy. In such a scenario, a proof supporting tool provides the user with a sense of high confidence. Of course, this applies only to the case of a *successful* proof. Indeed, as illustrated by our discussion, a proof failure is not necessarily indicative of the program's incorrectness.

The above facts are not too encouraging for one can claim that, if a great amount of user involvement is needed, the proof can be completed without a costly and generally difficult to use supporting tool. Certainly, such a claim may well be justified for new programming problems where no previous experience is available. This is not the case, however, for a class of related problems involving the same or similar domain of discourse. There, the accumulated experience can be captured by the rule data base for the domain. In that way, a new project can partially benefit from the use of a proof supporting tool.

3.6 Does the Loop Terminate? Variants

Note that so far only partial correctness of our loop has been shown. To prove its total correctness termination has to be established. Intuitively, a counted loop always terminates, unless an undefined operation within the loop is encountered. For a general loop, however, a separate procedure for establishing termination is necessary.

Problem 3.5 *Consider the following two simple loop programs A and B and decide whether they terminate for any positive integer x:*

```
A: x:=0;
     while x >= 0 loop
        x:=x+1;
     end loop;

B: get(x);
     while x <> 1 loop
        if even(x) then
           x := x div 2;
        else
           x := 3 * x + 1
        end if;
     end loop;
```

In the case of loop A both intuition and a rigorous mathematical analysis, lead to the conclusion that the loop does not terminate. An experiment on a typical computer reveals, however, that it does, with the final value of x equal to $-$(Integer 'Last $+1$), where Integer'Last is the maximal integer that can be represented by the machine word. Why is it so? Simply, for a typical two's complement machine representation of integers, when the variable x reaches the value of Integer'Last, the next addition of 1 to *Integer'Last* does not result in *Integer'Last*$+1$ but in $-$ (*Integer'Last*$+1$)! This illustrates the difference between the arithmetic of integer numbers and that of programming language-supported integers. In the latter case, the operation *Integer'Last*$+1$ is simply undefined. The implementation, however, may provide a "default" definition of that operation or the program involved may be aborted.

Loop B generates a sequence of numbers (assigned to the variable x) that is known as the *Ulam sequence*[5]. The claim that for any initial positive x the sequence eventually ends with $x = 1$ is known as *Ulam's conjecture*. To the best of the Author's knowledge, no case of nontermintaion has yet been found albeit there is no known proof of that property. Unfortunately, unlike the case of acyclic programs, one cannot prove termination by showing that some path will always be executed. Rather, one has to show that for any valid input the number of iterations is always finite. A relevant technique involves the notion of a *well-founded* set, i.e., an ordered set with a smallest element in it. A function, associated with the cut point, is defined on that set. Such a function is known as a *variant* to indicate that, unlike the invariant, it describes properties that *do change* at each iteration. It is required that the variant function monotonically decrease with iterations of the loop. Since the function cannot return values smaller than the smallest element in the well-founded set, the number of iterations must be finite.

3.7 Conclusions

Recall from Chap. 2 that the path analysis method for program proving is reliable: If all paths through the program are correct so is the entire program, otherwise it is surely incorrect. In contrast, the assertion method is not reliable and this is not only due to the natural fallibility of human reasoning. Clearly, other things being equal, the success of the assertion method depends on the *assertions correctly mirroring design decisions*. Again, if the proof succeeds then the program is correct. However, if the proof fails, one cannot claim that the program is incorrect! This is because the assertions might have been chosen improperly, while the program is actually correct. It is then obvious that the synthesis of assertions is the most creative step in the proof. However, that task is aggravated by the fact that there can be several designs of the same program, as illustrated in the Introduction.

---

[5] Stanislaw Ulam, the Polish mathematician (1909–1984). Among purely mathematical achievements (e.g., the Monte Carlo method), he significantly contributed to the development of the H-bomb while working in the US.

Moreover, even if the assertions are correct, the difficulties in carrying out the proof might be too big an obstacle to use the technique in every day programming. If carried out by hand, proofs tend to be even *more* cumbersome as programming itself. Proof supporting tools are a great help but they are few and far between and mastering them requires highly specialized skills. Does this mean that program proving should be viewed as an interesting yet impractical activity? Far from it. Since program proving is the only reliable technique to show the program's correctness, it should be used whenever correctness is of utmost importance, as in *safety-critical systems*. Fortunately, not all programs need to be that perfect. Moreover, even in the case of safety critical systems usually a relatively small part of the code is responsible for its reliability, thus making the formal proof an economically feasible task. Having said that, it does not mean that formal verification should not be used for less critical software. It is useful to at least attempt a formal proof for noncritical programs by deriving the verification conditions and synthesizing the assertions involved, even if that effort is only partially successful. The rewards are significant: A better understanding of the program and an improved documentation. Also, the difficulty in proving some verification segments *might mean* that the segment is incorrect. Indeed, a recent study indicates that failed proving is superior to testing in fault detection [4].

Most promising, however, seems to be the prospect of moving the verification effort up toward earlier stages of software development. Essentially this would involve the verification of high-level design thus helping detect the most expensive early-stage faults. And again, it appears that verification of abstract models, is superior to unit testing and code proving [4]. This should not come as a surprise since, as demonstrated in Chap. 1, it is easier to reason in terms of the user-defined abstract data types than in terms of concrete types of a programming language.

Exercise 3.1 *Derive the goal invariant, the termination assertion and synthesize the exit condition for the following "downto" while loop:*

```
k := X'Last;
s :=0;
loop
    -- Invariant I
    exit when ??? ;
    s := s + x( k );
    k := k - 1;
end loop;
```

Exercise 3.2 *Derive the Verification Schema for (1) a nested while loop and (2) for a program with a procedure call. Identify the cut points where assertions will have to be inserted.*

References

1. R. C. Backhouse, Program Construction and Verification, Prentice-Hall, Upper Saddle River, NJ, 1986.
2. D. Gries, The Science of Programming, Springer-Berlin, 1982.
3. J. Barnes, High Integrity Software, The SPARK Approach to Safety and Security, Addison-Wesley, Reading, MA, 2003.
4. S. King, J. Hammond, R. Chapman, A. Pryor, Is proof more cost-effective than testing? IEEE Transactions on Software Engineering, 26(8), 675–686, 2000.
5. H. Mills, The new math of computer programming, Communications of the ACM, 18(1), 43–48, 1975.
6. D. D. Dunlop and V. Basili, A comparative analysis of functional correctness, Computing Surveys, 14(2), 229–244, 1982.
7. J. Laski, An approach to loop programs debugging, SIGPLAN Notices, 14(1), 27–36, 1982.

Chapter 4
Prepare Test for Any Implementation: Black-Box Testing

Abstract Program testing is a run-time experiment whose *main* objective is the *detection* of faults in the program. A Black-Box (BB) test is synthesized using the specification of the program and thus is applicable to *any implementation* of the programming problem involved. So understood, the derivation (as opposed to the actual execution) of a BB-test falls into the realm of reasoning about the programming problem at hand, rather than into dynamic analysis proper. We show that every component of the declarative specification can be used in the test synthesis (the operational specification is actually an abstract program that can be tested according to the rules of structural testing, discussed at length in Chap. 8). These components give rise to the functionality and the partition testing. BB-testing is quite often the most powerful fault detecting technique: Unlike structural, code-based testing, BB-test can uncover flaws in the specification. Moreover, as is later demonstrated in Chap. 8, BB-testing is the ONLY practical testing method: Structural testing can only serve as a measure of adequacy of BB-testing. Thus we argue that in an ideal scenario (1) a BB-test should be prepared before an implementation of the problem is undertaken, rather than as an afterward activity, (2) BB-test should be synthesized in terms of User-Defined or Abstract Data Types pertinent to the problem at hand, and (3) random testing is infeasible in the absence of automatic "test oracle," such as the operational interpretable model of the problem.

4.1 Testing Principles

In the preceding chapters, we have demonstrated that the formal top-down design paradigm, in which the program and its proof are developed hand-in-hand is, perhaps, the ultimate approach to the development of correct software. Under ideal circumstances, the method is *supposed* to yield programs that are *correct by construction*, thus rendering testing obsolete. Unfortunately, in the imperfect world, there are problems with that method, too.

First, formal verification techniques involve *assertions* about the intended behavior of the program at some selected internal points. These, however, are usually difficult to derive. Second, the inevitable flaws in human reasoning might lead to flawed

J. Laski and W. Stanley, *Software Verification and Analysis*,
DOI: 10.1007/978-1-84882-240-5_5, © Springer-Verlag London Limited 2009

conclusions. Third, some assumptions about the primitives used (e.g., library or user-defined procedures) in the proofs, might be false. Therefore, the process becomes only partially reliable, leading to programs that are "almost" correct. Consequently, there might exist "subtle" faults detectable only by testing. Ironically, the detection of those faults appears much harder than those in programs developed by the traditional methods. Indeed, in the latter case program failures are *the* norm; in the former, one has to be quite imaginative and, let us admit it, somewhat lucky, to synthesize a test on which the program fails. One can safely claim, therefore, that testing will always be with us, as an inescapable and legitimate part of the design process and that, paradoxically, the difficulty of fault detection is inversely proportional to the progress in software design technology. The objective of testing is the opposite to that of proving, however: It is to *show incorrectness*, rather than correctness, of the program! In other words, when a test "passes" it simply *fails* to detect an error. Observe, however, that when a considerable number of tests fail that way, our confidence in the program does increase, even if its correctness cannot be guaranteed.

The essential problems in testing is the synthesis of the test suite. Ideally, the *test suite* is a *finite* set of *test cases*; a test case is a pair (Input, Expected-Output). However, in practice, it may be rather hard to find the expected, correct output even if a formal specification is available. For example, if one tests a sorting procedure it is very tedious and error prone to find by hand the sorted version of a large array. It is obvious then that this *test evaluation* must be automated. It appears that there are (at least) two possibilities here. First, assume the program under test (PUA) is a modified version, say more efficient, of an already existing and *trusted* implementation of the problem at hand. Then the old version can be run together with the new version and the results are compared. Second, an automatic *test oracle* can be implemented that can pass judgment on the results without necessarily being capable of producing them. For example, it is much cheaper to write a program that simply checks whether an output array is sorted than to actually produce a correct sorted array value.

In the literature on the subject, it is often postulated that the test suite have a great error detecting potential and its size do not exceed an economically acceptable level. Observe that the first postulate is, of course, one of those well-*undefined* wish concepts in software engineering. Without a sound model of programming faults and errors it has no meaning. The size of the test suite is essential albeit *not* because of the machine time needed to run the suite. It is because of the human intensive effort of test evaluation.

In general, test selection is inspired either by the specification (Black-Box testing) or by the implementation (White-Box or structural testing) according to some *testing strategy*. Of course, there are situations when tests are simply selected because it is relatively easy to evaluate the correctness of the results. In the remainder of this chapter, only Black-Box testing is discussed; Structural testing is dealt with in Chap. 8.

In Black-Box testing (*BB-testing*, for short), also referred to as *behavioral* or *functional testing*, tests are selected on the basis of the requirements or their formalized version, the specification. In the former case, BB-testing is obviously not well defined, in the sense that it is nonsystematic, i.e., there are no well-defined requirements for the tests[1]:

---

[1] In contrast, structural testing is systematic but cannot be carried out on its own, see Chap. 8.

Intuition, experience, a good understanding of the problem and of the possible solutions to it, all come into play. In the latter case, formal specification of the problem offers a *possibility* of a systematic synthesis of a BB-test. We say "a possibility" for not only formal methods are not widely used in practice but also their very promise, the deliverance from evil, makes research into testing something bordering on the heretical. Thus, the synthesis of a Black-Box test does not easily lend itself to automation. This is a serious drawback because the role of Black-Box testing cannot be overestimated, to consider only some of its most important advantages:

BB-testing appears in almost all stages of software development. To illustrate this, assume that program P is the sequential composition of two units Q and R, i.e., $P = Q; R$. Ideally, P and Q have their own specifications say, $\{pre\}Q\{A\}$ and $\{A\}R\{post\}$ where pre and post are the pre- and postcondition of P. Certainly, the main beauty of the independent specification of Q and R is the fact they may be developed independently. Now, even if the correctness of the design (understood as the correctness of combining just the specifications of Q and R) can be proved formally, Q and R can be verified through their independent testing (see Sect. 4.6).

BB-testing provides a means to check not only the implementation (i.e., the code) but also the specification itself. Indeed, as shown in Chap. 1, testing an assertion can reveal whether the assertion faithfully captures the requirements. This is especially important when the implementation "misses" some parts of the specification.

It is relatively easy to synthesize and apply *some* BB-test. As shown later in Chap. 8, it is virtually impossible to apply structural testing on its own. In contrast, it is relatively easy to synthesize some requirement-based test, however, imperfect. The structural code coverage induced by the BB-test can be then treated as a proxy measure of its reliability.

BB-testing quite often exhibits the best fault-detecting potential. Experience reports seem to indicate that many "subtle," hard to detect faults, are detected more often by a "judicial" BB-test than by a structural test.

We offer two, admittedly unorthodox, reasons for the superiority of BB-testing. First, the intellectual underpinning of BB-testing has nothing to do with testing proper as a run-time experiment. Indeed, it is a particular *semantic* analysis of the requirements or its specification. Its objective is to select a set of pairs (X,Y) such that (1) X satisfies the program precondition, X and Y together satisfy the postcondition, and (2) there is a reasonable expectation that, for the input X, the implementation may return a value Y', $Y' \neq Y$, that violates the postcondition. It is obvious that the success of this task is directly dependent on the understanding of the problem and of its possible implementations which, in turn, make it easier to identify the hardest parts of the problem at hand that are most likely to be incorrectly solved. Second, structural (white-box) testing is sort of a myth. In Chap. 8, we demonstrate that at the current state of the art, owing to the difficulties in the synthesis of tests, structural testing can be used only as an indirect way of checking the completeness of BB-testing rather than as a stand-alone activity. Therefore, for all intents and purposes, successful tests (i.e., ones that reveal the fault) are really BB-tests.

Recall from Chap. 1 that the goal of testing an assertion is to check whether it correctly represents the concept it is supposed to. If the tests reveal that the current formulation of the assertion is "not what we want" then the assertion has to be modified. That objective is also valid for the BB-test. Let us refer to this as the *specification testing*. The other objective is to detect faults in the implementation (that is, the program), under the assumption that the specification *is* correct. Ideally, specification testing should be completed *prior* to code development. In practice, however, more subtle errors in the specification may be detected during code testing. Indeed, it may well be that the program is correct for the wrong specification! As stated earlier, at the current state of the art there are neither hard rules how to go about the synthesis of a BB-test in general nor how to meet the two objectives of specification and implementation testing. Thus, rules of thumb and intuition have to be used in the process, hoping that in reality the test will catch *most* of the bugs. Nevertheless, the use of formal specification does make easier to synthesize some tests, even if it is not known what faults, if any, will be detected by those tests. Toward that goal, either the program input space, the output space, or both can be used to derive a BB-test. In the case of *input (domain) test,* one selects valid inputs (according to the strategy at hand) and finds for them the correct (expected) results. For the *output (range) test*, one selects a set of valid outputs and finds valid inputs that produce those outputs. The synthesis of an output test is, generally, more difficult than that of an input test because the output values involved have to be mapped back to find the corresponding inputs. It has to be made clear that any test case ultimately involves an input and an output; the concept of input/output test refers to the way the tests are synthesized, rather than how they are applied.

Black-box strategies differ in the way the specification is used to generate test data. Following the discussion in Chap. 1, we assume that the specification, whether formal or narrative, provides the following pieces of information:

Functionality (signature) of the problem. By this we mean the pair (X,Y) where X and Y are, respectively, the sets of possibly overlapping input and output variables of the program.

Precondition, i.e., restrictions on the initial values of the input variables in X before execution of the program.

Postcondition, i.e., the postulated relationships between, respectively, the initial values of the input variables in X and the final values of the output variables in Y.

One can employ these either separately or in some combination, to synthesize the BB-test. The objective of *functionality* (or *signature*) testing is to check the behavior of the program on data that characterizes the program domain and range *regardless of the actual processing*. That is, that kind of test will be the same for any program that accepts same type of inputs and produces same type of outputs. It follows then that functionality testing can be partially automated by cataloging some typical values in the domain, which can be used to test any program of the same signature, regardless of the actual processing. Although functionality testing is quite effective in detecting programming faults that are problem- independent (e.g., division by 0 or referencing out-of-bounds arrays) it fails to address problem-dependent faults.

The pre- and postcondition give rise to *Partition Testing*. In it, the domain (or, less likely, output range) of the program is partitioned into classes whose members are believed to be processed in the same way by a hypothetical implementation; "representatives" of those classes are then selected as elementary tests.[2] An input (domain) partition test uses information about the program's domain to identify *input classes*, which group elements that satisfy some relationships between valid inputs. The goal of testing here is to check whether the program correctly identifies and processes the classes; the postcondition serves only as a correctness criterion. The program postcondition can be used to synthesize an output (range) test by identifying *output classes*, which group elements that meet some relationships between valid outputs and valid inputs. To find a relevant test, however, each output class has to be mapped back onto the program domain as a class whose elements, when processed by the program, produce results that fall into the class. Thus, output classes can be used as a refinement of the input classes.

Of all these three kinds of tests, only input classes test guarantees that all its elements "make sense," i.e., the input is always valid; after all, that test is derived on the basis of the precondition itself. In contrast, the functionality and range partition test might contain elements that are either *invalid* or infeasible. A test is invalid if it violates the program precondition. For example, the value 0 might be prescribed by the functionality test but it becomes invalid if excluded by the precondition. Similarly, some outputs can be produced only by invalid inputs. Our natural inclination would be to discard those inputs. However, some of those inputs could be run as a *stress test*, which checks the program's reaction to invalid data and its potential ability to generate invalid output. In the case of invalid data, one gets some idea about the way the program fails; and if there is a fault in the program, infeasible outputs might actually occur.

In the following sections, some strategies for the synthesis of BB-test are discussed. Although the discussion does assume the availability of formal specification, the methods are useful even when only partial formalization of the specification is available.

4.2 Functionality Testing

Functionality or *signature* test is applicable to any program of the same signature, that is, one with the same number of input and output objects of the same type. It is evident that the information on whose basis the test data are derived is rather limited. It is the types of objects and their number, regardless of the way they are used (input objects) or generated (output objects). This limitation is partially offset by the functionality test being amenable to automation since, for most data types in the programming language at hand, a standard functionality test can be synthesized and stored for general use.

---

[2] In reality every testing strategy, including structural testing, involves some domain partitioning.

4.2.1   Special Values

It has been observed that many errors in programs are caused by improper handling of such values as 0 and 1 for numerical domains, logical values *true* and *false* for Boolean domains, empty string for sequence, zero and unitary matrices for two-dimensional arrays, and so on. It is recommended, therefore, that these "special values" be supplied to the program input, whenever applicable; hence the name of the strategy, "special values" testing. It is not required that these values explicitly appear in the specification: It is believed that the program, being an implementation of the specification, might actually react to them in a way that might be symptomatic of a fault. It is equally possible that the specification itself is either incomplete or inconsistent for those values (we use those terms in a rather loose fashion here).

It is also recommended that a special value test be derived for the output of the program. The underlying justification here is this: Under what circumstances does the program produce special values? Still another generalization of this approach is possible. If some parameters appear in the intermediate concepts in the specification, tests should be supplied to force those parameters to assume "their" special values. As expected, the synthesis of the output and the intermediate special values tests is, generally, more difficult than that of an input test. In the realm of informal programming there is no clear concept of what makes a value "special." In fact, however, they can be given a solid mathematical definition. One class of special values are the identities or zeros of certain algebras on the domain of interest. For the purpose of this discussion, an algebra is understood as some set, the *carrier* of the algebra, and a binary operation * on the carrier. A distinguished element **1** of the carrier is an *identity* for * iff **1** $*x = x$, for every x in the carrier. For example, the number 0 is the identity for the addition operation + on numerical domains. A distinguished element **0** of the carrier is a zero for * iff 0 $*x = 0$, for every x in the carrier. For example, 0 is the zero for the multiplication operation *.

Figure 4.1 shows special values for some typical algebras. Observe that the operation * is not necessarily commutative,[3] i.e., $x *y = y *x$ does not always hold as is, for example, in the case of the division or exponentiation operations. In such a case, the concept of the *left* (L) or *right* (R) identity (or zero), if only defined for the algebra, is used.

4.2.2   Fixed Points

Observe that binary operators are two-argument functions on the carrier with the result also in the carrier; special values are unique *constants* in the carrier. A class of special values that are not necessarily unique or even constants, are fixed points, a concept relevant to functions. Let f be a function, either user-defined or intrinsic. An element x is a *fixed point* of f, if $f(x)=x$. For example, 0 and 1 are fixed points

---

[3]The infix notation is assumed here, although those concepts can be generalized for other notations, too.

TYPE	OPERATION	IDENTITY	ZERO
integer/real	+	0	undefined
integer/real	*	1	0
integer/real	/	1 (R)	0 (L)
Boolean	AND	true	false
Boolean	OR	false	true
String	concatenation	empty string	undefined
Set	∩	∅	universal set
Set	∪	universal set	∅

Fig. 4.1 Special values for some data types

for the √ (square root) function. In general, the number of fixed points can be infinite, e.g., for the following sorting function

$$sort: \texttt{Array} \ \texttt{->} \ \texttt{Array}$$

that for an array argument returns a sorted version of the array, any already sorted array is a fixed point of *sort*. If the number of fixed points is small, all of them should be included in the functionality test; otherwise, they should be used to define "special classes" introduced in Sect. 4.2.3.

4.2.3 Special Classes

A *Special Class* of the domain contains elements that are distinguished by their importance for some theories in the domain. For example, the even, odd, positive, negative, and prime numbers are special classes in numerical domain; bipartite and acyclic graphs are classes of the set of all directed graphs. Special values returned by some functions defined on the domain may be used to identify a class, e.g., classes of strings of length 1 and 0. If it is plausible that the class property (e.g., that the numbers are prime) can have some impact on the computation, a representative of the class should be selected for the test.

4.2.4 Boundary Analysis

If a variable ranges over some finite ordered set, it is reasonable to expect programmers to make errors when manipulating elements lying on or close to the set boundaries. Those boundary values should be included in the test. There are two possible sources of boundary conditions namely, the restrictions on data in the specification and the restrictions imposed by the implementation. The following comments might be useful in defining a functionality strategy in practice:

(a) Assume that there are k objects $o_1, o_2, \dots, o_k$ (variables, functions, operators) and that the object o_i has n_i special or fixed values. Then there are $n_1 \times n_2 \times \dots \times n_k$ combinations of special values. This combinatorial explosion calls for a practical approach to reduce the number of tests. One way of achieving this is to require that each value appear only once in the test. Observe, however, that the logical structure of the specification may render some combinations invalid; therefore, the number of valid combinations of special values might still be manageable. It is strongly recommended that such combinations be included in the test for their fault-detecting power is much greater than that of their individual components.

(b) Intrinsics and user-defined functions should be analyzed for the existence of zeros, identities, and fixed points. This should include the domain of the function (input arguments) and its range (result) as well.

(c) For structured types (e.g., arrays) usually no meaningful special values can be defined at the concrete, programming language level. Nevertheless, the special values 0 and 1 of the *size* of arrays can be considered, perhaps requiring recompilation, if the language does not support dynamic arrays. Similarly, empty linked lists, lists of length 1, empty and singleton trees should be considered.

(d) One should not restrict one's interest to the concrete, language-supported types. As concrete types are often used to *represent* Abstract Data Types (ADT), it is recommended to look for special "things" at the abstract, rather than concrete, level. For example, a unary matrix as the identity for matrix multiplication, is easily identified at the abstract level but hard to justify at the representation, array level. There is evidence that the abstract approach leads to much more powerful tests than the concrete one.

4.3   Partition Testing

In partition testing, the program domain is divided into classes and "representatives" of each class are selected as elementary tests. It is hypothesized or, more correctly, hoped for, that all elements in a class are processed by the program in the same way with respect to the postulated fault, i.e., the program is either correct or incorrect over the entire class, Thus, elements in the partitioning are expected to have the same "error detecting potential" in the sense that all of them detect an error or none of them does. That premise is based upon the belief that there is no reason for a "typical" solution to the problem to process the elements in the class in different ways. If there is such a reason, however, then the class should be further refined. Naturally, such a premise is of purely heuristic nature and by no means does it guarantee that the partitioning will be valid for arbitrary faults. If, however, the premise is true then one deals with a *fault-induced equivalence partitioning*. Now, recall (from, say, your favored course on Discrete Mathematics) that a *partitioning* (or *stratification*) of set *S* is a family $\{S_1, S_2, \ldots, S_n\}$ of *nonempty* sets S_i referred to as *classes* (or *strata*), $i=1, \ldots, n$, such that: cf[5]

1. Every S_i is a subset of *S*
2. The union of the classes is *S*
3. The classes are mutually disjoint, i.e., for every $i, j, i \neq j$, the intersection $S_i \cap S_j$ is an empty set

The synthesis of test cases for a partition test consists of two stages:

1. The identification of the classes
2. The selection of test cases that *cover*, or *represent*, the classes

To identify the equivalence classes one can follow the following rules [4], (pp. 46–47):

> *"take each input condition (usually a sentence or phrase in the [narrative] specification) and partition it into two or more groups. If there is any reason to believe that elements in an equivalence class are not handled in an identical manner by the program, split the class."*

Although intuitively sound, the above process is hardly clear or systematic. Moreover, it appears to have been defined only for program input. However, classes can be defined for the output range, too, although in that case the underlying premise is that elements in an output class are all correct or incorrect being the results for inputs coming from, perhaps different, input classes. In practice, the output approach is less attractive because of the difficulties of finding the corresponding inputs.

The partitioning is defined according to a single criterion. In practice, several criteria may be used giving rise to a family of partitions that, in the basic scenario, are treated independently. The intersection of partitions is also a partition. Combining classes induced by different criteria leads to a more powerful testing strategy but may result in an unacceptably large number of tests. To obtain an economically acceptable test suite, tests can be selected that cover several partitioning criteria. However, more than one test might be selected from a class if partition testing is combined with other strategies. For example, if partition test is also to meet the requirements of boundary analysis, test points lying on and around the class borders will have to be selected.

4.4   An Example

Most interesting programming problems are specified in abstract, rather than language-supported concrete data types. The reason for this is quite obvious: To express the problem in terms of say, arrays, records, and pointers is a recipe for a guaranteed failure. The problem is best understood if expressed in terms of ADTs aka User-Defined Types, applicable to *any* implementation of the problem. This means that the BB-test must not make assumptions about either of the two main aspects of any solution to the problem at hand. The actual algorithm and the data representation used model the

ADTs used in the specification. To illustrate the derivation of a BB-test consider the following narrative specification of a well-known programming problem:

> *Derive a BB-test for a program (call it POSTFIX) that converts an infix expression to its postfix[4] form, e.g., a+b is to be converted to ab+. The input string must be an infix expression that is syntactically valid in the obvious way, e.g., the number of left and right parentheses must be the same, no operators without operands, etc. Identifiers are lower case single letters, constants are single digit integer numbers.*

The above narrative is quite typical in that it is expressed in terms of abstract data rather than in a concrete, language-supported data types. Clearly, "Infix Expressions," and "Postfix Expressions" are ADTs that have yet to be suitably defined in terms of the primitives of the programming language at hand, most likely strings. The string type, if not directly supported by the language at hand, has in turn to be represented by some other data types, typically arrays of characters.

Figure 4.2 shows the grammar of the language of simple infix expressions in the form of a set of *rewriting* or *production* rules. The vertical bar | ("or") separates alternative rules in a production; for instance, addop (addition operator) can be + or −. Observe that punctuation characters such as blanks or semicolons are not part of the language. The grammar is *left recursive*, i.e., a recursive call to a production, if any, occurs immediately after the ::= symbol as, for example, in production (2) exp ::= exp addop term.

```
exp ::=      term |                                    (1)
                exp addop term        -- "addition" operator    (2)

term ::=     factor |                                  (3)
                term multop factor  -- "multiplication"      (4)

factor ::=  identifier     |                          (5)
               constant     |                          (6)
               (exp)                                   (7)

addop ::=    + |                                       (8)
             −                                         (9)

multop ::=   * |                                       (10)
             /                                         (11)

identifer ::= a|b|...|z                                (12)

constant ::= 0|1|...|9                                 (13)
```

Fig. 4.2 A left-recursive grammar for simple arithmetic expressions

---

[4]The postfix notation is also called Reversed Polish Notation (RPN), due to the Polish logician Jan Lukasiewicz (1878-1956) who (successfully!) studied the possibility of eliminating parentheses in arithmetic expressions.

```
exp  ⇒²  exp(a+b*c) addop(-) term(2)
     ⇒²  exp(a) addop(+) term(b*c) addop(-) term(2)
     ⇒¹  term(a) addop(+) term(b*c) addop(-) term(2)
     ⇒³  factor(a) addop(+) term(b*c) addop(-) term(2)
     ⇒⁵  identifier(a) addop(+) term(b*c) addop(-) term(2)
     ⇒¹²  a addop(+) term(b*c) addop(-) term(2)
     ⇒⁸  a+ term(b*c) addop(-) term(2)
     ⇒⁴  a+ term(b) multop(*) factor(c) addop(-) term(2)
     ⇒³  a+ factor(b) multop(*) factor(c) addop(-) term(2)
     ⇒⁵  a+ identifier(b) multop(*) factor(c) addop(-) term(2)
     ⇒¹²  a+b multop(*) factor(c) addop(-) term(2)
     ⇒¹⁰  a+b* factor(c) addop(-) term(2)
```

Fig. 4.3 The *leftmost* derivation of $a+b*c-2$; the syntactical categories ("syntactical variables") are shown with their values, i.e., parts of the expression, in *parentheses*

Consider, for example, the expression $a+b*c-2$. Figure 4.3 shows the unique leftmost derivation of that string. A derivation is *leftmost* when every production replaces only the leftmost nonterminal metasymbol (syntactic category or variable); in that fashion the expression is *recognized* in piece-meal way starting from its beginning. The superscript k in $\Rightarrow^k$ shows the production number used in the derivation; several productions are sometimes combined to make things shorter.

Several observations are in place. First, the grammar forces addition and subtraction to be derived first. Thus the multiplication and division appear further down the parse tree, corresponding to the usual conventions for operator *precedence*. As a result, expression $a+b*c$ is parsed as $a+(b*c)$ rather than as $(a+b)*c$. Second, production (7) causes parenthesized expressions to be treated as Factors, thus forcing their evaluation first. Third, the left-recursive nature of the grammar leads to *left-to-right associativity* of operators at the same precedence level. Observe that every output must be derivable by the following grammar for postfix expressions:

```
postfix ::= constant | identifier | postfix postfix op,
```

where op is any operator in $\{+,-,/,*\}$. However, that requirement is too weak for it does not take into account the input infix expression. It is precisely the purpose of writing the specification for the problem to properly represent the input–output relationships. The specification is shown in Fig. 4.4 in a VDM-like style. The predicates is_expression(e) and is_converted(e,p) are defined, respectively, in Figs. 4.5 and 4.6; they are, of course, a straightforward translation of the grammar in Fig. 4.2. For example, the meaning of the predicate is_expression(e) in Fig. 4.5 is "e can be derived using the grammar for arithmetic expressions." The definition makes use of predicates is_term, is_factor, etc., which are true if their arguments are, respectively, a term and a factor, etc.

The definition of is_converted is shown in Fig. 4.6. The definition ensures that an expression inside parentheses is converted on its own and the parentheses are removed. Observe that the clause

```
Postfix(e: string) p: string
pre is_expression(e)      -- predicate is_expression(e) is
                          -- true when string e is a valid
                          -- arithmetic  expression
post is_converted(e,p);   -- is_converted(e,p) is true when
                          --  p is a Postfix version of e


Values                    -- test cases
e = "(a+7)*(c+4)";        p = "a7+c4+*";
e = "(a+7)*(c+4)";        p = "a7+c4+*";
e = "a+7*c+4";            p = "a7c*+4+";
```

Fig. 4.4   A VDM-style implicit specification of function Postfix

```
is_expression(e) ⟺ is_term(e) ∨ is_add_exp(e)

is_add_exp(e) ⟺       -- e is concatenation of e1, + or -, and t
     ∃ e₁,t: String, op: AddOps • e = e₁ op t
     ∧ is_term(t) ∧  is_expression(e1).

is_term(t) ⟺ is_factor(t) ∨ is_mult_exp(t)

is_mult_exp(t) ⟺ ∃t₁,f: String, op: MultOps •
       t= t₁ op f ∧ is_factor(f) ∧ is_term(t₁).

is_factor(f) ⟺ is_identifier(f) ∨ is_constant(f)
       ∨ is_parenthesized_exp(f)

is_parenthesized_exp(f) ⟺ e₂: String • f = ( e2 )
       ∧ is_expression(e2).


AddOps  = {'+', '-'}.
MultOps = {'*', '/'}.

is_identifier(id) ⟺ id  {'a', 'b',...,'z'}.
is¬_constant(c)   ⟺ c ∈ {'0', '1',...,'9'}.
```

Fig. 4.5   Recursive definition of is_expression(e), according to the grammar in Fig. 4.2; quotes around strings have been dropped

$$e = a \; op \; b \Rightarrow p = a' \; b' \; op \wedge \text{is\_converted}(a,a') \wedge \text{is\_converted}(b,b')$$

covers both add as well as mult expressions since the grammar for infix expressions parses e in a unique way. For example, for e=a+b*c, e is parsed as exp(a) addop(+) term(b*c), so e is the concatenation of a,+ and b*c rather than of a+b, * and c. Thus, the valid result p is abc*+ rather than ab+c*. However, for

```
is_converted(e,p) ⇔                      -- p is postfix version  of e
   (is_expression(e) ∧ is_postfix(p)
      ∧ (is_operand(e) ⇒ p=e)     -- e is identifier or constant
      ∧ (∃a: String • e=(a)       --  e is parenthesized expression
      ⇒  is_expression(a) ∧ is_converted(a,p))
                                    -- e is rooted in an operator
      ∧ a,b: String, op: Operators• e = a op b ⇒ p = a' b' op
      ∧ is_converted(a,a') ∧ is_converted(b,b').


is_postfix(p) ⇔ is_identifier(p) ∨ is_constant(p)
   ∨∃p₁,p₂: String, op: Operators•
      p=p1 p2 op ∧ is_postfix(p1) ∧ is_postfix(p2).

is_operand(e) ⇔ is_identifier(e) ∨ is_constant(e).

Operators = {'+', '-','*', '/'}.
```

Fig. 4.6 The definition of is_converted(*e,p*)

$e=(a+b)*c$, e is parsed as the concatenation of a+b, $*$ and c and the valid p is
ab+c$*$. Thus, in the definition of is_converted(e,p) one does not need to
bother with operator precedence, since the structure of valid input expressions has
the precedence built in it. Observe also the redundancy of the definition in Fig. 4.6.
First, in the quantified formula

∃a: String• e=(a) ^ is_expression(a) ⇒ is_converted(a,p),

the condition is_expression(a) is not really needed since it must hold if
e is an infix expression, due to the precondition. Second, the predicate
is_postfix(p) can be shown to hold if the other rules, which show how *p* is
actually build, are considered. Nevertheless, that kind of redundancy might be help-
ful as an emphasis of what is actually needed. Clearly, if one of the rules is wrong,
e.g., is_converted(a,a') is misspelled as is_converted(a',a), one
could use is_postfix(p) to detect the error.

It has to be noted that the structure of the input expression as specified by the
infix grammar does not necessarily apply to the implementation of the problem!
Clearly, the implementation can use code-wired operator precedence, rather than
parsing the input and produce results according to the input production rule. In
other words, the infix *grammar is used as a specification concept*, without preempt-
ing the implementation. Thus, the formal specification of the Postfix can be used to
derive a BB-test for any implementation. First, let us try to synthesize the signature
(functionality) test for the problem.

Observe that at the abstract level there are no "special" values of neither the
input nor the output type. However, since an expression can be *modeled* as a
sequence of characters one can select special value 1 of the length of the expression; observe that the length 0 corresponds to an invalid empty expression, which

may be used as a *stress test*, showing the program's reaction to invalid inputs. Any single operand can be selected as such a special value of either type of expressions. Thus, a constant say "3," or an identifier, say "*e*," are both valid special values. If one assumes that the sequrences will be implemented as arrays it makes sense to derive boundary test, including characters "1," "9," "0," "*a*," and "*z*." Incidentally, each of the above tests is also a *fixed* point of the postfix problem.

The precondition of the problem is one source of information on the basis of which input classes can be derived. Toward that goal, recall the top level definition of the predicate is_expression:

$$\text{is\_expression(e)} \Leftrightarrow \text{is\_term(e)} \lor \text{is\_add\_exp(e)}.$$

Since the above predicate is the disjunction ($\lor$) of two constituent predicates the class of expressions can be, in principle, refined into three classes: One whose elements satisfy, respectively, the is_term(e), is_add_exp(e) and both predicates (each of them is referred to as the *characteristic predicate* of the corresponding class). Observe, however, that is_term(e) and is_add_exp(e) are mutually exclusive; that fact should be obvious without a formal proof. Therefore, is_expression can be refined only into the two following classes of inputs:

$$T = \{e| \ \text{is\_term(e)}\}$$

and

$$A = \{e| \ \text{is\_add\_exp(e)}\}.$$

Both classes can be further refined according to their definitions. Class T can be split into two classes F and M defined as follows:

$$F = \{e| \ \text{is\_factor(e)}\}$$

$$M = \{e| \ \text{is\_mult\_exp(e)}\},$$

where, again, the constituent classes F and M are mutually disjoint, and thus their union is T, i.e., they constitute a partition of T. Class F can be partitioned into mutually disjoint classes I, C, and P that correspond, respectively, to the expression being an identifier, a constant, or a parenthesized expression. Since there are no inner predicates in the definition of I and C, they cannot be refined any further.

In contrast, classes M, A, and P are both conjunctions of conditions and, therefore, the only way one can refine them is to refine their constituent predicates. M involves the two-element class of multiplication operators $\{*, /\}$ and already defined classes F and T. While $\{*, /\}$ can be naturally split by considering $*$ and $/$ separately, the use of T in the definition of M, however, leads to recursion. Similar considerations apply to class A, whose only nonrecursive refinement is that of class $\{+, -\}$ of addition operators. Class P can be refined according to the definition of is_expression, i.e., of the entire domain E. That, in turn, involves the refinement of class A and, since the parenthesized expression can be a term, recursion. Obviously, recursion opens up the possibility of infinite number of refinements depending on how many recursive calls one is willing to consider. Consequently, the number of recursive calls has to be limited, needless to say in a rather arbitrary way. For example, the requirement

Each production rule should be used at least once

limits the number of *required* recursive calls to one. The following are tests that *together* meet this strategy:

$$3, d, (3), (5), a+b, a-b, a*b, a/b.$$

Observe that each of the above tests covers the classes of single operands be they constants or identifiers. This fact is even better illustrated by the expression a+b*c-2 parsed in Fig. 4.3. Observe that the expression forces the parser to invoke all production rules with the exception of rules 7 and 11!. Thus, if the strategy "fire each rule at least once" is adopted, two tests will be adequate for the strategy: The expression a+b*c-2 and, say, (a/b) to activate rules 7 and 11. Even a single test can be derived to satisfy the strategy e.g., a+b*c-2+(a/b)! This brings up the following question that is important for *most* testing methods, including structural testing (see Chap. 8):

Is it better to design a few complex test cases that meet the strategy at hand instead of a greater number of simpler tests?

The answer to the question depends on the perceived goal of testing. If the goal is only to *detect* bugs, then a few complex test cases are appropriate. They do not have to be cheaper, however, since the human cost of test evaluation might be much higher for complex tests. If, however, one would also like to get some *diagnostics* information when tests fail, a *sequence* of simple tests, *partially ordered* by their complexity, is a better solution; besides, it also might be a cheaper approach.

Finally, some comments on the synthesis of an output partition test. It is easy to see that the general form of the postfix output

```
Operand | Expression Expression Operator
```

Leads to output classes which are to be covered anyway if the correct results are computed for the input partitioning. For instance, observe that for the postfix expression p = ab+ the inputs that are mapped into that result are a+b, (a)+b, a+(b), (a+b), at least one of which will be selected as an input class representative. Of course, this is a coincidence, rather than a general case.

4.5 Random Testing

There have been many reports in the literature about the power of, or the lack thereof, random testing. Unfortunately, most of those reports are based on understandably unrealistic assumptions that render the discussion rather academic. It has to be kept in mind that randomness is just one (albeit the best developed and used in practice) technique for dealing with *uncertainty*. Now, that kind of random testing has been with us since time immemorial. Indeed, the early approach to testing (and let us be honest: Still practiced these days!) has been to arbitrarily select some inputs to see "what's going on." However, "arbitrariness" is not the same as "randomness" even if both carry the flavor of dealing with uncertainty.

The objective of random modeling proper is to derive the probability of the event of interest, e.g., the detection of a programming fault. However, it is meaningful to ask about the probability of the event only in the context of a given *sampling space*. In the case of computer programs, such a space would have to include the class of all possible programming problems, all programs solving the problems, the class of all possible faults in the programs, and the class of all possible input distributions. That is clearly not feasible and is of course the major philosophical problem for statistical modeling of most software engineering problems. Thus the question arises, "Can statistical methods be used in software engineering at all?" The answer to this question is a qualified "Yes" and is based on the premise that one always deals with a single and unique software artifact, rather than with a collection of artifacts. Thus a program *is* or *is not* correct for its specification. Consequently, a statement about the program's correctness is a *deterministic* proposition. Thus, random testing is rather a Monte Carlo method whose *main* objective is the detection of the fault in the program through random sampling of inputs and the evaluation the correctness of the program's response. If a fault has been detected the testing is deemed successful; otherwise it is a failure that brings up the secondary objective: What is the probability that an existing fault has escaped detection?

It has been a mantra among advocates of random testing that tests be selected according to the operational input probability distribution. On the face of it, that seems a reasonable requirement: After all, let us care about situations that are most likely to happen, right? Not quite. Critics of that approach point to the difficulties of obtaining the distributions in question. That is true, but the problems are getting even worse. First, except for some classes of stationary and ergodic[5] processes it is very hard to *assume*, letting alone to build, a probabilistic model in the general case. Second, we argue that software designers do have in mind the typical, most likely situations. It is, however, precisely the "special situations" (yes, very much like the special values in the functionality testing), which *may* happen but are not very likely – that tend to be neglected in the implementation. But Murphy's Law is merciless – things may go smooth till some unexpected situation causes a catastrophe. Therefore, we argue, it is important to test for situations that are less, rather than more, likely.

Statistical inferences underlying random testing require running a large number of tests. Now, each of those tests has to be evaluated, that is, it has to be determined whether the result produced by the implementation is correct or not. That is the most costly, heavily labor intensive part of the testing process that certainly runs counter to the principle of economy of testing. Consequently, the only practically

---

[5]A stochastic process is ergodic if its properties across a set of its realizations are the same as those of any particular realization over time or other coordinate involved.

feasible kind of random testing is the one which employs *automatic evaluation of test results*. The reader will recognize that the test oracle here is simply an executable postcondition of the program's specification! Indeed, such an approach seems the best around, particularly if applied at the abstract level since the postcondition at the implementation-language level tend to be very complex. We have carried out some experiments that support the viability of the approach. For instance, we have designed a high-level VDM-SL model (cf. Chaps. 1 and 6) of the not-so-trivial decomposition of a directed graph into dicliques [1]. The model included a declarative specification with interpretable postcondition and a direct operation providing a solution to the problem. More than 220,000 uniformly distributed random tests have been generated and automatically evaluated, with no error detected. Now, we cannot claim on that basis that the solution is correct but the probability that this is indeed the case is obviously very high. Observe, however, that if an abstract interpretable postcondition is to be used as a test oracle of an *executable* program, a run time mapping of the abstract data representation into the abstraction has to be implemented (cf. the *retrieve* or *abstraction function* in [2]).

4.6 Conclusions

The discussion in this chapter shows that Black-Box testing is rather ill-defined and its success in fault detection to a large degree depends on the creativity and sheer luck of the programmer. The main reason for this is the fact that the BB-test is typically synthesized on the basis of informally stated requirements. It is thus to be hoped that a wider use of formal specifications will result in more disciplined testing strategies utilizing the structure of formal specifications. In Chap. 1, we presented two approaches to formal specification: The *declarative* (indirect, declarative) specification using the pre- and postcondition and the *explicit* one, in the form of abstract algorithm. The latter gives rise to a systematic test selection strategy according to the principles of structural, white-box testing as discussed in Chap. 8. Further research is needed to synthesize the BB-test on the basis of the indirect specification. The importance of BB-testing cannot be overstated for all intents and purposes; it is the *only* testing technique that can be used on its own. Clearly, in Chap. 8 we demonstrate that structural testing can only be used as a *side-effect* and an *indirect* measure of the adequacy of BB-testing, rather than a stand-alone activity.

As BB-test is applicable to *any implementation* of the programming problem at hand, a BB-test could be synthesized before the design and implementation stages begin. In fact, synthesizing the functional test *prior* to the design should be a standard procedure. This is because BB-testing, besides being a method for the detection of faults in the implementation, is also an invaluable tool for the identification of flaws in the specification itself. Thus, an early use of BB-testing in program development limits the costly consequences of having to change the specification in the middle of, or after, the design stage. This principle can be naturally extended onto *all* stages of software development, as illustrated in [3]. According to that approach, the program and a test for it, rather than the proof, should be developed hand in hand. Of course, the attained degree of confidence is that that can be achieved through testing: On a successful completion of the design process, we can only state that "There are no grounds for the rejection of the hypothesis that the program is correct." Taken literally, this might not seem too encouraging. Every design method is based upon the underlying reasoning, however, informal the latter. The absence of errors during testing together with the reasoning that explains that fact provide sound justification for a high confidence in the final product.

Finally, a rather important practical observation has to be made. In general, elementary tests in a BB-test can be applied in any order. Indeed, existing theories assume that this is the standard procedure underlying, for instance, the very notion of random testing. Practicing programmers, however, know better: They usually start with some simple cases and only when those work do they move toward more complex cases. In that way some diagnostic information is gained when a test fails; indeed, it is likely that the most recently included specification feature has failed. A general scenario of such *sequential* testing would require an estimate of the likelihood of an *abstract fault*, by which we mean the potentially incorrect value of an exported parameter. Typically, the specification restricts the values of the exported parameters by some predicate in the postcondition. It is reasonable to expect that the more complex such a predicate the more difficult to establish it by an implementation and, therefore, the more likely the fault that violates the predicate. Unfortunately, it is not clear how to measure the predicates' complexity and how to synthesize tests that maximize the likelihood of their failure. Consequently, it is not clear how to formulate a theory of systematic synthesis of a BB-test that meets its stated objectives.

Exercise 4.1 *Derive a BB-Test for the Monotone function in the introduction. Do it both for the implementation-based specification and for the abstract specification of the problem in Chap. 1.*

Exercise 4.2 *Derive a random test for the Monotone function in the introduction. Generate randomly the length of the sequence in the array and its elements. Use the correct version of the function as a test oracle. Report on the probability of the detection of the fault.*

Exercise 4.3 *Complete the definition of function Postfix in* Fig. 4.4 *by converting the definitions of* Figs. 4.5 and 4.6 *to the VDM-SL notation.*

Exercise 4.4 *Write a VDM-SL operation that, given infix expression e, converts e into its postfix counterpart.*

References

1. R.B. Haralick, The diclique representation and decomposition of binary relations, Journal of ACM, 21(3), 356–366, 1974.
2. C.B. Jones, Systematic Software Development using VDM, Prentice-Hall, Upper saddle River, NJ, 1990.
3. J. Laski, Testing in program development cycle, Software Engineering Journal, 95–106, 1989.
4. G.J. Myers, The Art of software testing, Wiley, New York, NY, 1979.
5. N. Nissanke, Introductory Logic and Sets for Computer Scientists, Addison-Wesley, Reading, MA, 1999.

References

Part II
Static Analysis

Chapter 5
Intermediate Program Representation

Abstract To be able to talk about the *principles* of program analysis it is necessary to use a language-independent Intermediate Software Representation. The form of such a representation depends on the objectives of the analysis. Two such representations are discussed. The program *Abstract Syntax Tree* provides an accurate program representation that is also connected to the source code. The control program structure can be abstracted into program *control flowgraph* that is fully language independent but cannot be used to identify the code. However, *labeled flowgraphs*, i.e., flowgraphs supplied with other information, are the basic tools for static *intra*procedural analysis and structural testing and they also facilitate formal verification. Control flow is the backbone of the program since it supports the program's executions. In particular, "things" happen on program traces, i.e., executed paths, so path analysis is of a special importance. Programmers frequently ask questions about the flow of control. Also, system programs that support SAT methods must use control flow analysis to solve any static analysis problem at hand. An easy method for the detection of the existence of paths and their identification has been proposed in terms of the powers of the arc relation in the flowgraph. Since the current version of STAD does not support path identification the relevant concepts are illustrated by the high-level VDM-SL-based modeling.

5.1 Introduction

In order to analyze the program in an automatic fashion, one needs an *Intermediate Software Representation* that is *language independent*, stripped of unnecessary syntax features, accurate, easy to manipulate, and possibly indexed to the program text. The choice of a particular representation depends on the objectives of the analysis. Compiler design is based upon the availability of the program parse and (abstract) syntax tree (AST, Sect. 5.2). In contrast, software engineering typically uses program flowgraphs as an intermediate analysis tool (Sect. 5.3). Since flowgraphs are a poorer representation than the ASTs, they are not sufficient for certain applications. Therefore, they have to be sometimes enriched in one way or another. One way of doing that is to provide node labels to provide information of variables

J. Laski and W. Stanley, *Software Verification and Analysis*,
DOI: 10.1007/978-1-84882-240-5_6, © Springer Verlag London Limited 2009

used and defined in the nodes of the flowgraph (Sect. 5.4). The derivation of the flowgraph has to take into account the idiosyncrasies of the programming language at hand (Sect. 5.5). Paths in flowgraphs are essential to the understanding of its operational semantics and to the various static analysis methods. Since the current version of STAD does not support program path analysis, the relevant concepts are illustrated by the high-level VDM-SL-based modeling in Sect. 5.6.

5.2   Program Parse and Syntax Trees

The program Parse Tree (PT) represents the syntactical structure of the code [1]. Since the tree is developed according to the rules of grammar of the programming language, it contains full information about the original code. To illustrate this, consider the program in Fig. 5.1 and the parse tree for the **while** loop in the program in Fig. 5.2. Observe that only the leaves of the tree contain tokens from the source code, i.e., the "real stuff." The internal nodes represent some *metalinguistic* (*or syntactic*) *categories*, such as Var-Identifier (a set of all valid variable identifiers), or Relop (a set of relational operators). This fact is the main reason for the large size of the parse tree. There are other reasons, too. First, the tree also contains a lot of information that is not essential to the program's semantics. For example, a sequence of empty statements ;;...;, if allowed by the language, will nevertheless be faithfully represented in the parse tree. Second, punctuation tokens such as **if, then**, or **while**, once recognized are no longer needed and may be eliminated from the tree.

Fortunately, the full parse tree is rarely needed for program analysis. The *Abstract Syntax Tree* (AST) is a simpler and space saving version of the parse tree that still accurately represents the meaning of the program, albeit without all of the "syntactic sugar." Figure 5.3 shows the AST for the same code fragment whose parse tree is shown in Fig. 5.2. Observe that operators in the AST are interior nodes while the leaves of the tree are operands, i.e., the identifiers and literals of the original source code. In contrast, in the parse tree operators and operands are always children of some metalinguistic interior node. Thus, it is economically feasible for a compiler to build explicitly an AST by eliminating parts of the parse tree that are no longer useful.

5.3   Program Control Flowgraph

Program flowcharting is a time-honored quasigraphic technique for the documentation of program *design*. The flowchart shows program actions and their sequencing (control flow) at some conceptual level of abstraction chosen by the programmer. Actions in the flowchart are usually described in a language-independent way. The *flowgraph* of a program can be viewed as a flowchart that documents the *implementation* of the program, rather than its design [2]. Clearly, the flowgraph is derived automatically from the source code of the program, usually using the

```
Program series;
     VAR k, s: integer ;

   Procedure sum(i: integer ; var S:  integer );
     VAR k: integer ;

   Function Sqr(n: integer) : integer ;
        begin { sqr }
{1}           { <STAD> Initialization of parameter n }
{2}           sqr := n* n;
{3}           { <STAD> EXIT USE OF sqr (FUNCTIONRESULT) }
{4}     end   ; { sqr }
        begin { sum }
{1}           { <STAD> Initialization of parameter n }
{2}           { <STAD> Initialization of parameter n }
{3}           s := 0;
{4}           k := 1;
{5}           whil k <= i do
                begin;
{6}               s : =s + sqr ( k );
{7}               k : =k + 1 ;
                end
{8}           k := 1;
{9}           { <STAD> EXIT USE OF S }
{10}          end ; { sum }
        begin    { program series }
{1}           write ('Enter an integer...' }
{2}           read ( k ); { split node 1- definition of k .
{3}           if k < 0then
{4}             k:=k* -1;
{5}           { sum (k,s); { split node 1- copy s to system
variable}
{6}           sum (k,s); { split node 2 - definition s. }
                {8}           k := 1;
{7}        write ('sum of square is ', s);
{8}     end.  { program series }
```

Fig. 5.1 The STAD-generated listing of Program SERIES; commented out *numbers* denote nodes in the corresponding separate flowgraphs for each block in the program. The flowgraph for procedure Sum is displayed in Fig. 5.6

Abstract Syntax Tree as an intermediate step. Consequently, the actions in the flowgraph correspond to statements in the program, rather than to some higher level abstractions. This is notwithstanding the fact that a flowgraph, like a flowchart, can be derived at an arbitrary level of "control abstraction," i.e., a box in the flowchart or a node in the flowgraph may correspond to a group of statements in the program. Nevertheless, in contrast to the flowchart, no abstract meaning can be automatically assigned to such a grouping in the flowgraph. The basic form of the flowgraph is

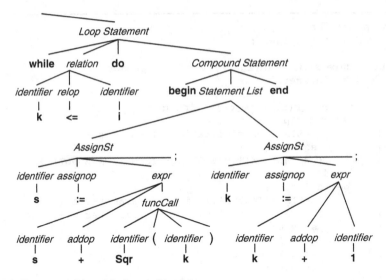

Fig. 5.2 Parse tree of the while loop in Fig. 5.1

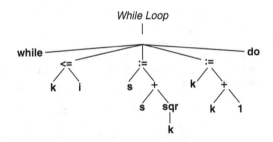

Fig. 5.3 Abstract Syntax Tree for the while loop in Fig. 5.1

one that identifies every elementary action in the program, that is, one that applies to the lowest level of program decomposition. Such an elementary action will be referred to as *instruction*, in contrast to the notion of a *statement*, which denotes a syntactically valid program construct. More precisely, an instruction is a smallest, further nondecomposable and *executable* part of a statement. Thus, at the most elementary level, an instruction can be an assignment statement, *read* or *write* statement, the Boolean expression COND in **if** COND... or **while** COND..., or a procedure call. In contrast to procedure calls, function invocations are not considered instructions, since they can only appear in expressions.

The flowgraph is an abstraction of the control structure of the program. Instructions in program correspond to *nodes* (or *vertices*) in the flowgraph. *Potential* flow of control from instruction *n* to instruction *m* corresponds to an *arc* (or *edge*) from *n* to *m*, denoted as the pair (*n m*). For arc (*n m*), *m* is a *successor* of *n* and *n* is a *predecessor* of *m*. A node that has only one successor is either a *processing node* or a jump node. A processing node performs data transformation, i.e., it affects the state of the program. A *jump node* changes the textually defined flow of control without affecting the state (**goto, break, exit,** or **continue**). If a node has more than one successor it is a *decision node*; arcs emanating from decision nodes are *branches*. For instance, node 5 in Fig. 5.1 is a decision node. Branches are uniformly labeled by the Boolean expressions which, if true, guarantee their traversal. Thus, for

if x>a **then** A **else** B;

the two branch labels are, respectively, $x>a$ and $x<=a$. Branches of multiway branch nodes (**case, switch**) are labeled by the corresponding selection expressions. However, branches emanating from a two-way decision node are typically labeled by the Boolean values *true* or *false* of the expression involved.

Consider the procedure Sum in the program Series in Fig. 5.1. Note that nodes 1, 2, 9, and 10 do *not* appear in the original source code; indeed, they have been inserted into the flowgraph by STAD. The role of the first three of them will be discussed in Sect. 5.4. Right now it is enough to state that node 10 is a dummy EXIT node that is inserted at end of the procedure. The EXIT node corresponds to the return to the calling unit which, in the case of the entire program, is the operating system. Sometimes it may also be convenient to introduce a dummy entry node.

Some clarifications are in place. Observe an important qualification in defining the meaning of the arc $(n\ m)$ between node n and m: It is a *potential*, rather than guaranteed, transfer of control from n to m. That qualification is due to the fact that for certain branches in the program there may exist no input data that causes their execution. For example, the **then** branch in the statement

if {1} x > x **then** {2}.. **else**...

cannot be executed, although the arc (1 2) does appear in the flowgraph. Such a branch is referred to as *infeasible* or *nonexecutable*. Note that even a purely sequential code may have infeasible arcs! For example, the **write** instruction in the sequence

x := -10; y := sqrt(x); **write**(x,y);

can never be reached due to the run-time error in the evaluation of sqrt(x). It has to be emphasized that infeasibility is a semantic problem that is *undecidable*, i.e., there is no algorithm which, for arbitrary program, can decide in a finite time whether an instruction or branch in the program can be executed.

The notion of the flowgraph presented so far has been rather intuitive, not sufficient to properly define the derivative concepts. Formal definition of the flowgraph is also needed to talk more precisely about other graph applications in programming, such as call graphs and dependency graphs. More advanced flowgraph problems will be revisited and discussed in more detail in Chap. 6; in the remainder of this section only the basic issues are discussed.

Let P be a program. The *(control) flowgraph* of P is a quadruple $G=(N,A,S,E)$ where (1) N is the set of *nodes,* each node corresponding to a single-entry single-exit executable code segment in the program, (2) A is a set of *arcs,* each arc $(n\ m)$ in A, n, m in N, corresponding to a potential transfer of control from n to m and (3) S and E are, respectively, the Start (entry) and Exit nodes such that there is no incoming arc to S and no outgoing arc from E. For example, the following is the formal definition of the flowgraph FG for procedure Sum in Fig. 5.1

```
FG  =  ({ 1,  2,  3,  4,5,  6,  7,  8,  9,  10},   -- set of nodes
        { (1 2),  (2 3),  (3 4),  (4 5),  (5 6),
          (5 8),  (6 7),  (7 5),  (8 9),  (9 10)}, - set of arcs
          1, 10)  -- Start and Exit nodes
```

The set of nodes N can be any finite set of distinct symbols that uniquely identify instructions in the program. In this text, however, a finite subset of consecutive natural numbers from 1 through some maximal value will be used. Mathematically, set A of arcs is a *binary relation* on the set of nodes N, symbolically denoted as $A \subseteq N \times N$, where $\times$ is the Cartesian product operator. Clearly, $N \times N$ is the set of all *ordered* pairs of elements coming from N and A is a subset of $N \times N$. Consequently, the set notation $(n\ m) \in A$, standing for "arc $(n\ m)$ is in set A of arcs" is equivalent to the relational one $n\ A\ m$, "node n is related to node m under relation A." Of course, either statement is true or false.

The above definition makes the flowgraph a particular version of a *directed graph*; the latter is simply a pair (N, A) without the entry and exit nodes explicitly identified. One may ask why is it necessary to specify the set of nodes explicitly, since they can seemingly be derived from the set of arcs. Unfortunately, that is not always the case. Consider, for example, the code and its flowgraph in Fig. 5.4. There is no arc involving node 2 (B), which is isolated and cannot be reached by any path starting at entry 1. Since the node does not appear in the set of arcs for the code its existence cannot be inferred from the latter.

Figure 5.5 shows the definition of the type flowgraph in terms of the VDM-SL notation, introduced in Chap.1. Observe the use of the *make* function mk_ in the

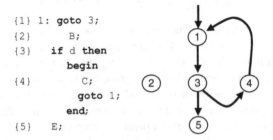

```
{1}  1: goto 3;
{2}      B;
{3}      if d then
            begin
{4}            C;
            goto 1;
            end;
{5}      E;
```

Fig. 5.4 Code with unreachable statement *B* (node 2)

```
types                       -- type definitions
  Node = nat1 ;             -- natural numbers
  Nodes = set of nat1 ;     -- sets of natural numbers

  inv N == N={1,...,card N}; -- type invariant: sets must
                             -- contain consecutive numbers only
  Arcs = set of (nat1 * nat1); -- set of pairs of nodes

  FlowGraph :: -- record with fields N, A, S, E
    N: Nodes
    A: Arcs
    S: Node
    E :Node

  inv G == (G.S in set G.N)   -- start node is in N
    and (G.E in set G.N)      -- exit node is in S
    and forall mk_(x,y) in set A
      & x in set N and y in set N;   -- arcs involve only
                                     -- nodes from N
values
  A = { mk_(1 2), mk_(2 3), mk_(3 4), mk_(4 5), mk_(5 6),
        mk_(5 8), mk_(6 7), mk_(7 5), mk_(8 9), mk_(9 10) }
  FG = mk_FlowGraph( {1,...,10}, A, 1, 10 );
```

Fig. 5.5 A VDM-SL definition of type flowgraph and the value FG of the procedure Sum in Fig. 5.1

creation of tuples of data. The type will be used in Sect. 5.6 to model path problems in the flowgraph.

5.4 Labeled Flowgraphs

The flowgraph of a program provides information only about the transfer of control between nodes and as such does not allow one to analyze the program's semantics. A richer program representation is obtained if nodes and arcs in the graph are labeled with additional information. For example, since nodes in the flowgraphs correspond to instructions in the program, instructions are "natural" node labels. In other words, node labels are viewed as the nodes' "contents." Mathematically, there is a total *node labeling function* nl: $N \rightarrow$ INSTR, from the set N of nodes to the set INSTR of instructions, which assigns an instruction to every node in N. Note that two nodes can have the same or different labels, e.g., the assignment x:=0 may appear more than once in the program. It is assumed that the exit node E in the flowgraph carries out no computations – it has a unique label EXIT. The assumption that there is exactly one exit node does not restrict the class of considered programs. Clearly, in the presence of multiple exit nodes (e.g., several **return** statements) an extra merging exit node that is *the* successor of those statements can be introduced into the flowgraph.

It might also be useful to associate some information with the arcs in the graph. That can be achieved by means of an *arc labeling function* al: $A \rightarrow$ Labels, which assigns unique labels to arcs in A. Function al can be partial or total, depending on the nature of the labels. For example, one may want to label every branch of a decision node with the logical value *true* or *false* of the Boolean expression (label of) in the node. Similarly, the branches of a **case** (**switch**) statement can be labeled with the value of the selector expression which, if satisfied, causes the traversal of the branch. In either case, the arc label function is partial, not defined for arcs emanating from purely processing nodes. A fully labeled flowgraph provides all information about the program's semantics, assuming that the semantics of the instructions (node labels) is known in the first place. Therefore, when "interpreted," i.e., traversed from the start S for some initial state, in principle the graph's behavior is equivalent to that of the original program. If such an equivalence is not needed and one is only interested in some purely structural properties of the program, a more restricted model can be used, that is particularly useful in the analysis of data flow in the program. In it, every node n in the graph is labeled with two sets of program variables: The set $U(n)$ of variables *used* (or *referenced*) in n and the set $D(n)$ of variables *defined* (assigned values) in n. Thus, U and D are functions from the set N of nodes to the power set of VARS, the set of program variables, i.e, they have the following signatures

$$U, D: N \rightarrow 2^{\text{VARS}}.$$

For programs without procedure calls, functions U and D can be determined statically, by analyzing instructions in the program: Variable v is *used* in node n if it appears on the right-hand side of an assignment statement, in the expression of a decision node, or as an IN or IN OUT argument to a predefined procedure or function call, as in *write(v)*. Variable v is *defined* in node n if it appears on the left-hand side of an assignment statement or as an OUT or IN OUT argument to a predefined procedure as in *read(v)*.

Unfortunately, the identification of used and defined variables for user-defined procedures and function calls is not that straightforward. As a first approximation, one would assume that every imported argument (VAL or VAR in Free Pascal, IN or IN OUT in Ada) is used in the computation of every exported argument (VAR or OUT in Free Pascal, IN OUT or OUT in Ada). Certainly this might be a rather crude model of what is actually going on. For example, a procedure with an empty body is perfectly valid syntactically although no actual dependencies between its parameters exist. Figure 5.6 shows the STAD-produced functions U and D for procedure SUM in Fig. 5.1. Unfortunately, that rather a crude approximation may lead to obviously spurious dependencies in the program. To alleviate the problem, STAD 4.0 employs a novel method of preprocessing procedure calls, which is discussed in Chap. 7.

```
LIST OF INSTRUCTIONS:
   1   { <STAD> Initialization of parameter i }
   2   { <STAD> Initialization of parameter s }
   3   s := 0
   4   k := 1
   5   k <= i
   6   s := s + sqr( k )
   7   k := k + 1
   8   k := 1
   9   { <STAD> EXIT USE OF s }
  10   { <STAD> EXIT }


CONTROL FLOW GRAPH:
~k --> set of nodes~  means: control can be passed from
                             node k to any node in the set.
~D~  means: set of variables defined at the instruction
~U~  means: set of variables used at the instruction


   1 --> { 2 }         D = { i }        U = { }
   2 --> { 3 }         D = { s }        U = { }
   3 --> { 4 }         D = { s }        U = { }
   4 --> { 5 }         D = { k }        U = { }
   5 --> { 6, 8 }      D = { }          U = { k, i }
   6 --> { 7 }         D = { s }        U = { s, k }
   7 --> { 5 }         D = { k }        U = { k }
   8 --> { 9 }         D = { k }        U = { }
   9 --> { 10 }        D = { }          U = { s }
  10 --> { }           D = { }          U = { }
```

Fig. 5.6 Used and defined variables in procedure SUM of Fig. 5.1 as produced by STAD

Yet another problem with procedures is the way one handles the initial values of the formal parameters. Consider again the procedure SUM in Fig. 5.1 but this time *without* instructions 1 and 2, which have been inserted by STAD. Now, since there is no definition of the parameter i in the original code, the use of an uninitialized i in the statement **while k<=i**... gives rise to a (spurious!) data flow anomaly. This is due to the fact that the initial assignment to i at the *call* of Sum, through the evaluation of the corresponding argument (actual parameter), has been ignored. To redress the problem, STAD inserts a *system* assignment node at the start of the new code (node 1 in our case), which assigns to the variable i some undefined value. The VAR parameter s is treated in a similar way in the system node 2. Finally, a system node 9 is a use of the exported parameter s. That process is referred to as the *elaboration*[1] or *expansion* of the original procedure and is discussed in depth in Chap. 6.

---

[1] Not to be confused with the elaboration of Ada programs.

5.5   Deriving the Flowgraph

The program's flowgraph can be derived automatically by traversing the program's AST. In the process, identified instructions can be given numbers according to the traversal order. The flowgraph is language independent in the sense that it can be derived for any program in a procedural language, such as Pascal, Ada, or C++. It is thus possible for programs in different languages to have the same flowgraph; this is also true for different programs written in the same language. However, the derivation of the flowgraph has to take into account the idiosyncrasies of the programming language at hand. The goal here is to ensure that the interpretation of the flowgraph replicates the actual run-time events during program execution. The degree of accuracy of that replication depends on the particular problem at hand, solution to which is to be supported by the flowgraph. The following examples illustrate that approach.

The C statement $j = ++i$ has to be represented by a sequence of two nodes with instructions $i := i+1; j := i$. The pathological (but unfortunately valid) condition in the C if statement

```
if (n=0){ ... }
```

also gives rise to a two-node sequence $n := 0; n == 0$, the second one being a decision node. A more contrived example is offered by the Pascal **for** loop in Fig. 5.7. While defining the meaning of a **for** loop, the latter is usually transformed into an implicit **goto** loop also shown in Fig. 5.7. However, for that transformation to be semantically equivalent to the original **for** loop, one needs to introduce new "hidden" constants and instructions. Thus, a hidden constant _ub1 has been introduced to account for the fact that, during execution of the for $i := expr1$ to $expr2$, both expressions are evaluated exactly once, on the very first entry to the

```
                    Program forloop;
                    VAR
                        c: char ;
                    begin { forloop }
{ 1-3, 5}       for c:= 'a' to 'z' do
{ 4}                write( c );
{ 6}            end . { forloop }


INSTRUCTIONS          SUCCESSORS
1 c := 'a'                {2}
2 _ub1 := 'z'            {3}
3 c <= _ub1             {6, 4}
4 write( c )            {5}
5 c:=succ(c)            {3} -- implicit goto 3
6 { <STAD> EXIT }       {}
```

Fig. 5.7 The STAD's flowgraph for a **for** loop

loop and the initial value of *expr2* is used in the test node. Instruction 5 :
c:=succ(c) is needed to explicitly increment the loop control variable. However,
even that hair-splitting approach is not entirely satisfactory. For one, if the loop
terminates "normally," the final value of loop control variable *c* is *undefined*, making it rather precarious to use it later by assuming, for example, that it is equal to
succ("z"). To alleviate this a "scrambling" instruction may be inserted on exit. In
contrast, if there were an exit in the middle of the loop, an arc from that exit to node
6 would have to be introduced, to preserve the current value of *c*.

However, even that approach might be insufficient. For example, if variable c
were declared as VAR c: 'a'..'z', rather than of type char, then on the last
iteration of the loop succ('z') would be undefined, violating the subtype range
(even if the implementation does provide such a successor, e.g.,'{'). Consequently,
instruction 5 would have to be replaced by

```
5': if (succ(c) is defined) then 5: c:=succ(c) else goto 6,
```

and the arcs (5' 5), (5' 6) should be added to the flowgraph. In contrast to Pascal,
in the following Ada loop;

for i in 1..N loop

. . .

end loop

the loop control variable *i* is always declared internally, then initialized to 1 and
incremented at the end of the loop body; however, *i* ceases to exist on the loop's
termination, rather than being left undefined. Such a treatment of the for loop is
similar to that of a *block* in Ada. Consider, for example, the Ada code with nested
blocks in Fig. 5.8.

Since an Ada block is always part of some other construct, it does not make
sense to derive a separate flowgraph for it. Rather, instructions are introduced to
capture the run-time *elaboration* of local declarations at the beginning of each
block and the destruction of local variables on the exit from the block. This is

```
declare              -- block $b1
    i,j: Integer;  -- $Create($b5.i); $Create($b5.j);
begin
    . . .
    declare              -- block $b2
        i:integer := 2; -- $Create($b2.i); $b2.i := 2;
    begin
        . . .
    end;                 -- $Destroy($b2.i)
    . . .
end;                 -- $Destroy($b5.i); $Destroy($b5.j);
```

Fig. 5.8 Handling of nested blocks in Ada

shown as comments in Fig. 5.8. The operations $Create(V)$ and $Destroy(V)$, respectively, create and destroy variable V. $bi denotes the ith block in the procedure and the dotted notation $bi.V$ stands for variable V declared in block $bi.

Yet another issue is the handling of **goto**s in the program. Although considered to be a rather unsavory way of expressing our programming ideas, it is given that every programming construct will be eventually used. However, since a **goto** is a pure transfer of control it can essentially be omitted without affecting the meaning of the flowgraph. On the other hand, it may be sometimes desirable to have an implicit **goto** node, even if it does not appear explicitly in the program text. Consider for example the following loop:

```
while p(x) do
    if c(x,y) then
        S₁
    else
        S₂;
    S₃;
```

where S_1, S_2 and S_3 are arbitrary statements. Technically, there exist arcs (S_1, p) and (S_2, p) in the corresponding flowgraph. However, this view does not convey the spirit of structured programming, i.e, the fact that an **if** statement is a single-entry single-exit construct. It might be then desirable to introduce a dummy merging **endif** node and the following arcs: $(S_1 \textbf{ endif})$, $(S_2 \textbf{ endif})$, $(\textbf{endif}, p)$. Observe that an Ada **null** statement gives rise to an explicit dummy (empty) node.

Usually, compound Boolean test expressions in decision statements, such as p and r in

```
if p AND r then
    S;
else
    Q
end if;
```

are modeled by single nodes since the order of evaluation of p and r is arbitrary (implementation defined). This may be insufficient, however, to correctly capture the semantics of *conditional* Boolean expressions where the order of evaluation *does* matter. For example, in the following Ada code

```
if p and then r then
    S;
else
    Q;
end if;
```

p AND THEN r is a *conditional* AND operator (CAND). Clearly, *r* is evaluated only
if *p* is true. Thus, two nodes *p* and *r* are needed to represent the compound predicate
and the arcs (*p r*), (*p Q*), (*r S*) and (*r Q*) are needed to capture the flow of control
between the nodes in the **if** statement.

Expressions, with the exception of Boolean ones, are not usually represented by
nodes in the flowgraph. However, if one wants to capture the order of evaluation of
an expression, then the expression can be represented by its own subflowgraph.
Such a subflowgraph can be obtained from the expression parse tree, with new
intermediate state variables needed to evaluate that tree. For example, the assignment z:=a+b*c can be given the following graph:

```
_1  :=  b  *  c  ;

_2  :=  a  +  _1  ;

z  =  _2  ;
```

where the underscored are system variables representing the intermediate storage
use by the compiler. Normally, the order of operand evaluation is not specified by
the semantics of programming languages. This may result in nondeterministic computations. Consider, for example, the following C code:

```
b  =  1;

x  =  ((a=b)  +  (b=2));
```

Depending on the chosen order of evaluation of the operands, one can derive two
flowgraphs for the code:

```
flowgraph 1:  b = 1; a = b; b = 2; x = a+b;

flowgraph 2:  b = 1; b = 2; a = b; x = a+b;
```

with different final results. The order of operand evaluation may be particularly
important for expressions involving calls to functions with side effects. For example, the Pascal assignment statement

```
x  :=  a  +  f(x);
```

where *f*(*x*) changes the global variable *a*, can be assigned the two following flowgraphs, potentially producing different results:

```
flowgraph 1:  _1 := f(x); _2 := a; x := _1 + _2;

flowgraph 2:  _1 := a; _2 := f(x); x := _1 + _2;
```

In general, a procedure call may define an arbitrary number of variables in the
calling program. However, most dataflow algorithms are based on the assumption that a node in the flowgraph has *at most* one variable defined in it. Thus,
to support those algorithms, a call with many defined variables has to be split
into *separate nodes*, in which exported (i.e., VAR or OUT in Free Pascal, IN
OUT or OUT in Ada) arguments to the call (actual parameters) are defined
individually, while the number of arguments used in the nodes is not restricted.

However, crucial here is the proper modeling of the dependencies between the variables defined in the split nodes and those used in them. A novel solution to that problem is offered in Chap. 7 in the form of the *Dependency Template* or *Output–Input relation*.

5.6   Paths in Flowgraphs

Programmers use the concept of a path in the program all the time, even if mostly informally. They need it to reason about the program to test and debug it. Consequently, it is necessary to define the notion of a path in an ambiguous and precise way. Toward that goal, the program flowgraph lends itself quite naturally. Consider, for example, the flowgraph in Fig. 5.9. It is intuitively obvious that the following sequence of nodes

$$1, 2, 3, 4, 6, 7, 8, 11, 12$$

is a valid path in the flowgraph and the sequence

Fig. 5.9   A flowgraph

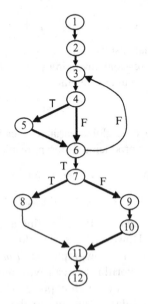

$$1, 3, 6, 2$$

is not while there may be some doubts how to classify the sequences

$$3, 4, 6, 7, \text{ and } 4$$

Problem 5.1   *Using the formal definition of the flowgraph in Sect. 5.3 define the concept of path in it.*

The following are the issues one should consider before choosing a useful definition of a path in the program. First, although some/most programmers would likely consider a valid path any that begins at the Start and ends at the Exit, in many problems in static analysis, testing, and debugging paths between two arbitrary nodes in the flowgraph have to be considered. Second, although it is plausible to view a path as a sequence of arcs such a definition would not allow a single node to be considered a path. Therefore, Definition 5.1 specifies a path as a sequence of nodes in the flowgraph.

Definition 5.1 (path in flowgraph)   *Given the flowgraph $G=(N,A,S,E)$ and two nodes n and m in the set N, a path p from n to m is a sequence $[n_1, n_2... n_k]$ of nodes from N, $k>0$, such that every pair $(n_i \, n_{i+1})$ of adjacent nodes in p, $i = 1, 2, ...k$ -1, is in the set of arcs A. The length len(p) of paths p is k-1, the number of arcs in the path.*

We adopt a convention that a path from n to m begins at the *top* of n and ends at the *top* of m. This assumption helps in the interpretation of the execution of the path; clearly, the first node on the path will be executed while the last one will not. Thus, if $p= [n_1, n_2 ... n_k]$, $k > 1$, $len(p) = k$-1. This quite well corresponds to the interpretation of the length of the path as the number of steps one has to take to move from n to m. Thus, for $k = 1$, $n = m$ and the length of the path is 0, meaning "one does not have to move from n to reach n." Therefore, by convention, there is a path of length 0 from every node in the flowgraph to itself. However, if there is an arc $(n \, n)$ in the set A of arcs, there also exists a path of length 1 from n to itself.

A path is *acyclic* if all nodes in it are distinct; otherwise it is *cyclic*. A cyclic path from n to n whose other nodes are distinct is a *simple cycle*. A path from Start to Exit is a *program path*. A path from n to m that has been executed is a trace from n to m; an executed program path is simply a *trace*. In what follows we use VDM-SL notation for a high-level modeling and interpreting of path problems.

Example 5.1   *Using the VDM-SL definitions of the type Flowgraph in Figure 5.5, consider the following VDM-SL definitions of some path concepts and the corresponding tests for the flowgraph in Fig. 5.9, defined as a Flowgraph value FG.*

```
types
   path = seq of Node;

functions
IsValidPath : Path * FlowGraph -> bool  -- returns true iff
                                        -- s is path in G

IsValidPath (s, G) ==
   s(1) in set G.N and              -- first and last node in
      s(len s) in set G.N and       -- s are in set N of nodes

      forall i in set              -- every pair of adjacent
         {1,...,len s - 1}         -- nodes in path
         & s(i) in set N and
      mk_(s(i),s(i+1)) in set G.A;  -- is an arc in set
                                    -- A of arcs

IsCyclic : Path * Flowgraph -> bool
IsCyclic(s, G) ==
   IsValidPath (s, G) and
      exists i,j in set {1,…,len s}& i<>j and
      s(i) = s(j).
```

The following are some tests of those concepts:

```
IsValidPath([2, 3, 4, 6], FG)  = true;
IsValidPath([2, 3, 6], FG)     = false;
IsCyclic([2, 3, 4, 5] , FG)    = false;
IsCyclic([2, 3, 4, 6, 3], FG)  = true;
IsCyclic([3, 2, 4, 6, 4], FG)  = false;
```

Node j is *reachable from* node i iff there exists a path from i to j. Node i is simply *reachable* if it is reachable from the start node S. The flowgraph is *connected* iff every node lies on some program path. In other words, if the program is connected then for every node in the graph, (1) the node is reachable and (2) there is a path from the node to the exit node E. It is obvious that if the graph is not connected then there exists a potential control anomaly in the program. Thus, if condition (1) is violated for some node, the node can never be executed; if condition (2) is violated, program exit is never reached if the node is reached on some computation.

It is intuitively obvious that the theoretical notion of a cycle is close to that of the programming notion of loop; these two, however, are not identical! This is illustrated in Fig. 5.10. It is not clear whether there is a loop around nodes 1, 2, 3, and 4 with an entry 2 in the middle or, rather, the loop is around nodes 2, 3, 5, 6, and 7 with an exit 3 in the middle! Clearly, the loop is a *language* concept rather than a graph-theoretical one.

Fig. 5.10   A code segment and its flow-graph; how many loops are there?

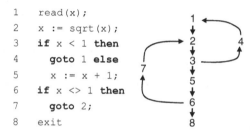

```
1    read(x);
2    x := sqrt(x);
3    if x < 1 then
4        goto 1 else
5        x := x + 1;
6    if x <> 1 then
7        goto 2;
8    exit
```

A yet another example of the difference between the language notion of a loop and that of a cycle is the following, admittedly pathological, piece of code:

```
while p loop
    S; -- straight line code
    << goto Next >> ;
    Q;
end loop;
Next:...
```

Clearly, in the above code, statement Q is not reachable, thus violating the connectivity property. Fortunately, static analysis can easily detect a control flow anomaly of this kind as shown in Chap. 7.

Problem 5.2   *How to determine whether there exists a path of length k from node n to m?*

Observe that we are not interested in showing a specific path from n to m; all we ask about is the *existence* of a path of length k from k to n. Certainly, for a small graph and small k we can answer this question by a simple inspection of the flowgraph. However, to answer the question in general, we need a more powerful tool, namely the power of relation.

Consider first $k = 1$. It is obvious that the path in question is simply an arc from n to m, and its detection is checking whether the pair $(n\ m)$ is in the set of arcs A. For $k = 2$, the path must consist of two arcs, one from n to some node, say p, and the other arc from p to m. To define this fact formally, we first introduce the concept of the composition of binary relations. Toward that goal, let Q be a binary relation from some set X to a set Y and R be a relation from the set Y to some set Z. The *composition* of Q and R, denoted $Q;R$ is defined as follows:

$$Q;R=\left\{(x\,z)\,\middle|\,x\in X,z\in Z\wedge\exists\,y\in Y\bullet x\,Q\,y\wedge y\,R\,z\right\}.$$

Now, for the paths problem there is $X = Y = Z = N$, where N is the set of nodes in the flowgraph and $Q = R = A$, where A is the set of arcs in the flowgraph. Thus, the composition of $A;A$ becomes the *second power* of A, denoted A^2. It is obvious that given two nodes n and m, there is a path of length 2 from n to m if and only if $(n\ m) \in A^2$ or, equivalently,

$$n\,A^2\,m \Leftrightarrow \exists p : N \bullet (n\,p) \in A \wedge (p\,m) \in A.$$

The existence of a path of an arbitrary length k, $k > 2$, can be established as the existence of path of length k-1 from n to some node p and of the arc $(p\,m)$ in A. This observation leads to the following recursive definition of the kth *power* of A:

$$A^1 = A$$

$$A^k = A^{k-1}; A$$

Clearly, if $(n\,m)\,A^k$ there is a path of length k from n to m in the flowgraph.

In some cases, one may be interested in the existence of a path from n to m of any length. This can be accomplished by establishing the fact that there exists some k, $k > 0$, such that $(n\,m) \in A^k$, or, equivalently, the truth of the following proposition

$$n\,A^1\,m \vee n\,A^2\,m \vee ... \vee n\,A^k\,m \vee ... \,.$$

The following union A^+ of all positive powers of relation A

$$A^+ = \bigcup_{k>0} A^k$$

is referred to as the (*irreflexive* or *positive*) *transitive closure* of A. In terms of this concept, there is a path from n to m if and only if $(n\,m)$ is in the set A^+. Intuitively, A^+ is the smallest superset of A that is transitive. Binary relation B on set N is *transitive* if and only if for any three nodes x, y, z from N, if $x\,B\,y$ and $y\,B\,z$ then there also is $x\,B\,z$.

Problem 5.3 *The definition of the transitive closure of a relation involves the infinite union of the powers of the relation. How, in practice, the closure can be computed by considering only a finite number of powers?*

If the arc relation A is acyclic, then there always exists some power k, smaller than the size of the flowgraph, for which A^k is the first empty power, i.e., all powers of A *less than* k are nonempty. Consequently, all powers equal to or *higher* than k are ultimately empty. Consider, for example, the flowgraph in Fig. 5.9 and its subgraph induced on the set of nodes {7, 8, 9, 10, 11, 12}, obtained if all other nodes and the arcs incident on those nodes have been removed. The set B of arcs of that subgraph is $B = \{(7\,8), (7\,9), (8\,11), (9\,10), (10\,11), (11\,12)\}$. To derive B^2 compose B with itself by inspecting every pair, say $(x\,y)$ in B, and identifying other pairs in B that start with the second element y of the first pair, say $(y\,z)$; then, $(x\,z)$ is in B^2. Thus, for our example one gets $B^2 = \{(7\,11), (7\,10), (8\,12), (9\,11), (10\,12)\}$. To derive B^3 compose in the same fashion B^2 and B to obtain $B^3 = \{(7\,11), (7\,12), (9\,12)\}$. Next, $B^4 = \{(7\,12)\}$ and finally $B^5 = B^4; B = \{\}$, since there is no path of length 5 in the subgraph. Consequently, all powers B^k, $k > 4$, are empty.

Now let us add the arc $(11\,7)$ to our subflowgraph. This introduces a cycle to the sublowgraph. However, this addition causes the sets of values of the powers of the new B={(7 8), (7 9), (8 11), (9 10), (10 11), (11 7) (11 12)} to be substantially larger and thus hard to handle by hand. Fortunately, the helping hand of VDM-SL's high-level notation comes to the rescue as illustrated below.

Example 5.2   *The following are the straightforward VDM-SL definitions of the composition and power of relation. The type BinRel is a renamed type Arcs in Fig. 5.5:*

```
Composition:BinRel * BinRel -> BinRel        -- returns R;Q
Composition(R,Q) ==
  {mk_(a,c) |
     mk_(a,b1) in set R, mk_(b2,c) in set Q & b1= b2};

power_of:BinRel * nat1 -> BinRel       -- Computes the x-th
power_of(R,x) ==                       -- power of relation R
  if (x = 1)
     then R
     else Composition(R, power_of(R, x-1))
pre x>0;
```

The function power_of (B, k) returns B^k, the *kth* power of B. B^1 through B^6, produced by the CSK VDM_SL Toolbox's interpreter, are listed in Fig. 5.11; recall that in VDM-SL a pair $(x\ y)$ is written down as **mk_**(x, y):

It is easy to see that for some high enough powers no new pairs are added to their *union*. Thus, even if B^2 contains all new pairs compared to B^1, B^3 contains all new but one pair: (7 11) (we drop the **mk_** constructor here), and B^4 has four new pairs: (8 10), (9 8), (9 9), and (10 10) while B^5 has no new arcs. Thus, B^5; B yields no additional pairs than those already in the union of B^1 through B^5. Clearly, the pairs added to the subsequent powers of B are "modulo" the length of simple cycles in the sublowgraph. There are three simple cycles of length three around nodes 7, 8, and 11 and four simple cycles of length four around nodes 7, 9, 10, and 11; all of them are in B^3 and B^4, respectively. Consequently, after a simple cycle say, from x to x, has been identified as a pair $(x\ x)$ in some B^k, $k > 1$, the subsequent powers greater than k contain simply those pairs emanating from x that appear in B^5. That fact allows one to formulate the following straightforward VDM-SL definition of the transitive closure:

```
Transitive_cl: BinRel -> BinRel
                -- Returns the transitive closure of R
  Transitive_cl(R) == dunion {Power_rel(R,k)
                   | k in set {1,..., card G.N}};
```

In the above dunion is the *distributed* (or *generalized*) set union, which takes as its (unary!) argument a family of sets and returns their union. Observe that the highest power of *R* included in this operation is the number of nodes in the flowgraph.

Example 5.3   *The following VDM-SL definitions use the transitive closure to test some properties of the flowgraph:*

```
B1 = { mk_(7, 8),    mk_(7, 9),   mk_(8, 11), mk_(9, 10),
       mk_(10, 11), mk_(11, 7), mk_(11, 12) }

B2 = { mk_(7, 10), mk_(7, 11), mk_(8, 7),    mk_(8, 12),
       mk_(9, 11), mk_(10, 7), mk_(10, 12), mk_(11, 8),
       mk_(11, 9) }

B3 = { mk_(7, 7),    mk_(7, 11),  mk_(7, 12), mk_(8, 8),
       mk_(8, 9),   mk_(9, 7),   mk_(9, 12), mk_(10, 8),
       mk_(10, 9), mk_(11, 10), mk_(11, 11) }

B4 = { mk_(7, 7),    mk_(7, 8),   mk_(7, 9),   mk_(7, 12),
       mk_(8, 10),  mk_(8, 11),  mk_(9, 8),   mk_(9, 9),
       mk_(10, 10), mk_(10, 11), mk_(11, 7), mk_(11, 11),
       mk_(11, 12) }

B5 = { mk_(7, 8),    mk_(7, 9),   mk_(7, 10),  mk_(7, 11),
       mk_(8, 7),    mk_(8, 11),  mk_(8, 12),  mk_(9, 10),
       mk_(9, 11),  mk_(10, 7),  mk_(10, 11), mk_(10, 12),
       mk_(11, 7),  mk_(11, 8),  mk_(11, 9),   mk_(11, 12) }

B6 = { mk_(7, 7),    mk_(7, 10),  mk_(7, 11),  mk_(7, 12),
       mk_(8, 7),    mk_(8, 8),   mk_(8, 9),   mk_(8, 12),
       mk_(9, 7),    mk_(9, 11),  mk_(9, 12),  mk_(10, 7),
       mk_(10, 8),  mk_(10, 9),  mk_(10, 12), mk_(11, 8),
       mk_(11, 9),  mk_(11, 10), mk_(11, 11) }.
```

Fig. 5.11 The first six powers of the relation{(7 8), (7 9), (8 11), (9 10), (10 11), (11 7) (11 12)}

```
IsPath : FlowGraph * Node * Node -> bool
                     -- Returns true if there exists
                     -- a path from n to m in G
IsPath (G, n, m) == mk_(n,m) in set Transitive_cl (G.A);
```

Testing of this function is left to the reader as an exercise. The above method for the identification of the existence of a path in the flowgraph can be modified to identify the path itself. Here is the rough algorithm. To find a shortest path from n to m, find the *smallest* power k such that the pair $(n\ m)$ is in B^k. Then, there must exist a *predecessor p* (not necessarily unique) of m such that $(n\ p)$ is in B^{k-1}, i.e., there exists a path from n to p of length k-1, meaning that $[p, m]$ is the last segment of the path from n to m. Continuing the process for k-2...1 allows one to recover the entire path or even a set of all shortest paths. Certainly, this method is, in general, rather inefficient and better, faster algorithms have been developed. However, as shown in Chap. 1, an inefficient, but *easy to understand* method may well serve as a direct specification of the problem!

5.7   Conclusions

The flowgraphs considered so far have been derived at the *instruction level*, where nodes in the graph correspond to the smallest executable units in the program. However, the flowgraph can be derived for any level of abstraction, provided that its nodes correspond to well-defined single-entry single-exit code segments. Thus, a node can correspond to a sequence of instructions, an entire **if–then–else** statement, or to a **while** loop. Consider, for example, the graph in Fig. 5.9. If the nodes in the graph are grouped as follows: $b1=(1,2)$, $b2 =(3,4,5,6)$, $b3 = (7,8,9,10,11)$, and $b4=(12)$ then one obtains a linear flowgraph that corresponds to the sequence of "macro" instructions $b1;b2;b3;b4$. Such a decomposition may be useful in some applications, to name only a few: Encapsulation of static or dynamic slices; Encapsulation of program modifications [3, 4, 5]; The localization of programming error; Display of the flowgraph in a finite-size space. However, care has to be taken to properly model the data used and defined in such macronodes; this, of course depends on the problem at hand. Path analysis is very important for static and dynamic program analysis, as demonstrated in the subsequent chapters. This brings up a need for a general and practical approach to paths problems, cf.[6]

Exercise 5.1 *Define a function that detects the existence of a path from node n to m, which traverses some node p, other than n and m.*

Exercise 5.2 *Define a function that detects the existence of a path from node n to m, which does NOT traverse some node p, other than n and m.*

Exercise 5.3 *Define a VDM-SL function that returns a finite set of paths from node n to node m that are either acyclic or simple cycle.*

Exercise 5.4 *The flowgraph is strongly connected if every node in it is reachable from the start S and can reach the exit E. Define predicate Is_Connected(FG: Flowgraph), which returns true if FG is strongly connected.*

References

1. A.V. Aho, R. Sethi, J.U. Ullman, Compilers: Principles, Techniques and Tools, Addison-Wesley, Reading, MA, 1985.
2. M.S. Hecht, Flow Analysis of Computer Programs, North Holland, New York, NY, 1979.
3. J. Laski, W. Szermer, Identification of program modifications and its applications in software maintenance, Proceedings of IEEE Conference on Software Maintenance, Orlando, FL, November 10–13, 1992, pp. 282–290.
4. J. Laski, W. Szermer, Regression analysis of reusable software components, Advances in Software Reuse, Second International Workshop on Software Reusability, Lucca, Italy, March 24–26, 1993, pp.134–141.
5. W. Szermer, Identification Of Computer Program Modifications Through Flow Graph Correction, PhD Dissertation, Oakland University Rochester, Michigan, 1995.
6. R.E. Tarjan, A unified approach to path problems, Journal of the ACM, 28(3), 577–593, 1981.

Chapter 6
Program Dependencies

Abstract Program dependencies model the ways program entities – statements, expressions, variables, control flow, etc. – interact with each other. Therefore, they are explicitly or implicitly the basis of static (source-based) and dynamic (execution-based) program analysis. The basic two are the Control and Data Dependencies. The former accounts for the selection of program statements for execution, while the latter models data exchange between program statements. Both are binary relations on the set of nodes in the flowgraph but they can be used as a basis to define other heterogeneous relations, e.g., between statements and variables. The discussion is illustrated by the actual results produced by STAD 4.0.

6.1 Motivations

From the *software engineering* perspective, the objective of program static analysis is to help understand the code. However, static analysis originated in the field of *code optimization* and, henceforth, some of its concepts are not necessarily directly useful in the field of software engineering. Moreover, it is not possible to arrive at a unique interpretation of the multifaceted and subjective notion of program comprehension. Nevertheless, it appears that in the realm of software engineering, two major areas of applications have emerged. One is the *proscriptive* analysis, which aims toward the detection of real or potential flaws in the program; the other is the *descriptive* analysis, which provides answers to the user's queries about "what's going on in the program." Fortunately, these two objectives share the same mathematical underpinning, that is, *program dependencies*. These are models of the way program entities – statements, expressions, variables, control flow, etc. – interact with each other. Here is a sample of questions about the program that can be answered in terms of program dependencies (Chap. 7 is devoted to that kind of analysis):

J. Laski and W. Stanley, *Software Verification and Analysis*,
DOI: 10.1007/978-1-84882-240-5_7, © Springer Verlag London Limited 2009

- Which imported variables are used to obtain the values of the exported variables?
- Which statements in the program are responsible for the value of variables of interest at a certain point in the program?
- Is there a possibility of a statement to refer to an uninitialized variable?
- Which statements have to be traversed to reach a statement of interest?
- If statement say, S, is modified, which parts of the program will be affected?

There are two basic types of program dependencies: *Data Dependencies* and *Control Dependencies*. The transitive closure of the union of these two is referred to as a *General Dependency*. All three are binary relations on the set of nodes in the flowgraph. However, they can be used to define dependencies between heterogeneous entities, e.g., statements and variables. Control dependency is much more complex affair than data dependency as it requires some, not so intuitively obvious supporting concepts, that is, dominance and attraction. The main ideas of control dependency are presented in Sect. 6.2–6.5, while data and general dependencies are treated in Sect. 6.6. However, one has to be aware that the discussion is restricted to *intra*procedural analysis, when the procedure is analyzed independently from the rest of the program. The more general *inter*procedural analysis, where a collection of procedure and functions is analyzed, is not fully covered in the text; a modicum of *inter*procedural analysis discussed here involves node splitting for procedure calls and procedure signature anomaly discussed in Chap. 7. Throughout, procedure P in Fig. 6.1, its elaborated version in Fig. 6.2 and the flowgraph of the latter in Fig. 6.3 will be used as an illustration of the discussion.

```
procedure P(
          x: integer;
       VAR z: integer);
    VAR
       p,
       q,
       r : boolean;
       y: integer;
    begin
      repeat
         if q then
            y := 1 ;
      until q;
      if r then
         y := 1
      else
         begin
            z := x + y;
            z := z + 2*x;
         end;
    end;     {procedure P}
```

Fig. 6.1 A Pascal procedure

```
          procedure P(x: integer;
                   VAR z: integer);
          VAR p,
              q,
              r : boolean;
              y : integer;

          begin
{ 1}        { <STAD> Initialization of parameter x - 3 }
{ 2}        { <STAD> Initialization of parameter z - 4 }
{ 3}        repeat
{ 4}           if q then
{ 5}              y := 1 ;
{ 6}        until q;
{ 7}        if r then
{ 8}           y := 1
            else
               begin
{ 9}              z := x + y;
{10}              z := z + 2 * x ;
               end;
{11}        { <STAD> EXIT USE OF z - 4 }
{12} end; { Procedure P }
```

Fig. 6.2 STAD's extended (elaborated) procedure *P* from Fig. 6.1

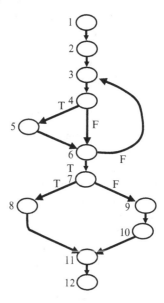

Fig. 6.3 Flowgraph of the procedure in Fig. 6.2

6.2 Dominators and Attractors

Consider the expanded procedure *P* in Fig. 6.2 and its flowgraph in Fig. 6.3 Suppose that one wants to monitor execution of *P* *without* placing breakpoints at every statement.[1] That is, one would like to place a minimal number of "strategically" chosen breakpoints which, if encountered during execution, allow one to identify other nodes that *had* to be executed. For example, if a breakpoint at node 6 is encountered one knows that nodes 1, 2, 3, and 4 have surely been traversed while node 5 just *may* have been traversed. We say that nodes 1–4 *dominate* node 6, while node 5 does not. The following definition formalizes the above observation.

Definition 6.1 (dominance) *For two (not necessarily distinct) nodes v, w ∈ N, if v lies on every path from the start node S to w, then v dominates w (or v is a dominator of w). If v≠w and v dominates w then v properly dominates w. If v properly dominates w and for every other dominator v' of w, v'≠w, v' dominates v, then v is the (unique) immediate or direct dominator of w.*

The above definition gives rise to the binary relation DOM on the set *N* of nodes in the flowgraph, DOM $\subseteq N \times N$, defined as follows: v DOM $w \Leftrightarrow v$ dominates w. The following are some properties of this relation [2]

- The start node *S* dominates all other nodes in the flowgraph,
- Every node dominates itself (n DOM n, *reflexivity*).
- If *n* dominates *k* then the reverse is not true
  (n DOM $k \Rightarrow \neg k$ DOM n, *antisymmetry*).
- If *n* dominates *k* and *k* dominates *m* then *n* dominates *m*
  (n DOM $k \wedge k$ DOM $m \Rightarrow n$ DOM m, *transitivity*).
- For any three distinct nodes *n*, *m*, and *k*, if *n* and *m* dominate *k* then either
  n dominates *m* or conversely, *m* dominates *n* (the dominators of a node
  form a *linear ordering* aka chain):

Fig. 6.4 shows the dominance relation for the flowgraph from Fig. 6.3 as generated by STAD; please note that the reflexive elements of the relation (i.e., pairs ($n\ n$)) are not listed for obvious reason.

Now, let us look at the immediate dominators. Intuitively, for every node *d*, the immediate dominator is the first merging point for all paths form the start *S* that reach *d*. Obviously, pairs ($n\ m$) such that *n* is the immediate dominator of *m* are members of the DOM relation. However, the very definition of the immediate dominance guarantees that for every node in the flowgraph there is at most one unique immediate dominator (the entry node is not dominated by any other node in the flowgraph). That means that the immediate dominance part of the relation DOM is a *function*, call it ID, from the set of nodes *N* in the flowgraph to *N*. That is, ID(*m*), if defined, is the unique immediate dominator of *m*. Owing to this fact, the dominance relation can be

---

[1]This problem is typical for structural (white-box) program testing, see Chap. 8.

conveniently represented by the *dominance tree*, rooted at the program start node. For every node n in the tree, node m is a child of n if and only if $n = ID(m)$. Fig. 6.5 shows the dominance tree for the control graph of Fig. 6.3.

Problem 6.1   *Assuming that the dominance relation has been derived, how to use it to compute the ID function?*

First, we know that the immediate dominator $ID(n)$ of node n is among dominators of the node. Second, we also know that dominators of n form a chain, i.e., a linear ordering. Therefore, $ID(n)$ is that node in the set of dominators of n that does not dominate any other node in that set. Thus, whenever defined, $ID(n)$ is the unique element of the following set

$$DOM(n) \setminus \bigcup_{x \in DOMS(n)} DOMS(x).$$

In the above, $DOMS(x)$ is the set of dominators of node x and $\setminus$ is the set difference operator. Clearly, $ID(n)$ is computed by removing from the set $DOMS(n)$ all dominators of nodes in it. The result is either an empty set (for the start node) or a singleton set containing the unique element $ID(n)$. For example, the set $\{1,2,3,4,6,7\}$ contains all dominators of node 8, the union of all dominators of nodes in that set is $\{1,2,3,4,6\}$

NODE	DOMINATED BY
1	{ }
2	{1}
3	{1 2 }
4	{1 2 3 }
5	{1 2 3 4 }
6	{1 2 3 4 }
7	{1 2 3 4 6}
8	{1 2 3 4 6 7}
9	{1 2 3 4 6 7 }
10	{1 2 3 4 6 7 9}
11	{1 2 3 4 6 7 }
12	{1 2 3 4 6 7 11}

Fig. 6.4 The dominance relation produced by STAD for the flowgraph in Fig. 6.3

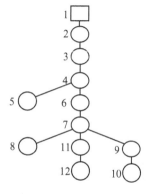

Fig. 6.5 The dominance tree for the flowgraph in Fig. 6.3

and thus ID(8) = 7. Of course, a literal implementation of that method could be quite inefficient. Again, however, this inefficient but straightforward solution may serve as a` direct *specification* of the problem. Now, assume we want to identify a path that reaches the exit 12 from, say, node 3. We know that any path from 3 to 12 will ultimately have to traverse nodes 4, 6, 7, and 11; this is because all of them *attract* node 3. The notion of attraction[2] is that of dominance applied to the inverse flowgraph, one in which the orientation of arcs has been reversed and the Start S and Exit E nodes swapped. Thus, for the original flowgraph $G = (N, A, S, E)$ its inverse version is $G^{-1}=(N, A^{-1}, E, S)$, where $A^{-1} = \{(n\ m)|\ m\ A\ n\}$. The following is the formal definition of the concept:

Definition 6.2 (attraction) *For two (not necessarily distinct) nodes v, w $\in$ N, if v lies on every path from w to the exit node E, then v attracts w (or v is an attractor of w). If v $\neq$ w and v attracts w then v properly attracts w. If v properly attracts w and for every other attractor v' of w, v'$\neq$w, v' attracts v, then v is the (unique) immediate or direct attractor of w.*

Fig. 6.6 shows the attractors produced by STAD for the flowgraph of Fig. 6.3. Let ATTR be a binary relation on the set of nodes in the flowgraph, such that

$$n\ \text{ATTR}\ m \Leftrightarrow n\ \text{attracts}\ m.$$

All formal properties of the DOM relation are satisfied by the ATTR relation in the context of the inverse graph (CAUTION: ATTR is not, in general, the inverse of

NODE	ATTRACTORS OF NODE
1	{2 3 4 6 7 11 12}
2	{3 4 6 7 11 12}
3	{4 6 7 11 12}
4	{6 7 11 12}
5	{6 7 11 12}
6	{7 11 12}
7	{11 12}
8	{11 12}
9	{10 11 12}
10	{11 12}
11	{12}
12	{}

Fig. 6.6 The attraction relation produced by STAD for the flowgraph in Fig. 6.3

---

[2] Attraction is often referred to as postdominance or reverse dominance. Since one word is preferred to two, and postdominance might be construed as a counterpart of nonexisting predominance, attraction seems to be a better choice as it also has a programming appeal.

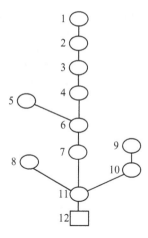

Fig. 6.7 The attraction tree for the flowgraph in Fig. 6.3

DOM!). In particular, let IA be the immediate attractor function, i.e., for any node n in the graph except for the exit E, IA(n) returns the immediate attractor of n. Intuitively, IA(n) is the *nearest merging point* of all paths from n to the exit E (in G). Like dominance, attraction is a partial linear ordering since for any three distinct nodes n, m, and k, if n and m attract node k then either n attracts m or conversely, m attracts n. The exit node E attracts all other nodes in the graph. Thus, ATTR can be represented by an attraction tree, rooted at the exit node E. Node m is a child of node n if and only if n is an immediate attractor of m. Fig. 6.7 shows the attraction tree for the flowgraph in Fig. 6.3; observe that to better capture the intuitive meaning of the tree, it has been drawn growing up, rather than down.

Similarly to the immediate dominators case, IA(n), the immediate attractor of node n, is the unique member of the following set (except for the exit node E):

$$\text{ATTRS}(n) \setminus \bigcup_{x \in \text{ATTRS}(n)} \text{ATTRS}(x).$$

where ATTRS(n) is the set of attractors of node n. Attractors are important to the definition and derivation of control dependencies for arbitrary control as illustrated in Sect. 6.3. However, we first introduce the concept for structured control.

6.3 Control Dependency: Structured Control

Whether, in a program run, a particular statement is executed or not, *may depend*[3] on the results of the evaluation of the predicates in the decision nodes encountered on a path leading to the node. In order to handle this in a more systematic way, two

---

[3] We say "may" for in some cases a decision node may always evaluate to a constant, e.g. **if** $3 > 2$ **then** ...**else**.

related concepts are introduced here: the Control Dependency (CD) and the Scope of Control (SC). Both are binary relations from the set N of nodes in the flowgraph to the set N_d of decision nodes in it, i.e., both are subsets of $N \times N_d$. The CD relation identifies the immediate, "*most recent*" decision nodes directly responsible for the selection of a node for execution; in contrast, the SC relation identifies *all* decision nodes that affect the selection of the node either directly or indirectly. To get a better understanding of the problem let us analyze some specific cases first. Consider the following compound Ada statement:

```
if d then
  Q;
else
  R ;
end if ;
S ;
```

Assume now that Q and R in the **if** statement above are single, further nondecomposable statements. It is obvious that, *assuming* the **if** statement has been reached, the execution of Q and R depends on the outcome of the run-time evaluation of d. Thus, Q and R are both control dependent on d, symbolically Q CD d and R CD d. In contrast to statements Q and R, execution of statement S does not depend on d since S is *always* executed whenever d is entered, *provided* that the entire **if** statement properly terminates, an issue discussed in earlier chapters.

It is rather obvious that the above findings apply also to the case when Q and R are both straight-line code segments, i.e., each is a sequence of one or more statements. Clearly, each component of Q and R is directly control dependent on d.

Problem 6.2 *Consider the following nested Ada if statement:*

```
if p then
if q then
  A;
else
B;
  end if;
else
  if r then
C;
else
  D;
  end if;
end if;
E;
```

Derive the direct control dependency relation CD for the statement.

Now the selection for execution of the statements A, B, C, and D above depends on the evaluation of two, rather than one, predicates: p and q (for A and B) and p and r (for C and D). When $p = true$ the only statement that is guaranteed to be executed is q, while execution of A and B is only potential, depending on the evaluation of q itself. Thus, there is

$$\begin{array}{ll} A \ \mathbf{CD} \ q, & B \ \mathbf{CD} \ q \\ C \ \mathbf{CD} \ r, & D \ \mathbf{CD} \ r \\ q \ \mathbf{CD} \ p, & R \ \mathbf{CD} \ p. \end{array}$$

Observe that the entire **if** statement offers an example of *two-level* control influence. Clearly, at the first level statements A and B are control dependent on q, C, and D are control dependent on r, and q and r are control dependent on p. Consequently, the latter has a second-level control influence over A, B, C, and D. Formally, that influence is the *second power* of the CD relation, i.e.,

$$X \ CD^2 \ p,$$

where X stands for any of A, B, C, and D. Thus, in this case, GCD is the union of CD and its second power. Now, if the entire **if** statement were nested in an outer **if** statement, the latter would give rise to the third level of decision control, modeled by the third power CD^3 of the control dependency relation CD. In general, the general control dependency (GCD) is the union of all positive powers of CD, i.e.,

$$GCD = \bigcup_{k>0} CD^k.$$

In words, if n GCD d, then n is control dependent on d either directly (n CD d) or indirectly (n $CD^k d$, for some $k > 0$). In other words, GCD is the *transitive closure* of CD, i.e.,

$$GCD = CD^+.$$

Observe that in theory the number of powers of CD contributing to GCD is not restricted. However, it is, in fact, bounded by the number of nodes in the flowgraph, an issue discussed earlier in Chap. 5.

Next, consider the following loop statement

```
While d loop
   B;
end loop;
   E
```

Since statement E is always reached (*provided* the loop properly terminates) its execution does not depend on the decision node d. If B is a single statement then certainly B is control dependent on d. If B is a sequence of statements, i.e., $B = S_1; S_2;...; S_k$, each S_i, $i = 1,..., k$, is also control dependent on d. However, if B is another loop or a conditional statement then not all the statements in B are control dependent on d. Clearly, for any node n in B to be control dependent on d, d must be the *last* decision node on a path from the start of the loop to n such that the selection of n for execution depends on the particular branch taken in d. Note that in the case of loops this requirement makes d *depend on itself*, since d

CD *d* holds! Indeed, if the loop body is entered, *d* itself will be executed again; otherwise it will not. Now we are ready to define CD formally for the conditional and loop statements

```
if d then              while d loop
  A;                     A ;
else           AND     end loop;
  B;                     C;
end if;
C ;
```

where *A* and *B* are single-entry single-exit code segments. Let N_A and N_B stand for the sets of nodes in the (sub)flowgraphs of *A* and B, respectively.

Definition 6.3 *(Control Dependence CD, structured control). For **if** d **then** A **else** B;C statement, every node in N_A and N_B that lies on every path from entry to A or B to C, with the exception of C, is control dependent on the decision node d. For a **while** d **do** A;C statement, every node in N_A that lies on every path from entry to A to C, with the exception of C, is control dependent on d. Also, d is control dependent on itself.*

Definition 6.3 properly captures our intuition about control dependence of nested structured control constructs, i.e., **if** and **while** statements: Node *n* is control dependent only on the decision node that immediately controls the selection of *n* for execution. This explains the requirement in Definition 6.3 that node *n* in the body of a loop or a branch of an **if** statement is control dependent on the decision node only if *n* lies on *all* paths through the body of the statement. Clearly, inner decision nodes in the statement's body have no effect on the selection of *n*. Fig. 6.8 shows STAD-generated CD and its second power for the flowgraph of Fig. 6.3. One element of the CD relation warrants some clarification: The fact that node 6 is control dependent on itself. This is due to the fact that after 6 is encountered the very first time its subsequent execution depends on the decision in 6 itself.

NODE	CONTROL DEPENDENT ON NODES
3	6
4	6
5	4 (6)
6	6
8	7
9	7
10	7

Fig. 6.8 Control dependency CD derived by STAD for the flowgraph in Fig. 6.3; its second power (*s* shown in *parentheses*)

6.4   Control Dependency: Arbitrary Control

The notion of CD for structured control can be generalized on arbitrary control (**goto**-licensed) as follows. Let d be a decision node and IA(d) be the immediate attractor of d. Consider node k in the flowgraph. If k is control dependent on d then there exist two arcs emanating from d, say (d n) and (d m), where n and m are two *distinct* successors of d, such that (1) k lies on every path from d to IA(d) that starts with one of the arcs, say (d n), and (2) k cannot be reached if the other arc, i.e., (d m), is taken. The following, equivalent definition of control dependence is borrowed from [1] it is also the basis for the algorithm to compute the dependencies.

Definition 6.4 (Control Dependence CD, arbitrary control [1]). *Let d be a decision node and k be any node in the flowgraph. Node k is* **control dependent** *on* d *(or, equivalently, d has* **direct control** *over k) iff*

   (1) there exists a path from d to k in the flowgraph such that any node on the path, with the exception of d and k, is attracted by k

and

   (2) d is not attracted by k.

Condition (1) states that there exists a path from d to k from which there is no branching to bypass k. Observe that this condition can be satisfied by a path consisting of a single edge, e.g., (d k). Condition (2) states that k may or may not be executed, depending on the branch taken in d, since not every path from d to IA(d) traverses k. If d is a loop exit, then d is dependent on itself. In that case, conditions (1) and (2) are trivially satisfied (the definition of attraction and empty path, respectively). Note that the definition refers to the possibility of the node in question being reached or not on a path from d to IA(d) on an *acyclic* path. Clearly, if d lies on a cycle, a node can be reached on a path that continues past IA(d), even if it could not be reached on a shortest path from d to IA(d).

Problem 6.3   *Using the appropriate definitions of the concepts involved, derive the CD relation for the flowgraph in Fig. 6.9.*

   Since the number of decision nodes is typically but a fraction of the set of nodes N in the flowgraph, it is more convenient to derive the Direct Control relation (DC), rather than the CD itself. DC is the inverse of CD, i.e.,

$$DC = CD^{-1}$$

or

$$d \text{ DC } n \text{ iff } n \text{ CD } d.$$

Fig. 6.9 A flowgraph with arbitrary flow of control

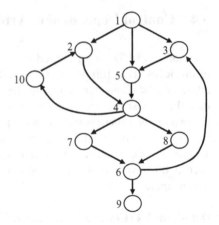

There are three decision nodes in the flowgraph in Fig. 6.9: 1, 4, and 6. It is easy to see that the immediate attractors of those nodes are the following:

$$IA(1) = 4$$
$$IA(4) = 6$$
$$IA(6) = 9.$$

Now, applying Definition 6.4 to the flowgraph we get the DC, represented by sets of nodes directly controlled by a decision node involved, i.e., $DC(d) = \{n \mid n \text{ DC } d\}$ (this kind of identifier overloading is well known to programmers, even if generally avoided by mathematicians):

$DC(1) = \{2,3,5\}$ -- set of nodes directly controlled by 1
$DC(4) = \{2,4,7,8,10\}$ -- set of nodes directly controlled by 4
$DC(6) = \{3,4,5,6\}$ -- set of nodes directly controlled by 6.

From the above one gets the CD relation:

$$CD = \{(2\ 1), (3\ 1), (5\ 1), (2\ 4), (4\ 4), (7\ 4),$$
$$(8\ 4), (10\ 4), (3\ 6), (4\ 6), (5\ 6), (6\ 6)\}.$$

The fact that nodes 1 and 9 do not depend on any decision node, indicates that they appear on *every* program path provided, of course, that every loop in the program properly terminates. Observe, however, that although nodes 4 and 6 also appear on every program path, they lie on cycles and, therefore, depend on themselves. Moreover, node 6 controls 4 but not the other way round. This is because if the branch (6 9) is taken, node 4 is not executed at all, while the execution of 6 is guaranteed regardless of the decision in 4, of course under the assumption that all loops terminate.

The last example illustrates the fact that, in general, a node can be directly control dependent on *more than* one decision node. It is easy, however, to see that in a structured flowgraph, every node is control dependent on exactly one, unique decision node! Therefore, *for structured flowgraphs, the CD relation is really a function.* Consequently, higher powers of CD are also functions although their union, i.e., the transitive closure CD^+ is, in general, a relation. Please recall from Chap. 5 that the very definition of the transitive closure of a binary relation R on set N of nodes

$$R^+ = \bigcup_{k>0} R^k$$

involves the infinite union of powers of R. However, the number of *distinct* powers of R is limited by the size of the graph. Again, in practice that number is much lower since usually either some higher powers stabilize or they render empty sets of nodes. For example, for the graph in Fig. 6.9

$$DC^2(6) = DC^2(4) = DC^1(4) = \{2,4,7,8,10\}$$
$$DC^2(1) = \emptyset.$$

Apparently, no new nodes can be derived for the higher levels of control dependence, since $DC^k(6) = DC^k(4) = DC^1(4)$, and $DC^k(1) = \emptyset$, for $k \geq 3$. Given decision node d, the union of all powers of DC(d) will be referred to as the Scope of Control of d and is denoted as SOC. Thus, one obtains

$$SOC(6) = DC^1(6) \cup DC^2(6) = \{2,3,4,5,6,7,8,10\}$$
$$SOC(4) = \{2,4,7,8,10\}$$
$$SOC(1) = \{2,3,5\}.$$

In words, if node k is in the SOC of some other node n, then the selection of k for execution depends directly of indirectly on the run-time evaluation of the predicate in n.

6.5 Computing Control Dependency

In this Section we discuss a method for the computation of DC(d), proposed in [1]. The method is based upon the analysis of the attraction tree, whose availability is thus assumed; that tree for the flowgraph in Fig. 6.9 is shown in Fig. 6.10.

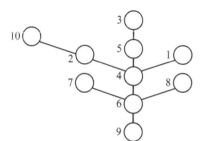

Fig. 6.10 The attraction tree for the flowgraph in Fig. 6.9

The first step in the process is the identification of the set S of arcs $(A\ B)$ in the flow-graph for which B is not an ancestor of A in the attraction tree, that is, B does not attract A. In the case of the graph in Fig. 6.9 those arcs are shown in the first column in Fig. 6.11.

Second, for each arc $(A\ B)$ in the set S, we identify the least common ancestor of A and B in the attraction tree. That ancestor, denoted L in Fig. 6.11, is the first merging node for all paths from A and B to the exit. Observe that L is always a decision node distinct from B, although it can be A in the case of cyclic (loop) dependence.

Third, we identify nodes that are under direct control of the decision nodes. Toward that goal, we use the property established in [1] that L is either A (when A and B are on a cycle) or L is the parent of A in the attraction tree (otherwise). That property leads to the following two rules:

1. if $L = A$, then all nodes on the path from A to B in the attraction tree, including A and B, are control dependent on A. This case captures dependence when A lies on a cycle and directly controls itself.

2. If L is the parent of A, then all nodes in the attraction tree on the path from L to B, including B but not L, are control dependent on A. This is the acyclic case.

Fig. 6.11 illustrates the procedure for the flowgraph in Fig. 6.9. Observe that the union of all sets of nodes nc(A) that are controlled by the decision node A is the set DC(A). Thus,

$$DC(1) = \{2\} \cup \{3, 5\} \cup \{5\}$$
$$DC(4) = \{7\} \cup \{8\} \cup \{2, 4, 10\}$$
$$DC(6) = \{3, 4, 5, 6\}.$$

The following is an outline of an algorithm for the identification of the nodes that are directly controlled by decision node A. Given arc $(A,\ B)$ in the set S, traverse the attraction tree backward until the parent of A (if one exists), marking all nodes visited before A's parent as control dependent on A. Observe that if $L = A$ (Case 1), A will be marked as control dependent on itself. On the other hand, if L is the parent of A (Case 2), A is not on the path from B to L and will not therefore be marked as dependent on itself. If the procedure is repeated for every arc in S, all control dependencies will have been determined.

Arcs (A B) in S (not B atrr A)	L (common ancestor of A, B)	Controlling node A	Nodes controlled by A, (nc(A))	Rule
(1 2)	4	1	2	ii
(1 3)	4	1	3, 5	ii
(1 5)	4	1	5	ii
(4 7)	6	4	7	ii
(4 8)	6	4	8	ii
(4 10)	4	4	2, 4, 10	i
(6 3)	6	6	3, 4, 5, 6	i

Fig. 6.11 Direct control dependencies for arcs in S

6.6 Data and General Dependency

In the preceding sections we discussed the concept of Control Dependency. Observe that the latter was expressed entirely in terms of the control flow in the program with no account of the data manipulated by the program. Now, the ultimate objective of the program is *not* traversing the flowgraph – it is to transform data, using the control as a *vehicle* supporting that objective. Therefore, to arrive at a full picture of dependencies in the program we have to finally account for the data manipulated by the program. That goal will be achieved in two steps. First, we define the Data Dependency between the nodes in the flowgraph in which the control flow will be essentially ignored. Second, the Data Dependency will be combined with Control Dependency as the General Dependency.

An intermediary step toward the notion of data dependency is that of *reaching definitions*. The following example illustrates the underlying intuition. Suppose that during debugging you suspend an execution of the program at some break point B and inspect the values of variables of *interest* (recall from the preceding chapters that to pass judgment about the correctness of variables at B you must have well, an intermediate *assertion* at B, however, informal the latter!). Further suppose that the value of variable, say X, is incorrect. The first question you may ask is, "Where does the value of X come from?" or, equivalently, "Which is the last assignment to X before B has been reached?" Surely, for a sequential deterministic program there is only one such assignment. Now, if you monitored the execution you could easily identify that unique place of the assignment; otherwise you have to consider *all possible* assignments to X that potentially can be used when control reaches point B. This is precisely the set of reaching definitions of X.

Definition 6.5 (Reaching Definition [2], [3]) *Let node p in the flowgraph be a definition of variable X. That definition reaches node q iff there exists a path from p to q along which X is not redefined.*

The above definition can be rephrased as follows: Definition of X in p reaches q iff there is a path from top of (entry to) p to (top of) q along which X is not *killed* (overwritten). Thus, the value of X at q *may* come from p, depending on the path taken from p to q. Fig. 6.12 shows the sets of reaching definitions for the procedure P from Fig. 6.2. Observe that since we allow at most one definition in a node, the node number uniquely identifies the variable defined in the node.

Also note that it is irrelevant whether X is manipulated in q or not. However , when X is used in q we say that q is *data dependent*[4] on p. Here is the formal definition of that notion:

Definition 6.6 *Data Dependency (DD) is a binary relation on the set N of nodes in the flowgraph, i.e., DD $\subseteq$ N $\times$ N, such that p DD q iff there exists a variable that is*

---

[4]This is also known as *a* definition-use chain, cf [2] and under such name is used in testing, see Chap. 8.

defined in p and used in q and there is a path from p to q along which the variable is not redefined.

Fig. 6.13 shows all data dependencies in procedure P from Fig. 6.2.

Now, nodes can be dependent on each other because of data dependency, control dependency, or any combination thereof. This give rise to the following definition of *General Dependency* (GD) as the transitive positive closure of the union of the control and data dependencies:

$$GD = (CD \cup DD)^+ = \bigcup_{k>0} (CD \cup DD)^k$$

In word, n GD k means that node n depends on node k either through data dependency, control dependency, or a combination of these two. The CD for the procedure in Fig. 6.2 is shown in Fig. 6.8; the GD relation for the procedure is shown in Fig. 6.14.

NODE	REACHED BY DEFINITIONS IN NODES
1	0
2	1 0
3	1 2 5 0
4	1 2 5 0
5	1 2 5 0
6	1 2 5 0
7	1 2 5 0
8	1 2 5 0
9	1 2 5 0
10	1 5 9 0
11	1 2 5 8 10 0
12	1 2 5 8 10 0

Fig. 6.12 Reaching definitions of procedure *P* in Fig. 6.2, as produced by STAD

NODE	IS DATA DEPENDENT ON NODES
9	1 5 0
10	1 9 0
11	2 10 0

Fig. 6.13 Data Dependency for procedure *P* in Fig. 6.2, as produced by STAD

NODE	IS GENERAL DEPENDENT ON NODES
1	0
2	0
3	6 0
4	6 0
5	4 6 0
6	6 0
7	0
8	7 0
9	1 4 5 6 7 0
10	1 4 5 6 7 9 0
11	1 2 4 5 6 7 9 10 0
12	0

Fig. 6.14 General Dependency for procedure *P* in Fig. 6.2, as produced by STAD

6.7   Conclusions

In [1] an algorithm is offered that computes the CD in $O(n^2)$ time, where *n* is the number of nodes in the flow graph. Applying an algorithm for the transitive closure e.g., Warshall's [5], the CD and SOC can be obtained in $O(n^3)$ time. An algorithm presented in [4] computes the immediate dominators in $O(|A| * \log n)$, where $|A|$ stands for the number of arcs in the flow graph. Similarly, immediate attractors for nodes in flow graph *G* can be determined by applying the algorithm for dominators in the reverse flow graph of *G* (the graph in which each arc (m, n) in *G* is replaced by arc (n, m) and the start and exit nodes swapped).

It is important to keep in mind that the concept of CD and its derivatives (e.g., scope) are expressed purely in terms of the control flowgraph and as such are "conservative," in the sense that they identify potential, but not necessarily real, dependencies. For example, in the following statement

```
if X = X then
   ...
else
   ... ;
```

the predicate $X = X$ has control over all other nodes in the statement while, in fact, no such control can ever be exercised. Unfortunately, in general, static analysis fails to identify cases like this one, since they fall into the category of undecidable problems. The above discussion is implicitly based on the assumption that all statements ultimately terminate. This is particularly important in the case of loops. To illustrate that fact, consider the following loop:

```
1: read(x);
2: while x > 0 do
3: x := f(x);
4: writeln;
```

According to the definition, node 4 is not control dependent on node 2. This is satisfactory if the loop terminates since in that case node 4 is always reached, regardless of the run-time evaluation of the control decision in node 2. Otherwise, one may claim that node 2 does have control influence on node 4, although in that case 4 can never be reached. It is not clear how to treat that situation formally. Here, we adopt a pragmatic approach to the problem. That is, the intended application of the dependency determines the choice of the definition. Typically, termination will be assumed.

Two observations are in order. First, the data and control dependencies can be used as a basis to define other relations of interest. For example, one may be interested in variables that may be used to compute the values of variables at certain points in the flowgraph. Second, the dependencies have to be ultimately extended on the system (program) level, to carry out interprocedural static analysis.

Exercise 6.1   *Provide the interpretation of the relation $DOM \cup ATTR^{-1}$.*

Exercise 6.2   *Provide the interpretation of the relation $DOM ; ATTR^{-1}$.*

Exercise 6.3   *Consider a program P consisting of several procedures. Define data and control dependency between statements in different procedures.*

Exercise 6.4   *Define a binary relation Variable Dependency VD on the set VARS of variables manipulated by the program such that v VD w if and only if variable v at the Start of the program may be used to obtain the value of the variable w at the Exit.*

References

1. J. Ferrante et al., The program dependence graph and its use in optimization, ACM Transactions on Programming Languages and Systems, 9(3), 319–349,1987.
2. M.S. Hecht, Flow Analysis of Computer Programs, North Holland, New York, NY, 1979.
3. A.V. Aho, R. Sethi J.D, Ullman, Compilers, Principles, Techniques and Tools, Addsion-Wesley, Reading, MA, 1986.
4. T. Lengauer, R.E. Tarjan, A fast algorithm for finding dominators in a flowgraph, Transactions on Programming Languages and Systems, 1,121–141,1979.
5. E. Nuutila, Efficient transitive closure computation in large digraphs, Acta Polytechnica Scandinavica, Mathematics and Computing in Engineering Series No. 74, Helsinki 1995, 124 pages, Published by the Finnish Academy of Technology, ISBN 951-666-451-2, ISSN 1237-2404, UDC 681.3.

Chapter 7
What Can One Tell About a Program Without Its Execution: Static Analysis

Abstract Static Program Analysis is a powerful method for the detection of program anomalies (the proscriptive analysis) and for the explanation of the events in the program (the descriptive analysis). Static analysis is also a prerequisite for structural, white-box program testing. Either kind of static analysis can be carried out at the procedural or at the system level. In this chapter, we first discuss the detection of control and data flow anomalies using the dependency models developed in Chap. 6. However, those models originated in the area of optimizing compilers and are not always suitable for problems germane to software engineering. Consequently, two novel methods are proposed in the chapter. First, it is the modeling of procedure calls by preprocessing the called procedure and identifying the actual dependencies of the exported (VAR and OUT) parameters on the imported ones (VAL and VAR). This significantly increases the accuracy of the modeling calls to the procedure and allows one to detect some signature anomalies. Second, a method is proposed to identify some events that take place on individual program paths and help detect some, otherwise hard to identify multidata anomalies.

7.1 Motivations

We all know that code inspection can be a very useful way to glean information about the program. However, there are fundamental limitations to the method due to the idiosyncrasies of the human mind: While we can be very successful in solving challenging semantic problems, e.g., synthesizing invariants, we utterly fail in simple clerical tasks like, for instance, identifying the reaching definitions in the program. Moreover, in either case the difficulties increase with the size of the program under analysis. Therefore, even for a program of moderate size, a tool support for code inspection is a must and is known as *Static Program Analysis*. As we shall see, this is a quite powerful method although tending to provide rather conservative results, due to the fact that many problems in static analysis are undecidable. In other words, while interpreting the results of static analysis we err on the side of *caution*.

J. Laski and W. Stanley, *Software Verification and Analysis*,
DOI: 10.1007/978-1-84882-240-5_8, © Springer Verlag London Limited 2009

Roughly speaking, the following are the three main objectives of static analysis. First, *proscriptive analysis* aims at the detection of real or potential flaws in the program. Usually, those are referred to as "*anomalies*", that is, things that either are clearly wrong or at least look so. Second, *descriptive analysis* provides *explanations* of "what's going on" in the program. Program dependencies introduced in Chap. 6 are a perfect example of that kind of analysis; indeed, even the derivation of the program's flowgraph falls into this category. Third, static analysis is a *prerequisite for structural (white-box) testing* to identify parts of the program (or combinations thereof) that are to be exercised during testing (cf. "*Required Elements*" in Chap. 8). Observe that the above classification refers only to the ways the results of the analysis are *used*, rather than to the way they are obtained; the mathematical underpinning of the analysis is similar in all three cases. Either kind of static analysis can be carried out at the procedural level (intraprocedural analysis) or at the system level (interprocedural analysis). Not surprisingly, most of the relevant research and practical results deal with the former, the latter lagging significantly behind. Consequently, the bulk of this chapter (and, indeed, of the whole text) is devoted to intraprocedural analysis while issues involving interprocedural events will be usually presented in a more general way.

The above remarks notwithstanding, in this chapter we do offer a *novel* insight into *some* aspects of interprocedural analysis. Specifically, this involves the modeling procedure calls that allows one to identify the input–output dependencies in the calling program as induced by the dependencies in the called procedure(s). That allows one to identify inconsistencies between the procedure's signature and the *actual* dependencies established by the procedure code.

Finally, we have to stress the importance of pragmatic issues. Our experience clearly shows that programmers want to know the rationale behind a warning about an anomaly. In particular, they want to know whether the anomaly is *guaranteed* (i.e., occurring on every execution) or *potential*, occurring on some executions only. That, however, is rarely offered by the supporting tool while manual efforts usually fail in the case of even moderate size program. Consequently, anomalies whose reason is hard to understand tend to be ignored. To appreciate the importance of that problem, imagine that you received a message "Statement Y is Data and Control Dependent on Statement X." If X and Y are close enough (textually, that is) you may see the reason for the message. However, if X and Y are separated by several pages of code your most likely reaction would be, "*Sorry, I can't see this.*" Now, you recall from Chap. 6 that typical algorithms for the derivation of program establish only the *existence* of the dependencies but not the underlying rationale. To alleviate the problem we postulate that an Explanation Feature be offered by the static analyzer. Typically, such a feature would identify a path (or a collection of paths) along which the anomaly involved occurs or, more correctly, *may* occur. For example, to explain data dependency of, say, node P on Q (assuming that some variable is defined in Q and used in P), one would produce a path from Q to P along which there is no definition of the variable involved. In contrast, to explain control dependency of statement S on some decision node *D* *two* paths would be needed: One from *D* to IA(*D*), the immediate attractor of *D*, that *bypasses* *S* and the other path, also from *D* to IA(*D*) that *traverses* *S*. That means that some kind of path analysis would have to be carried out. Although STAD does not yet offer such a feature we will sometimes outline the methods that can be employed to develop one. Moreover, STAD *does* identify some events on program paths if not necessarily the paths themselves. Those are *Data Contexts* used for the identification of quite tricky anomalies described in Sect. 7.7 and for testing in Chap. 8.

Summarizing the above discussion, here are the following three, not necessarily disjoint, stages in the handling of program anomalies:

– The *detection,* i.e., a positive statement that "something is suspect"
– The *localization*, i.e., pinpointing the detected event to a concrete
place in the code
– The *explanation*, i.e., the reformulation of the preceding two steps
in user-friendly terms

In what follows we discuss some of the better recognized anomalies plus a few ones not yet in the general (sub)consciousness of the programmers. However, since human ingenuity in erring seems to be unlimited (we believe it really is *so*) there is hope that many more anomalies will be identified in the future.

7.2 Control Flow Anomalies

Consider the following Ada function *f*:

```
function f(x: integer) return integer is
begin
    if x>0 then
        return 1;
    end if;
end f;
```

The flowgraph of the function is *ill-formed* since there is only one successor of the $x > 0$ instruction: When that condition is not true, i.e. if $x \geq 0$, a run-time control error *may* occur. Clearly, the real exit of an Ada function is a dummy, system-defined merging point of *all* **return** statements in the function, rather than the end of the function's body. Such an **exit-function** dummy node should be reachable by *all* paths originating at the start. Thus, every executable path through the function should end with a **return** followed by the (system-defined) exit-function node. In other words, if the precondition of the program is x > 0 then no control error can occur for a *valid* invocation of the function. Observe, that in Pascal, the Ada return(expression) statement roughly corresponds to the assignment function_name := expression. Thus, our Ada function *f* when transliterated into Pascal becomes the following function *f*_pas:

```
function f_pas(x: integer): integer;
begin
    if x>0 then
        f_pas:=1;
end;
```

However, in contrast to Ada, the flowgraph for the Pascal version *is* well-formed, since in Pascal the end of the function's body is indeed also the exit point! That means that for x ≤ 0 the function might terminate with an undefined returned value (it is again an open question whether the compiler at hand would detect that anomaly). Observe, however, that if the statement *f_pas:=2* were inserted at the very end of the function, *f_pas* would always return the constant value 2, thus overriding the assignment *f_pas:= 1*, even if the latter is executed.

Consider now the following Ada procedure *p*:

```
procedure p(IN OUT x: integer) is
begin
    if x >0 then
        <<A>> goto B;
        x:=x+1;
        x:=x-1;
        <<B>> goto A;
    end if;
end p;
```

Two anomalies can be identified in the procedure. First, there is an infinite loop around the two **goto** statements. Second, the two assignment statements in *p* are *unreachable*. Observe, however, that if the **goto** B statement is removed and the label <<A>> is assigned to the first assignment statement, there is still an infinite loop albeit the assignment statements become reachable. Now, it is an open question whether the compiler at hand will detect those flaws. It is instructive to convert *f* and *p* into the language of your choice and check whether the compiler issues a warning or an error message.

Problem 7.1 *Propose a flowgraph-based method for the detection of the anomalies in functions f, f_pas and procedure p.*

One quite obvious candidate for such a method would be the lack of connectedness of the flowgraph. The flowgraph is *connected* if and only if every node in it lies on some path from the start *S* to the exit *E*. In plain words, every node should be reachable from the start and it should be possible to continue from that node to the exit. This leads to a straightforward algorithm for the detection of the lack of connectedness: Compute the transitive closure A^+ of the arc relation A (see Chap. 5) and check whether, for every node n in the flowgraph, there exist the pair (Start, n) and the pair (n, Exit) in A^+. If the answer is "Yes" then the flowgraph is connected; otherwise, it is not.

Checking for the connectivity is a quite powerful tool for the detection of *some* anomalies. For example, it *successfully fails* for the procedure *p* above. However, it is easy to see that this test *passes* (i.e. *fails to detect* the anomaly) both for the Ada function *f* and the Pascal function *f*_pas. Toward that goal, the following solutions can be offered. For an Ada function, each path from the start must end with a **return** statement. For a Pascal function, each path from the start to the exit must traverse an assignment to the function name. An explanation of the anomaly would simply be the display of the offending path(s).

7.3   Data Flow Anomalies

The control flowgraph of a sequential program is its backbone that has to be fleshed out for the program to do its job, whatever that may be. That is of course achieved by manipulating the data while traversing the flowgraph. The generic term *data flow* (or the more general notion of *Information Flow*) refers to various aspects of defining and using data in the program. Whenever a data flow pattern is outright wrong or just potentially wrong, an error or warning message should be issued.

Before we proceed with the detection of data flow anomalies we need an auxiliary notion of *Live Variables*. To understand the rationale behind that notion consider the program segment in Fig. 7.1 and the following.

Problem 7.2. *Assume that in the process of debugging the code you have suspended its execution at the breakpoint labeled 1, and want to validate your ideas about the bug in the program by changing the values of some variables before resuming the execution. Which variables can potentially affect the resumed computation?*

A brief inspection of the code in Fig. 7.1 shows that the value of variable y at the breakpoint 1 has no influence on the execution of the code for that value is always

```
            begin
         1: if q then
                 y := 1
            else
                 y := 2;
            if r then
                 y := 1
            else
                begin
                    z := x + y;
                    z := z + 2 * x;
                end;
            end;
```

Fig. 7.1 A code segment

overwritten by the first if statement. In contrast, the initial values of variables x and z may influence the final values of these variables. We say that x and z are *live at* the breakpoint. Formally, given a point p and variable X in the program, X is live at p if and only if there is a node q such that (1) X is used in q and (2) there is a path from p to q along which X is not redefined. In other words, the value of X at p may

```
        procedure sum(i : integer; var s : integer);
            var k : integer;

            function sqr(n : integer) : integer;
              begin
{ 1}            {<< STAD >>VALUE PARAMETER INITALIZATION of n }
{ 2}            sqr := n * n
{ 3}          end;

        begin
{ 1}        { << STAD >> VALUE PARAMETER INITALIZATION of i }
{ 2}        s := 0;
{ 3}        k := 1;
{ 4}        while k <= i do
              begin
{ 5}              s := s + sqr(k);
{ 6}              k:= k + 1;
              end;
{ 7}        k := 1;
{ 8}        { << STAD >> EXIT USE OF VAR PARAMETERS s    }
{ 9}      end;
```

Fig. 7.2 A STAD-elaborated Pascal procedure

```
            LIST OF LIVE VARIABLES of sum

            node  2   live variables: i
            node  3   live variables: i, s
            node  4   live variables: i, s, k
            node  5   live variables: i, s, k
            node  6   live variables: i, s, k
            node  7   live variables: s
            node  8   live variables: s
```

Fig. 7.3 Live variables for procedure SUM of Fig. 7.2; Only nonempty sets are shown

be used without changes in q. To get a better understanding of the concept consider procedure sum in Fig. 7.2 and the list of its live variables in Fig. 7.3.

7.3.1   Undefined-Referenced (UR) Anomaly: The Use of Uninitialized Variables

A rather typical programming error, to which nobody is immune *regardless* of the number of years in the profession, is the reference (use) of a variable without its prior definition. In contrast to the imported parameters (VAL or VAR) which are *assumed*[1] to be initialized at the call, local variables are *undefined* at the start of the procedure. This assumption is true even if the programming language at hand provides a means to initialize them at the time of the declaration as, for example, do the following Ada and Free Pascal declarations of local variable X:

X: integer := 0; -- Ada
X: integer = 0; // Free Pascal

Clearly, when building the flowgraph, the initialization of X will be represented as a node in which X is defined.[2] Consequently, the following discussion applies only to local variables that are *not* initialized at the time of their declaration (even if the language supports the initialization).

Consider a statement K: $Y := X+2$, where X is a *local* variable. A use of undefined variable X occurs when there exists a path from the start S to K along which X is not assigned a value.

Problem 7.3 *Propose a method for the detection of the UR anomaly.*

Observe that our standard model of program dependencies developed in Chap. 6 does not offer a straightforward tool for the detection of a UR anomaly since the missing initialization simply does not exist. Thus a more contrived approach is called for. Toward that goal, the following method offers a fast and quite efficient solution to the problem. Compute the set LV(S) of Live Variables at the Start node; in STAD 4.0, that information is computed for every block in the program. Now, if LV(S) is empty there is no UR anomaly in the block. Otherwise, there is an UR anomaly involving every variable that is in the set LV(S).

The localization of the detected UR anomaly is more intricate. Assuming that the existence of an UR anomaly has already been established by the method proposed above, the following method offers a quite attractive solution to the localization problem. For every X in the set LV(S), identify all places in the program that use X. Let K be such a place. Now, compute the set RD(X,K) of definitions of X that reach K. If RD(X,K) is empty then certainly there is a *guaranteed* anomaly at K, with respect to the variable X.

---

[1] To establish whether arguments to a call are indeed defined requires interprocedural analysis.
[2] STAD 4.0 does not support declarations with initialization.

Problem 7.4 *Assume that the set RD(X,K) of definition of X that reach K is not empty. Can we claim that there is no UR anomaly at K with respect to X?*

The following example illustrates the fact that such a claim is, in general, unjustified.

```
VAR x,y: integer;   //local variables
begin
    x := 1;
1: while p(x,y) do
       begin
2:        y := x + 2
       end;
  end;
```

Observe that the set RD(y, 1) of definitions of y that reach the entry 1 to the loop is not empty for the definition of y in 2 does reach 1. Nevertheless, there is for sure a guaranteed anomaly at 1 on the very first execution of 1, since the variable y is not yet defined! We can generalize this fact as follows. Let K be a node in which variable X is used and M be a definition of X that reaches K. Now, if K *dominates* M (cf. Chap. 6) the definition of X in M always follows K on any execution and, consequently, on the very first time K is traversed the definition of X in M is not available. Thus, if there is no other definition of X that reaches K there is a guaranteed UR anomaly at K.

Finally, as an *explanation* of a UR anomaly it would be sufficient to identify a path from the Start node to K that does not traverse a definition of X. One way of achieving that is to compute the *transitive closure* of the set of arcs A *without* arcs that are incident on the existing definitions of X (an arc is *incident* on a node if it is either outgoing or incoming to the node). Clearly, if the arc (S,K) is in the transitive closure of so modified set A of arcs there is a UR anomaly at K; the path itself can be then identified using an approach discussed in Chap. 5. Alternatively, we can insert special "undefinition" nodes of local variables into the beginning of the flow-graph, i.e., dummy nodes in which the variables are assigned special *defined* value, say *nil*. Clearly, with that modification of the flowgraph, the existence of data dependency of K on the corresponding "undefinition" node establishes a UR anomaly at K. In either case, a path from the start S to K that does not traverse a definition of X provides an explanation of the anomaly. Conversely, the absence of such a path is an evidence of the absence of the anomaly itself.

Problem 7.5. *The above definition of an UR anomaly does not distinguish between a potential one, where, besides an offending path along which no definition of X reaches K, there also exists a path from S to K along which a definition of X is traversed, and a guaranteed UR anomaly where X is not assigned a value on every path from S to K. Propose a method for the detection of a guaranteed anomaly.*

It is enough to establish that for all paths from Start to K, no definition of X can be traversed before the very first occurrence of K on the path. An explanation of such anomaly would simply state the fact in a perhaps, user-friendly way: "*One cannot execute any assignment to X without prior execution of node K.*" An explanation of a potential anomaly would entail the display of *two paths* from the start to K: One that traverses a definition of *X* before reaching *K*, and the other which does not. Observe that if an offending path (one along which there is no definition of *X*) is nonexecutable (infeasible) then the anomaly is actually harmless.

Problem 7.6 *If an undefined variable is used in an operation, its result is usually also undefined (except for operations like X*0, if X is numerical). How to identify all objects in the program that may be directly or indirectly affected by undefined values of variables?*

First one has to identify the nodes in the flowgraph that *directly* use the undefined values; those are exactly the nodes that meet the criteria for an UR anomaly. Then, the nodes that are *indirectly* affected by the undefined values are those that are *General Dependent* (see Chap. 6) on the directly affected nodes.

7.3.2   Double Definition (DD) Anomaly

That kind of anomaly occurs when a definition of a variable is followed by another definition of that variable *without* a prior use of the variable. For example, given the assignment $K: Y := X+2$, if there is a path from K to say, $L: Y := X+4$, along which Y is *not* used, then there is a DD anomaly *at L*. Obviously, the anomaly may be entirely innocuous but, nevertheless, it warrants a warning, just in case. The detection of a DD anomaly is left to the reader as an exercise.

7.3.3   Redundant Statement (RS) Anomaly

This anomaly (referred to as *Ineffective Statements* in [1]) refers to statements (in our case nodes in the flowgraph) that do not contribute to the computation of values of any exported (VAR or OUT) variable in the program. The detection of such anomaly is simple: Node K is redundant if there is no export node that is generally dependent on K. Observe that if K is a definition of a variable, that variable may be used in other nodes but that use does not affect the value of any exported variable.

7.3.4   Loop Analysis

While iterative processes offer obvious irreplaceable computing power they also give rise to new kinds of suspicious situations. To illustrate that consider the code segment in Fig. 7.4.

Observe that the values of some variables in the program do not change after some iterations. Clearly, the variable C cannot change after one iteration; Y cannot change after two iterations; X after three iterations. This phenomenon, referred to as *stability* of expressions in the groundbreaking paper [1] has been put to good use in SPARK's Examiner. Stability is symptomatic either of a programming error a flaw in the

```
       z := 1;
       c := 5;
       a:= 3;
       b := 4;
       y:= 4;
       while c > 0 do
          begin
            x := y + c;
            w := z - x * z;
            y := c;
            c := a;
            z := b;
            b := w;
          end;
```

Fig. 7.4 A while loop, inspired by [1]

programming style or both. For example, in the above example either the loop iterates once or it never terminates. This strongly suggests a programming error, albeit a rather eccentric programming style cannot be ruled out. Observe, however, if the loop test is replaced by c+w > 0, then the above conclusion is no longer valid. Stable variables or, more general, expressions containing such variables within the loop can be hoisted out of the loop, a technique known in optimizing compilers.

7.4   Modeling Procedure Calls

Nodes in the flowgraph are the basic building elements of dependencies in the program; consequently, the accuracy of the node dependency model is essential for the accuracy of the static analysis of the entire program. Consider, for example, a node in which variable Y is defined and variables A and B are used. It is reasonable to assume that Y depends on *both* A and B, even if in practice this may not necessarily be the case. For example, for the assignment $Y:= A-A+B$, due to the inherent limitations of static analysis, Y will be identified as depending on both A and B although obviously the initial value of A has no impact on the value of Y. The situation gets even more difficult in the case of procedure calls. To illustrate the problem consider the procedure Sum in Fig. 7.5.

Consider the call sum (a + b, c, d, e, f). If the body of the procedure is not available only the procedure's signature can be used to build a flowgraph model for the call. Again then one can only *assume* that the defined variables in a node depend on *all* of the variables used in the node. In practice, however, this conservative approach may lead to spurious dependencies. For instance, in our example that approach gives rise to four nodes that (1) define the exported arguments c, d, e, and f, respectively, and (2) *all* use the imported arguments a, b, c, and d. It is easy to see, however, that neither assumption is necessarily warranted. Clearly, neither the exported parameters have to be actually defined by the procedure nor the imported parameters have to be used to obtain the final value of an exported parameter.

```
              procedure sum(
                     i : integer;
                 VAR v,
                     s : integer;
                 OUT t,
                     w: integer);
              VAR
                 k : integer;

              begin
                 s := 0;
                 k := 1;
                 while k <= i do
                     begin
                         s := s + sqr(k);
                         k := k + 1
                     end;
                 k := 1;
                 t := k;
                 w := s + v;
              end;   { Procedure SUM }
```

Fig. 7.5 A Pascal procedure

Praxis's SPARK offers a solution to the problem albeit by putting an extra burden on the user, who has to supply a DERIVES *annotation* as a prerequisite to static analysis. The DERIVES annotation specifies the Input–Output dependencies as *intended by the programmer*, thus not necessarily representing the actual dependencies. For example, the programmer may write the following annotation for Sum, involving only the parameters *s*, *w* and *v* (*assuming* it's a SPARK, rather than Pascal, code):

```
--# DERIVES s from s, -- final value of s depends on the
                      -- initial value of s
--# v from i, v -- final value of v depends on the
                      -- initial values of i and v
--# w from i; -- final value of w depends on the
                      -- initial value of i
```

Conceptually, the DERIVES annotation defines a set $\{d_1, d_2, ..., d_k\}$, where each d_i, $1 \le i \le k$, is a pair $(V\ U)$, where (1) V is an exported parameter of the procedure, (2) U is a *set* of parameters of the procedure and (3) the final value of V *may* be obtained using the initial values of the variables in the set U. In Free Pascal, the sets IMP and EXP of, respectively, *imported* and *exported* parameters are defined as follows:

$$IMP = VAL \cup VAR$$

$$EXP = VAR \cup OUT.$$

We say V "*may be* obtained," rather than "*is* obtained" to emphasize the fact that some statically identified dependencies may be spurious, as illustrated previously. In the case of the above example annotation the *postulated* dependency set is the following:

$$\{(s\{s\}), (v\{i\ v\}), (w\{i\})\}$$

Now, SPARK checks the consistency of the annotation against both the signature of the procedure and its body, *if* the latter is available. Thus, the first dependency in the DERIVES annotation (s is derived from s) does not violate the signature, since s is a VAR parameter. However, the dependency is inconsistent with the code for the initial value of s is overwritten ("killed") in the procedure by the assignment $s:=0$. Thus, *if* the code is correct, the mode of s should be OUT, rather than IN OUT. The second dependency (v is derived from i and v) violates the actual dependency in the code since v is not defined in sum at all and thus its initial value is *preserved*. However, SPARK classifies this case as v being dependent on v because, technically, the final value of v may be (actually *is* in this case) obtained from the initial value of v; in contrast, the postulated dependence on i is reported as spurious. Finally, the third dependency (w is derived from i) violates neither the procedure's signature nor its code. However, it is incomplete since w also depends on v.

  In what follows a novel solution, incorporated into STAD 4.0 is discussed. It is based on the *preprocessing* of the called routine, and creating a Dependency Template (DT) for the routine, which is next used to compute the *actual* dependencies in the calling program. The approach is restricted to *acyclic call graphs* only. However, in contrast to SPARK, it allows arbitrary flow of control within procedures and does not require user annotations. Here is the essence of this approach.

  Given procedure P, its *Dependency Template* (or Output–Input Dependency) is a binary relation DT from the set EXP of exported parameters to the set IMP of imported parameters. A pair $(Y\ X)$ is in DT if and only if the imported parameter X *may be* used in P to obtain the final value of the exported parameter Y. Recall from Chapter 5 that in the flowgraph every imported parameter, say Z, has a unique *initial definition node* $idn(Z)$, while every exported parameter, say W, has a unique *exported use node* $eun(W)$. Thus, the DT relation can be defined in terms of the General Dependency GD introduced in Chap. 6 as follows:

$$Y\ DT\ X\ \Leftrightarrow\ idn(Y)\ GD\ eun(X).$$

The following is the DT relation for the procedure Sum in Fig. 7.5 as produced by STAD 4.0, *represented* as a set of pairs $(Y\ U)$, such that $U = \{X\mid Y\ DT\ X\}$:

$$DT = \{(v\ \{v\}), (s\ \{i\}), (w\ \{i\ ,v\}), (t\ \{\})\}.$$

Some explanations are in place. The VAR parameter v is not redefined in the procedure; therefore, its initial value is preserved. That fact can be modeled by the assignment $v:=v$ which, consequently, establishes $v\ DT\ v$. The VAR parameter s depends only on the initial value of i, and does *not* depend on the initial value of s itself, since that value is killed by the assignment $s:=0$. Consequently, either there is an error in the body of the procedure or the mode of *s* should be OUT, rather than VAR. The OUT parameter *w* depends on *i* (control dependency) and *v* (data dependency) and thus there is *v* DT *i* and *w* DT *v*. The OUT parameter *t* is defined in the procedure but depends on no imported parameter. Technically then there is no *x* such that *t* DT *x* , the exact meaning of the term (*t* {}) in the DT above. Now, to derive the part of the flowgraph of the calling procedure that corresponds to a call, the actual parameters (arguments) of the call are substituted into the formal ones and then the dependencies between the arguments to the call are derived on the basis of the DT. For example, the call

```
Sum(a+b, c, d, e, f)
```

gives rise to the following substitutions:

```
a, b → i
c → v
d → s
e → t
f → w.
```

Using the Dependency Template DT = {(*v* {*v*}), (*s* {*i*}), (*w* {*i* ,*v*}), (*t* {})}, one gets the following four nodes in the flowgraph for the *calling* program:

```
1.  Defined: c
    Used: c

2.  Defined: d
    Used: a, b

3.  Defined: f
    Used: a, b, c

4.  Defined: e
    Used:
```

Take note of the empty list of variables used to define the variable *e* in node 4. This is due to an assignment of a constant to *e* in the call to Sum. However, in general case, an empty set of used variables may as well be due to the variable involved being undefined; in Sect. 7.4 we discuss this subject in some detail.

In the above example, the DT relation is *acyclic*. To illustrate the problems caused by the existence of *cycles* in the relation, consider the following procedure Swap:

```
procedure Swap (
        VAR i,
    j : integer);
        VAR
    temp : integer;
      begin { swap }
      temp := i;
      i := j;
      j := temp;
      end; { Swap }
```

The DT for Swap

$$\{(i\ \{j\}),\ (j\ \{i\})\}$$

contains a cycle. Now, consider the call Swap(t, s). After substituting the arguments for the formal parameters one gets the following two nodes corresponding to the call (the ordering of nodes is, of course, arbitrary):

```
1. Defined: t
   Used: s

2. Defined: s
   Used: t
```

When interpreted sequentially in the above order the final value of s appears (falsely) dependent on the initial value of s; when the order of nodes 1 and 2 is reversed, t appears dependent on t. The problem is due to the fact that the nodes in the dependency template are to be interpreted in *parallel*, rather than sequentially. To allow sequential interpretation needed for the dependency analysis, we introduce two additional *system variables* t_1 and s_1 which, respectively, store the initial values of t and s. Then, all references to VAR imported parameters, in the *use* sets of the DT, are replaced by the corresponding system variables while the VAR exported parameters remain unchanged. Applying the approach to the call Swap(t, s) results in the following four nodes in the flowgraph of the calling procedure:

```
1. Defined: t__1
   Used: t

2. Defined: s__1
   Used: s

3. Defined: t
   Used: s__1

4. Defined: s
   Used: t__1.
```

Observe that nodes 1 and 2 above initialize the system variables, while nodes 3 and 4 substitute system variables into the use sets of the DT, wherever applicable. Now the dependency analysis yields correct results. Note that the order of pairs of nodes (1 2) and (3 4) can be reversed, i.e., the DT is indeed interpreted in parallel after the substitutions are in place.

The following is a summary of procedure call modeling:

1. During parsing the program, the Routine Call Graph (RCG) for the program is derived. The nodes in the RCG are user-defined procedures and functions. An arc (Q, R) from Q to R means that there is a *possibility* of Q calling R. This means that there is a call to R in Q.

2. It is required that the RCG be *acyclic*. Under that assumption, a Topological Sort of the RCG provides the order of preprocessing the routines in it.
3. For every routine R in the RCG, which has no successor in the RCG, the DT is derived.
4. For every call to routine R,

   (a) Every VAR parameter (*regardless* whether it is used that way or not) is copied into the corresponding system variable; this gives rise to the initial nodes generated by the call, whose number is equal to the number of VAR parameters.
   (b) The actual parameters (arguments) are substituted into the corresponding formal parameters in the DT; however, all references to the VAR parameters in the use sets in the DT are replaced by references to their copies. References to the VAR exported parameters remain intact.

Example 7.1 *Consider again procedure Sum in Fig. 7.5 and its Dependency Template DT = {(v {v}), (s {i}), (w {i,v}), (t, {}) }.*

Although in this case the DT is acyclic and there is no need to store the initial values of the VAR parameters, we nevertheless do it to assure the consistency of the approach. Thus, the call Sum(a + b, c, d, e, f) *gives rise to the following two copy operations of the VAR arguments into their corresponding system variables*

$$c \rightarrow c\_1$$
$$d \rightarrow d\_1$$

and the call-modified DT in which the VAR arguments in the **use** *sets, if any, have been replaced by their corresponding system variables:*

$$DT = \{(c \{d\_1\}), (d \{a, b\}), (f \{a, b, c\_1\}), (e, \{\})\}.$$

Consequently, we obtain the following six nodes for the call

Sum(a+b, c,d,e,f):

```
        1. Defined:  c__1
           Used:  c

        2. Defined:  d__1
           Used:  d

        3. Defined:  c
           Used:  d__1

        4. Defined:  d
           Used:  a,  b

        5. Defined:  f
           Used:  a,  b,  c__1

        6. Defined:  e
           Used:
```

Observe that the only ordering requirement here is that the first two nodes (the copy operations) precede the remaining DT-generated nodes. Otherwise, the interpretation of the augmented DT and the copying of the VAR arguments is fully parallel. Moreover, to simplify things an implementation may actually copy *all* arguments to a call, rather than only the VAR arguments.

7.5   Signature Anomalies

The DT relation is from the set of exported to the set of imported parameters, where both sets are derived from the procedure's signature. However, the real code does not necessarily have to conform to the signature. For example, an exported parameter may depend on an OUT parameter even if the latter must be assumed undefined. Ada compilers will usually detect that kind of anomaly, while other compilers (e.g., Free Pascal) may allow the use of OUT parameters at any time.

Before we formulate the rules of consistency of the procedure's signature with its code, some comments are needed. Consider a VAR parameter Y. According to our definition of the DT relation, Y depends on itself (Y DT Y) if there is a path from the Start to the Exit of the procedure along which either Y is *not* redefined (thus preserving its initial value, the latter *assumed* to be defined on every call) or it is assigned a value that itself depends on the initial value of Y. Y depends on another imported parameter, say X, (i.e., Y DT X, $Y \neq X$) if there is a corresponding path through the procedure that traverses an assignment of a value to Y and that value depends, respectively, on X. In either case, the involved definition of Y must reach the exit of the procedure. However, Y may also be assigned a constant or an (undefined!) value of a local variable; in such a case Y is correctly reported as not being dependent on any imported parameter. Observe that all four cases may occur together, depending on the path taken through the procedure. Now, if Y is an OUT, rather than VAR, parameter it is *assumed* undefined on the call to the procedure. Thus, in contrast to VAR case, if there is no assignment to Y it remains undefined on the return from the procedure. The above observations are summarized by the *Consistency Conditions* for the signature of the procedure. These are shown below assuming the STAD's way of building a flowgraph for the procedure discussed in Chap. 5, notably the fact that VAL and VAR parameters are initialized in the flowgraph; as usual, Imp stands for the set of VAL and VAR parameters and Exp stands for the set of VAR and OUT parameters:

1. Every exported parameter depends on at least one imported parameter, or formally
$$\forall v: \text{Exp} \cdot \exists w: \text{Imp} \cdot v \, \text{DT} \, w.$$

2. Every imported parameter is used to compute at least one exported parameter, i.e.,
$$\forall w: \text{Imp} \cdot \exists v: \text{Exp} \cdot v \, \text{DT} \, w.$$

3. No exported parameter depends on an OUT parameter, i.e.,

$$\forall v: \text{Exp} \bullet \neg \ \exists z: \text{OUT} \bullet v \ \text{DT}.$$

4. No OUT parameter can be used before being defined in the procedure, i.e., cannot be live at the entry to the procedure.

$$\forall z: \text{OUT} \bullet \neg \ z \in \text{LIVE (Start)}.$$

The detection of the violation of the above conditions involves the inspection of the General Dependency relation GD (conditions 1 and 2) and of the GD and the mode of the parameter (conditions 3 and 4). Now, if the above conditions are indeed violated, perhaps the code *is* correct and only the signature should be adjusted accordingly. In such a case, the calling (directly or indirectly) procedures can be analyzed using the actual DT with a warning to the user. Alternatively, the processing of the callers may be suspended until the user corrects the code and, if needed, the signature. A similar approach may be taken in the case of other code anomalies discussed in this chapter, e.g., the use of uninitialized variables.

Problem 7.7 *Let Y be an exported parameter. If there is a path through the procedure along which Y is assigned a constant or an undefined value of a local variable that fact will not be recorded in the Dependency Template DT. Propose a method for the detection of these two events.*

The detection of the above situation is quite straightforward: All definitions of Y reaching the exit are assignments to Y of constants or undefined local variables.

The above discussion illustrates the fact that the *Proscriptive Analysis*, aimed towards the detection of flaws in the code, may be carried out at the flowgraph building stage. In contrast, the *Descriptive Analysis*, offering explanations of events in the program, is an *on-request* activity.

Example 7.2. *Consider the program FIVE_CALLS in* Fig. 7.6. *Derive the (partial) flowgraphs that correspond to all procedure calls in the program.*

The call graph for FIVE_Calls is shown in Fig. 7.7; its topological sort is the following:

ONE, TWO, THREE, FOUR, FIVE, FIVE_CALLS.

Let DT(P) stands for the Dependency Template for procedure P. Then the DT(P) for procedures P that do not call other procedures, One, Two, Three, are the following:

$$\text{DT(One)} = \{(\text{One\_}A, \{\})\}$$
$$\text{DT(Two)} = \{(\text{Two\_}A, \{\text{Two\_}A\})\}$$
$$\text{DT(Three)} = \{(\text{Three\_}B, \{\text{Three\_}A\})\}$$

Now, here are the nodes in the flowgraph for procedure FOUR that correspond to the calls to procedures ONE, TWO, and THREE in procedure FOUR:

```
Program Five_Calls;
  VAR i, j : integer;

    Procedure One (VAR One_A : integer );
      begin
        One_A := 1;
      end; { ONE }

    Procedure Two (VAR Two_A : integer );
      begin
        Two_A := Two_A + 2;
      end; { Two }

    Procedure Three (Three_A : integer;
                VAR Three_B : integer );
      begin
        Three_B := Three_A + 3;
      end; { THREE }

    Procedure Four (VAR Four_A,
                        Four_B : integer );
      begin
        One  ( Four_A      );
        Two  ( Four_A      );
        Three( Four_A, Four_B);
      end; { Four }

  Procedure Five (VAR Five_A : integer;
                  VAR Five_B : integer);
      begin
        Four( Five_A, Five_B );
        Two ( Five_A      );
      end; { FIVE }

begin  { program Five_Calls }
  One  ( i   );
  Five ( i, j );
  Two  ( j   );
  Four ( i, j );
end.    { program Five_Calls }
```

Fig. 7.6 A program with procedure calls

Fig. 7.7 The call graph for the progam in Fig. 7.6

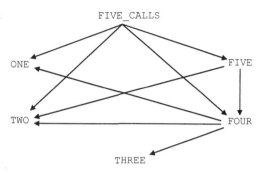

One(Four_A)

        1. Defined: Four_A_1
           Used : Four_A

        2. Defined: Four_A
           Used: None

Two(Four_A)

        1. Defined: Four_A_1
           Used : Four_A

        2. Defined: Four_A
           Used : Four_A_1

Three(Four_A, Four_B)

        1. Defined: Four_B_1
           Used : Four_B

        2. Defined: Four_A_1
           Used : Four_A

        3. Defined: Four_B
           Used : Four_A_1

Observe that the above nodes are parts of the sequential flowgraph for the procedure Four. That allows one to apply the standard dependency analysis to synthesize the DT for procedure Four. That template is needed for any procedure that calls Four; observe that the DT involves only the formal parameters of Four.

DT(Four) = {(Four_A, {Four_A}), (Four_B, {Four_A})}.

Now we use the above template to analyze the calls to Two and Four in the procedure Five.

Two(Five_A)

        1. Defined: Five_A_1
           Used : Five_A

```
                      2. Defined: Five_A
                         Used : Five_A_1
```

Four(Five_A, Five_B)

```
                      1. Defined: Five_A_1
                         Used : Five_A

                      2. Defined: Five_B_1
                         Used : Five_B

                      3. Defined: Five_A
                         Used : Five_A_1

                      4. Defined: Five_B
                         Used : Five_A_1
```

The nodes of the last two calls establish the core of the flowgraph for procedure Five. The DT for the latter is then the following:

DT(Five) = { (Five_A, {Five_A}), (Five_B, {Five_A})}.

Finally, here is the flowgraph for the main program, which corresponds to the four calls in Five_Calls:

One(i)

```
                      1. Defined: i_1
                         Used : i

                      2. Defined: i
                         Used : i_1
```

Five(i,j)

```
                      1. Defined: i_1
                         Used : i

                      2. Defined: j_1
                         Used : j

                      3. Defined: i
                         Used : i_1

                      4. Defined: j
                         Used : i_1
```

Two(j)

```
                      1. Defined: j_1
                         Used : j

                      2. Defined: j
                         Used : j_1
```

Four(i, j)

1. Defined: i_1
   Used : i

2. Defined: j_1
   Used : j

3. Defined: i
   Used : i_1

4. Defined: j
   Used : i_1

Now, since the main program has no parameters the standard dependency analysis may be used to identify dependencies between variables.

7.6 Descriptive Static Analysis

The objective of Descriptive Static Analysis is to glean information about the program to support *reasoning* about it, rather than to detect anomalies. The obtained insight can be used in debugging, testing, or documenting the program. The current version of STAD provides some of that in the form of the *Basic Program Structures* introduced in Chap. 6 – the reaching definitions, dominators, attractors, control and data dependencies and live variables introduced in this chapter. Moreover, the procedure modeling method introduced in Sect. 7.4 is also of descriptive nature. That information is automatically computed for every block in the program under analysis and it can certainly be potentially very useful; please note that even the flow-graph itself is a valuable help in the understanding the program.

Having said that, the Basic Program Structures are needed primarily to support the proscriptive static analysis – that is why they are derived automatically for all blocks in the program in the first place. However, the most prevailing questions about *any* program asked by *any* programmer, *regardless* of his/her experience are not necessarily those about the general views of the entire program or even of selected blocks but rather those that help debug, understand, or test the program. Unfortunately, that kind of *queries* about the program are hard to categorize for they frequently are more a product of frustration rather than of a sound recognition of the needs. However, some form of query categorization is necessary if a tool support is to be provided. Perhaps the rational way of going about it is to provide the user with tools that allow one to *customize the query support* according to one's needs. Indeed, the data bases provided by STAD 4.0 can be a reasonable starting point here. Thus, in the remainder of this section we offer a brief and naturally imperfect attempt at such a categorization. Moreover, since the current version of STAD does not offer a query support, the discussion will be quite general, offering only an outline of a solution, if any. Here are the main group of queries; answers to

them can be derived by processing the *Basic Program Structures* produced by
STAD, rather than being simply found there:

– *Control Flow Queries*
– *Data flow and Dependencies Queries*
– *System (Program) and Visibility Queries (aka Program Browsing)*
– *Structural (White-Box) Testing Queries*

7.6.1   Control Flow Queries

At the *Procedural Level* the following control flow queries seem potentially useful
as indicated by the comments in the parentheses:

1. Is there a path from node p to node q? (test synthesis, dependence of action in q
   on the action in p)
2. Show all the shortest paths from node p to node q, including simple cycles, if
   any (structural testing)
3. Is there a path from p to q that goes through a set K of nodes? (Want to get to q
   from p guaranteeing at least one actions in K is taken)
4. Is there a path from p to q that does NOT go through a set K of nodes? (testing,
   debugging)
5. For set K of nodes, show their common "entry gate," i.e., the nearest node that
   always has to be traversed on any path from start to any node in K (the *Nearest
   Common Dominator* of the set K; the placement of monitoring breakpoints)
6. For set K of nodes, show their "exit gate," i.e., the nearest node that always has
   to be traversed on any path from any node in K to the exit (the *Nearest Common
   Attractor* of the set K).
7. For node p show decision nodes that have scope of control over p (testing).

7.6.2   Data Flow and Dependency Queries

Queries of this kind refer to data manipulation in the program; it is assumed that
the *scope* and *visibility* of variables in question have been determined by suitable
system level queries.

1. For variable X defined in node p, show all places where X can be used without
   being changed (*direct* propagation of modifications of node p and of possible
   errors in X). Observe that it is not enough here to know that X is live at p – that
   fact establishes only the *existence* of a use of X rather than its exact location.
2. For variable X defined in node p, show pairs (Y, q) such that variable Y is
   computed in q using the value of X defined in p (direct and indirect dependence
   on X at p and the propagation of errors in X).

3. Show all nodes that directly or indirectly can affect the computation of a set *V* of variables at some point in the program (debugging, program comprehension). This query leads to the derivation of a partial program [1] aka(backward) *program slice* [10].
4. Given node *p*, if *p* is modified, which other nodes may potentially be affected? (debugging, program comprehension; similar to point 3).
5. Given node *p* and set *S* of variables, show all nodes in the program that are potentially affected by the values of *S* at *p* (*forward* static slice, 9.
6. Is there a path through the routine on which an IN or VAR parameter is not used ?
7 Is there a path through the routine on which an OUT or VAR parameter is not defined?

7.6.3 Structural Testing Queries

A query of this type derives the sets of *Required Elements,* which have to be covered during testing, according to the adopted test selection criteria. This is covered in greater detail in Chap. 8.

7.6.4 System (Program) and Visibility Queries

1. For variables sharing the same identifier *X*, show all their places of declaration, possibly using the fully dotted notation (program comprehension).
2. For variable *P.X*, declared in block *P*, show all the areas of *scope* and *visibility* (program comprehension, whenever applicable).
3. For types *T*, show their place of declarations, possibly using the fully dotted notation (program comprehension).
4. Given type *T*, show the tree (or the Directed Acyclic Graph DAG) of definitions of *T*, i.e., types used in the definition.
5. For a declared type *T*, show all variables of the type.

7.7 Events on Program Paths

As presented so far, "traditional" static analysis is, to large extend, based on the ideas developed for the optimizing compilers and as such is not always well suited to the problems germane to Software Engineering [2]. For example, the lynchpin of static analysis, program dependencies involve *all* possible paths through the program while the operational semantics of the program is naturally defined in terms of the execution traversing *individual paths* or a group of paths. To illustrate the problem

```
Procedure NoContext( u: Integer; w: Integer);
                { partially inspired by Exercise 9.14 in [GJM02] }
    VAR a, b, z, y: Integer;

        begin
{ 1}      { <STAD> PARAMETER INITIALIZATION - u }
{ 2}      { <STAD> PARAMETER INITIALIZATION - w }
{ 3}      a := 1;
{ 4}      b := 2;
{ 5}      if u > 0 then
{ 6}          z := a+b
          else
{ 7}          y := a+b;
{ 8}      w := z +y;
{ 9}      if u > 0 then
{10}          w := z
          else
{11}          w := y;
{12}  end; { Procedure NoContext}
```

Fig. 7.8 A procedure with a multidata anomaly

```
At Node: 5  Variables Used: u   - Contexts: 1
At Node: 6  Variables Used: a b - Contexts: 3 4
At Node: 7  Variables Used: a b - Contexts: 3 4
At Node: 8  Variables Used: z y - Contexts:
At Node: 9  Variables Used: u   - Contexts: 1
At Node: 10 Variables Used: z   - Contexts: 6
At Node: 11 Variables Used: y   - Contexts: 7
```

Fig. 7.9 U-Contexts for the procedure in Fig.7.6, node 8 without U-contexts is *highlighted*

consider the procedure NoContext in Fig. 7.8. Conventional static analysis of the procedure shows that either variable z or variable y *may* be undefined when the assignment to the variable w in node 8 is reached, indicating the existence of a *potential* data flow anomaly at node 8. However, a human analysis shows that one of these variables is *always* undefined whenever node 8 is reached, indicating thus the existence of a *guaranteed* anomaly. Unfortunately, "standard" static analysis is ill-suited to handle events that take place along program paths. Fortunately, STAD[3] offers its helping hand here by supporting the notion of U-Contexts, see Chap. 8.

STAD, in its "standard" scope of analysis, issues the following warning:

---

[3] To the best of our knowledge, at the time of this writing STAD is the only tool that offers that kind of support.

```
possible use of variable "y" and "z" before definition.
```

At best, standard static analysis can establish the existence of a potential UR anomaly involving a *single* variable used in a statement. However, during program execution, whenever node 8 is encountered, the values of *both* y and z have to be defined for the entire assignment to be also defined. Clearly, the two definitions of y and z must come from two distinct nodes in the flowgraph. Now, a *U(se)-Context* at node in which variables say, V_1, V_2,... ,V_K are used, is a K-tuple of definitions of these variables that reach the node *together* on the same path.

All U-Contexts for the procedure in Fig. 7.8 are listed in Fig. 7.9. Observe that in this simple code, for nodes in which only single variables are used, their U-contexts are the same as single-tuples of reaching definitions. However, the most telling thing about Fig. 7.9 is the fact that there is no context for node 8. Clearly, a *guaranteed multidata anomaly* at 8 has been detected!

The above very simple example has been chosen to illustrate the concept of U-contexts. However, one should not conclude that a U-Context is simply an element of the Cartesian product of the sets of definitions of variables used in a node that reach the node. Clearly, some combinations of those definitions do not reach the node on a same path.[4]

Originally, U-Contexts have been identified as a specific multidata testing strategy [4, 6], which *appears* to be the strongest structural testing technique around that is still practically acceptable (see Chap. 8).

The above discussion, even as a first step in handling events on program paths, does illustrate the possibilities of the approach. However, further research is needed to establish its full potential. To illustrate some of the difficulties let us consider the procedure NoContext *without* node 8, i.e., with the assignment w:=z+y either removed or changed to an empty statement (to keep the numbering intact). Now, (single-variable) potential UR anomalies may be identified at nodes 10 and 11 but no guaranteed anomaly can be detected. For one, there is no real anomaly in the code now for the test u > 0 is the same in both conditional statements thus ensuring the use of defined values in the second conditional. However, if we replace the test u > 0 in the second conditional by u ≤ Ø then we get a guaranteed UR anomalies at 10 and 11. Unfortunately, it does not seem possible to detect such an anomaly with any degree of certainty but it might be possible to identify it as a suspicious situation warranting a warning.

Such a possibility is offered by the notions of codefinitions and couses. The former is a generalization of the notion of U-Contexts. A *codefinition* at node K in the flowgraph is a *maximal* set of definitions that reach K on the same path [5]. Recall that every definition in a codefinition is essentially a pair (Variable, Node-Where-Defined). Now, when the nodes in the definitions are ignored one gets simply the set of variables that are *codefined*, i.e., their definitions reach K on the same path. For example, for the procedure NoContext in Fig. 7.8 with an empty statement 8, there are two sets of codefined variables at node 9: $\{a,b,z,u\}$ and $\{a,b,y,u\}$.

---

[4]Experimental data suggest that the ratio of U-Contexts is approximately 50% of all tuples in the Cartesian product of the sets of Reaching Definitions of the variables used in a node.

Now, a set C of variables at node K is **colive** if and only if all variables in C are live on the same path, i.e., there are uses of all variables in C on the path before their definitions. For the procedure NoContext, the colive variables at node 9 are singleton sets $\{z\}$ and $\{y\}$. It is obvious that to avoid a multidata UR anomaly every potentially executable set CD of codefined variables should be followed by a set CU of coused variables such that CU $\subseteq$ CD. Since the sets CD and CU are associated with a single path or a set of paths through the code, anomaly-free execution paths can be identified.

7.8   Conclusions

We believe that static analysis should be part of every software quality assessment process. Moreover, we believe it should be carried out as a *prerequisite* of all other verification techniques, such as program proof or testing proper (dynamic testing). Indeed, the programmer should first correct any reported anomalies or make sure that they are harmless before starting testing or attempting a proof. However, for that strategy to gain general acceptance several problems both of substantive and of pragmatic nature have to be solved first, to name only a few.

First, both proscriptive and descriptive static analysis should be extended onto the system, interprocedural level. In this chapter, we offered a modicum of such analysis in the form of modeling procedure calls by identifying the Output–Input dependencies of the called procedure and using those to derive the dependencies in the caller incurred by the call. There is no doubt that in general this approach does provide a more precise model of the dependencies than the naïve "Every exported parameter depends on all imported parameters" paradigm. But that is only a first step: Both the detection of anomalies and query support system have to be developed for the entire program. Second, static analysis involves *all* possible paths through the program along which the event in question can occur. For example, the set of reaching definitions contains all definitions of variables that reach the node of interest on all possible computations. In reality, however, only some definitions from that set reach the node on a *particular* computation. After all, path events are the essence of *operational semantics* of the program. In Sect. 7.7 we illustrated the potential of *path analysis* by offering a U-Context method for the detection of multidata Undefined-Referenced anomalies. In Chap. 8 we show the unfortunate case of the L._(Live) Context testing strategy whose inadequacy is a direct result of the lack of a suitable path analysis support. Consequently, further research into that kind of analysis should be of the highest priority. Elsewhere, some attempts have been made to formulate a theory of *multipath analysis* [7, 8, 9]. It is obvious, however, that much more work is still needed here. In Chap. 9 we intimate that dynamic, execution-based analysis be used as a refinement of static analysis. Finally, from the pragmatic point of view it is essential that and an *explanation* is offered for any proscriptive or descriptive message, perhaps on request. Otherwise, harder to understand and, consequently, more dangerous, warnings may be ignored by the user.

Exercise 7.1 *Propose a method for the detection, identification and explanation of a DD anomaly.*

Exercise 7.2 *Propose a method for the detection of stable loop variables. HINT: Review the solution in 1 for goto-less programs.*

Exercise 7.3 *Propose a method for the identification of variables used and defined on a path through the program.*

Exercise 7.4 *Propose an algorithm for the detection of a forward program slice, i.e., set of nodes affected by a subset of imported variables to the program.*

Exercise 7.5 *Derive a program slice (forward or backward) with an explanation feature, by connecting the nodes in the slice with arcs corresponding to the flow of control within the slice.*

References

1. J.F. Bergeretti, B.A. Carre, Information flow and data flow analysis of while-programs, ACM Transactions on programming Languages and Systems, 7, 37–61,1985.
2. A.V. Aho, R. Sethi, J.D. Ullman, Compilers: Principles, Techniques, and Tools, Addison-Wesley, Reading, MA, 1986.
3. C. Ghezzi, M. Jazayeri, D. Mandrioli, Fundamentals of Software Engineering, Prentice-Hall, Upper Saddle River, NJ, 2002
4. J. Laski, B. Korel, A data flow oriented program testing strategy, IEEE Transaction on Engineering, SE-9(3), 347–354, 1983.
5. J. Laski, An algorithm for the derivation of codefinitions in computer programs, Information Processing Letters, 23, 85–90, 1986.
6. J. Laski, Data flow testing in STAD, Journal of Systems and Software, 12, 3–14,1990.
7. J. Laski, W. Stanley, J. Hurst, Dependency analysis of ada programs, Proceedings ACM SIG Ada Annual International Conference (SIGAda98), Nov. 8–12, 1998, Washington, DC, pp. 263–275.
8. J. Laski, W. Stanley, P. Podgorski, Beyond ASIS – program data bases and tool-oriented queries, Proceedings of ACM SIGAda Annual International Conference, Sept 30–Oct 4, 2001 Bloomington, MN,(SIGAda 2001), pp. 81–90.
9. J. Laski, Programming faults and errors: Towards a theory of program incorrectness, Annals of Software Engineering, 4,79–114,1997.
10. M. Weiser, Program slicing IEEE Transactions. On Engineering, SE-10, 352–357,1984.

Part III
Dynamic Analysis

Chapter 8
Is There a Bug in the Program? Structural Program Testing

Abstract As Black-Box (BB) testing (see Chap. 4), *Structural* (White-Box) program testing is an experiment with the program, in which the actual program results are compared with the expected ones, prescribed by the testing "oracle," ideally the program specification. However, in structural testing, tests are synthesized on the basis of the code itself, rather than its specification. A structural testing strategy is defined in terms of *Required Elements*, i.e., program statements, or combinations thereof, that are to be exercised. The best known coverage criteria are expressed in terms of simple properties of the flow of control: These are *statement* and *branch* coverage. Less known, but potentially more powerful are data flow coverage criteria: *Definition-Use Chains* (Data Dependency in Chap. 7) and its generalization *U(se)-Context*. All four strategies are supported by STAD. However, due to the difficulties of test synthesis structural testing as a stand-alone method is currently out of the question. It can only be used as a measure of completeness of BB-testing. The main weakness of structural testing is the lack of sound theoretical foundations. To remedy this situation, an attempt has been made to (1) define formally the notions of program faults and errors in terms of the program verification schema and (2) formulate testing strategies in terms of program dependencies. Also, it has been suggested that besides the standard "main" objective of program testing, the detection of the fault, testing also offers a measure of fault localization and, for a passing test suite, the degree of confidence that the program is indeed correct.

8.1 Introduction

Recall from Chap. 4 the two basic problems in program testing. First, it is the "judicial" selection of test cases that have high potential for fault detection, the *main* objective of testing under the healthy assumption that *"There is always one more bug."* Second, it is the definition of a *completeness* criterion that allows one to decide when to stop testing under the assumption that no program failure has been observed. The former problem is essentially of intellectual nature; the latter is of economic one. Both, black-box and white-box testing offer solutions to either problem. Recall that a *Black-Box* (BB)-test, inspired (if not *exactly* derived from) by the program's specification applies to any implementation of the problem at hand. By the same token, a *White-Box* (WB)-test, while indeed derived from the code (rather than simply inspired by it) is *independent of any specification* that may possibly be assigned to the program (as long as the signature of the program is observed). Clearly, the rules for the synthesis of a WB-test involve only purely structural properties of the program. A testing strategy here is defined in terms of program statements, or combinations thereof, that are to be exercised. We use the generic term of *Required Elements* to refer to those statements; this is a generalization of the term required K-Tuple introduced in [11].

Essentially, any white-box testing strategy is an approximation to *path coverage*, which requires that all paths through the code are executed at least once. Since the number of paths through the program is usually infinite any realistic strategy must lead to the selection of a well-defined finite set of paths. Toward that goal, a plethora of WB strategies has been proposed in the literature, none of them based on any sound theory. Rather, intuition, common sense, and, sometimes, sheer faith were the source of inspiration. How else one could judge a rule, according to which a loop should iterate zero, one, and four times? Why not seven or 13 times? Like the medieval problem of the number of angels dancing on the top of a pin, the irrationality of many of the proposals for path selection for structural testing stems from the same source: The lack of sound understanding of the issues involved – that is, the lack of a *theory* – which, in turn, raises false hopes in activities bordering on magic. (To be fair, the Authors of this text have also contributed to this sad state of affairs, as evidenced later in this chapter when the L_Context coverage is discussed).

For better or worse, Black-Box testing has been the prevailing practice in industry, with structural testing and static analysis tools rarely used. To the extent, however, that testing tools are used the coverage criteria supported are usually limited to statement and branch testing. These and other, relatively new data flow testing strategies are introduced in the Sect. 8.2. Then, in Sect. 8.3, a typical testing scenario under STAD is presented. The main lesson learned there is the fact that structural coverage on its own is out of the question and can only be used as an indirect measure of the quality of Black-Box testing. In Sect. 8.4, we discuss the origin and propagation of programming errors, using the formal framework of the program Verification Schema (see Chap. 2). The results of that section are then used in Sect. 8.5 to discuss the error-detecting power of white-box testing. The discussion shows clearly that structural testing lacks even a modicum of a sound theory and it is a sad conclusion that we do not really know what we are doing. Section 8.6 offers some ideas about putting structural testing on a more solid ground using the vehicle of program dependencies introduced in Chap. 6. In Sect. 8.7 we briefly address the general scenario of testing in an integrated program verification system.

8.2   Code Coverage Criteria

The basis for structural (white-box) testing is the program's flowgraph. The most popular are the *instruction* and *branch* coverage. The former requires that every instruction in the program be exercised at least once; the latter stipulates that every

```
        Procedure Weird(
                    i: integer ;
                VAR s: integer );
        VAR k, a, b, c, d: integer ;

           begin     { Procedure Weird }
{   1}        { <STAD> Initialization of parameter i }
{   2}        { <STAD> Initialization of parameter s }
{   3}        c := 1 ;
{   4}        d := 2 ;
{   5}        s := 0 ;
{   6}        k := 1 ;
{   7}        if k > c + d THEN
{   8}            a := c
              ELSE
{   9}            b := d ;
{ 10}         s := a + b ;
{ 11}         while k <= i do
                  begin
{ 12}                 s := s + k ;
{ 13}                 k := k + 1 ;
                  end ;
{ 14}         if d > 0 THEN
{ 15}            a := s + a
              ELSE
{ 16}            b := k + a ;
{ 17}            { <STAD> EXIT USE OF s }
{ 18}     end ;     { Procedure Weird }
```

Fig. 8.1 The STAD-elaborated procedure Weird

branch be exercised at least once. Recall that a branch is an arc (edge) in the flow-graph if it emanates from a *decision node*, i.e., one with at least two outgoing arcs. It is obvious that for the **if** C **then** A **else** B; statement, either strategy requires the statement to be executed at least twice, the condition C evaluating alternately to *true* and *false*. A more refined version of branch coverage is the *condition coverage*, which requires that the primitive predicates of a compound statement also take on the two logical values. For example, in the statement

if (p **or** q **and** r) **then** A **else** B;

the constituent predicates *p*, *q*, and *r* should, *if* possible, take on all eight vectors of Boolean values. In the remainder of this section, three data flow testing strategies will be discussed: Chain Coverage, U_Context, and L_Context coverage. These will be illustrated by the STAD's outputs for the procedure Weird in Fig. 8.1 and its abridged flowgraph in Fig. 8.2.

```
 1 --> {   2 }           U = { }               D = { i }
 2 --> {   3 }           U = { }               D = { s }
 3 --> {   4 }           U = { }               D = { c }
 4 --> {   5 }           U = { }               D = { d }
 5 --> {   6 }           U = { }               D = { s }
 6 --> {   7 }           U = { }               D = { k }
 7 --> {   9, 8 }        U = { k, c, d }       D = { }
 8 --> {  10 }           U = { c }             D = { a }
 9 --> {  10 }           U = { d }             D = { b }
10 --> {  11 }           U = { a, b }          D = { s }
11 --> {  12, 14 }       U = { k, i }          D = { }
12 --> {  13 }           U = { s, k }          D = { s }
13 --> {  11 }           U = { k }             D = { k }
14 --> {  16, 15 }       U = { d }             D = { }
15 --> {  17 }           U = { s, a }          D = { a }
16 --> {  17 }           U = { k, a }          D = { b }
17 --> {  18 }           U = { s }             D = { }
18 --> {   }             U = { }               D = { }
```

Fig. 8.2 An abridged control flowgraph of procedure Weird from Fig. 8.1

```
DEFINITION-USE CHAINS (DATA DEPENEDNCIES)

   4 ---> 7 (d)     3 ---> 7 (c)     6 ---> 7 (k)
   3 ---> 8 (c)
   4 ---> 9 (d)
   9 --->10 (b)     8 --->10 (a)
   1 --->11 (i)     6 --->11 (k)    13 --->11(k)
  10 --->12 (s)    12 --->12 (s)     6 --->12(k)    13 --->12 (k)
   6 --->13 (k)    13 --->13 (k)
   4 --->14 (d)
  10 --->15 (s)
  12 --->15 (s)     8 --->15 (a)
   8 --->16 (a)     6 --->16 (k)    13 --->16 (k)
  10 --->17 (s)    12 --->17 (s)
```

Fig. 8.3 Definition-Use chains (data dependencies) for procedure Weird in Fig. 8.1.

Observe first that full lists of Required Elements can be obtained by requiring STAD to display the coverage report *without* running any test at all. Proceeding that way one gets the following sets of instructions and branches in the program:

INSTRUCTIONS: 1, 2, …, 18
BRANCHES: (7 8), (7 9), (11 12), (11 14), (14 16), (14 15)

The STAD-generated Definition-Use Chains, U-Contexts, and L-Contexts are shown, respectively, in Figs. 8.3–8.5. The following is a discussion of these criteria.

```
at node: 7
   used variables: c d k
   contexts:     1: 3  4  6
at node: 10
   used variables: a  b
   contexts:        NONE
at node: 11
   used variables: i k
   contexts:     1:  1  6
                 2:  1 13
at node: 12
   used variables: k s
   contexts:     1:  6 10
                 2: 13 12
at node: 15
   used variables: a s
   contexts:     1:  8 10
                 2:  8 12
at node: 16
   used variables: k a
   contexts:     1:  6  8
                 2: 13  8
```

Fig. 8.4 Nontrivial (i.e, involving at least two used variables) U_contexts for procedure Weird in Fig. 8.1

```
AT NODE: 11
Live variables: i d k a s
contexts:     1: 1 4 6 8 10
              2: 1 4 13 8 12
AT NODE: 12
Live variables: i d k a s
contexts:     1: 1 4 6 8 10
              2: 1 4 13 8 12
AT NODE: 13
Live variables: i d k a s
contexts:     1: 1 4 6 8 12
              2: 1 4 13 8 12
AT NODE: 14
Live variables: d k a s
contexts:     1: 4 6 8 10
              2: 4 13 8 12
AT NODE: 15
Live variables: a s
contexts:     1: 8 10
              2: 8 12
AT NODE: 16
Live variables: k a s
contexts:     1: 6 8 10
              2: 13 8 12
```

Fig. 8.5 Nontrivial L_contexts for procedure Weird in Fig. 8.1; the live variables involved are also listed

The notion of *Definition-Use Chains* testing strategy was put forward apparently *independently* in [2], [11] and [3]. That fact is perhaps an indicator of its intuitive appeal. To see why is this, consider the chain 13 --->16 (k) from Fig. 8.3. The notation n ---> m (v) means here "the variable *v* is defined in node *n*, is used in node *m*, and there exists a path from *n* to *m* along which *v* is not redefined." Indeed, the variable *k* in the procedure in Fig. 8.1 is defined in node 13 and there is a path [13, 11, 14, 16] from 13 to 16 along which *k* is not modified. We immediately recognize that the existence of the chain 13 --->16 (k) is due to the fact that node 16 is *Data Dependent* on node 13, a notion defined formally in Chap. 6. In the sequel, we will thus use these two terms interchangeably.

The notion of U_Context is a generalization of Data Dependency onto *all* variables used in a node. To illustrate this consider node 12 in Fig. 8.1, in which the variables *s* and *k* are used. There are two definitions of each of these variables that reach node 12 – that is, the definitions of *s* in 10 and 12 and of *k* in 6 and 13. These are duly reported in Fig. 8.3. Now, Definition-Use Chain testing treats the reaching definitions of *s* and *k* *separately* while in reality an execution of the statement s:=s+k requires definitions of *s* and *k* to reach the statement *simultaneously*. This requirement gives rise to the following definition [3].

If an instruction in the program, say *K*, uses variables V_1, V_2, ..., V_p, then a *U(se)_Context* at *K* is a *p*-tuple of definitions of these variables that reach *K* on the *same* path.

It is clear from the above definition that if in a node only one variable is used, then U_contexts at the node are simply Definition-Use Chains that target the node; consequently, we will be interested only in *nontrivial* U_Contexts, i.e, those involving more than one variable used in the node. A full list of nontrivial U_contexts for the procedure in Fig. 8.1 is shown in Fig. 8.4. The entry for node 12 has the following two U_Contexts at the node displayed as two-element sequences of definitions of the variables *k* and *s*:

$$1: \quad [6, \quad 10] \quad 2: \quad [13, \quad 12].$$

Thus, at any execution of node 12, the values of, respectively, *k* and *s* may come either from 6 and 10 or from 13 and 12 but neither from 6 and 12 nor from 13 and 10. This example illustrates the fact that the set of U_Contexts at a node is *not*, in general, equal to the Cartesian product of the sets of respective definition-use chains at the node. That happens because some combinations of those definitions do not reach the node on the same path. Of particular importance is the case when *no* such a combination does so as happens at node 10 in procedure in Fig. 8.1. Clearly, there is no path from the start to 10 along which the variables *A* and *B* are *both* defined. Consequently, there is no U_Context at the node or, using the terminology coined in Chap. 7, there is a *multidata anomaly* at node 10 in the flowgraph. Our experience suggests that typically about 50% of the Cartesian product of the sets of definition-use chains at a node constitute U_Contexts. This is an anecdotal evidence as is the observation that U_Context testing *appears* to be the strongest structural testing that is practically acceptable, as discussed in Sect. 8.3.

Fig. 8.6 Live variables for procedure Weird at nodes not shown in Fig. 8.5

```
LIVE VARIABLES of Weird

node  1      b  a
node  2      i  b  a
node  3      b  a
node  4      i  c  b  a
node  5      i  d  c  b  a
node  6      i  d  c  b  a
node  7      i  d  c  b  a  k
node  8      i  d  c  b  k
node  9      i  d  a  k
node 10      i  d  b  a  k
```

Finally, we discuss the L_Context testing strategy. As noted earlier, the notion of U_Contexts at a node in the flowgraph is an extension of Definition-Use Chains onto all variables used in the node. Similarly, the notion of L_Contexts is an extension of U_Contexts onto all variables that are *live* at the node, rather than only used in it. Recall from Chap. 7 that a variable, say X, is *live* at node k, if and only if there is a potential execution path from k to the exit, along which X is used *before* being assigned a new value, *if at all*. To identify L_Contexts at instruction k, we are looking for a path that (1) traverses all definitions of variables that are live at k and (2) those definitions reach k on that *same* path. Observe that a variable used in an instruction is also live at the instruction but not necessarily the other way round. Thus, L_Contexts involve tuples of variables that are usually much larger than the corresponding U_Contexts. Consequently, it might appear that L_Context testing is more demanding than U_Context testing, the way U_Context testing is more demanding than Chain testing. Unfortunately, this is not necessarily the case for the two following reasons: L_Context may not exist where Chains and U_Contexts do and may be infeasible for an otherwise correct program.

Fig. 8.5 shows all nontrivial L_Contexts for the procedure Weird in Fig. 8.1 while Fig. 8.6 shows live variables for the procedure not listed in Fig. 8.5. Observe that there are no L_Contexts at nodes 1–10.

Earlier in the section we showed that if, for an instruction that uses at least one variable, there exists no U_Context there is a data flow anomaly at the instruction. This is not necessarily the case of L_Contexts, an issue we explore further in Sect. 8.3.

8.3 Testing Scenario

In a purely structural testing scenario, an activation of a required element involves executing a path in the program that traverses the element. Thus, any structural test is ultimately expressed in terms of a set (typically not unique) of paths that are to be exercised. Therefore, testing a program, according to a coverage criterion, consists of the following main steps:

1. *The identification of the REs involved by means of static analysis of the program.*

   For each RE:

2. *The identification of an execution path along which that RE may be activated; such a path will be referred to as a constructor of the RE*
3. *The synthesis of a test, i.e., an input that causes the traversal of the constructor*
4. *Finding the expected result for the test*
5. *Test execution and monitoring*
6. *Test result evaluation*

An attempt to follow the above steps to synthesize a structural test suite for the "complex" program in Fig. 8.1 appears to be a rather daunting prospect. Steps (1) and (5) can be fully automated and, indeed, are supported by STAD. Step (2) can also be potentially automated and, in fact, a relevant solution for Data Flow Chains has been found, although not yet included in STAD [5]. In contrast, the synthesis of test data for a constructor of a RE is a difficult problem, further aggravated by the fact that some constructors may be infeasible. If all constructors of a RE are infeasible then the RE itself is infeasible, too. That is too bad, but nothing can be done about it: The detection of path (in)feasibility is *undecidable* and thus does not lend itself to automation. Consequently, since the programmer's creativity (possibly helped by heuristics) is the main tool here, this step is human labor intensive. All things considered, it is safe to conclude that at the current state of the art, *structural testing on its own is out of the question!* Thus, until partial automation of the test synthesis becomes reality, structural coverage can only be used as an indirect *measure of the adequacy of Black-Box testing* (see Chap. 4). However, if the BB-incurred coverage is inadequate, the programmer is well served by trying to synthesize structural tests for the remaining *uncovered* REs. That effort significantly increases the understanding of the program. Indeed, our experience with STAD confirms an earlier observation in [2] that many "interesting" *errors are discovered not necessarily through actual testing but during the synthesis of test data!* One explanation of this phenomenon is that the test synthesis process directs the programmer's attention to some aspects of the program that might have been otherwise overlooked. If anything else, this confirms the importance of static program analysis and illustrates the unintended benefits of manual approach to test synthesis! So, rather than to embark on the torturous path of the synthesis of a purely structural test, the reasonable approach is to synthesize some BB-test and identify the required elements activated by that test. The outcome is shown in Fig. 8.7 for the three values 1, 2, and 0 of the input argument i.

In the case of our example, no criterion has been covered in 100% and further Black-Box inspired attempts to increase the coverage fail; therefore, a *BB-saturation* has been achieved and now one should try to apply the purely structural testing scenario outlined earlier in this section to the remaining uncovered Required Elements. Toward that goal, STAD reports that the following instructions and branches in procedure Weird have not been activated during testing:

Uncovered Instructions: 8, 16
Uncovered Branches: (7 8), (14 16)

TESTING STRATEGY	PERCENTAGE COVERAGE	INCREASE
i=1		
INSTRUCTIONS	88.89%	88.89%
BRANCHES	66.67%	66.67%
CHAINS	56.00%	56.00%
U_CONTEXT	50.00%	50.00%
L_CONTEXT	7.14%	7.14%
i=2		
INSTRUCTIONS	88.89%	0.00%
BRANCHES	66.67%	0.00%
CHAINS	68.00%	12.00%
U_CONTEXT	62.50%	12.50%
L_CONTEXT	7.14%	0.00%
i=0		
INSTRUCTIONS	88.89%	0.00%
BRANCHES	66.67%	0.00%
CHAINS	76.00%	8.00%
U_CONTEXT	68.75%	6.25%
L_CONTEXT	14.29%	7.14%

Fig. 8.7 Cumulative Coverage of Procedure Weird of Fig. 8.1 after tests $i = 1$, $i = 2$, and $i = 0$

```
3 ---> 8 (c)
8 ---> 10 (a)
8 ---> 15 (a)
8 ---> 16 (a)
6 ---> 16 (k)
13 ---> 16 (k)
```

Fig. 8.8 Uncovered Definition-Use chains (data dependencies) for procedure Weird in Fig. 8.1

The uncovered definition-Use Chains and U_Contexts are shown, respectively in Figs. 8.8 and 8.9. It appears that not a single L_Context from Fig. 8.5 has been activated and thus they are not listed in the figure.

Problem 8.1 *Figure 8.6 illustrates the cumulative coverage induced by testing under STAD procedure Weird from Fig. 8.1 for the values 1, 2, and 0 of the VAL parameter i. Attempts to increase the coverage by more BB-testing fail. How to go about the synthesis of additional tests to increase the coverage?*

It is reasonable to start the process of the synthesis of additional structural tests with the *simplest* REs and proceed toward the more complex ones. Clearly, if an

Fig. 8.9 Nontrivial uncovered U_contexts for procedure Weird in Fig. 8.1

```
at node: 15
   used variables: a   s
      contexts: 1:   8   10
                2:   8   12

at node: 16
   used variables: k   a
      contexts: 1:   6   8
                2:  13   8
```

additional instruction gets executed that usually leads to the execution of a new arc; if a new Definition-Use Chain gets covered this *may* result in the covering of additional U_ and L_Contexts. Consider, for instance, the uncovered instructions 8 and 16 in the procedure Weird. Indeed, a successful execution of these instructions would also lead to the execution of the branches: (7 8), (14 16). Moreover, it may potentially also cause the coverage of Definition-Use Chains and contexts that involve the definition of the variable A in node 8. Now, observe that any test (i.e., the value of the parameter *i*) causing the execution of node 8 must ensure the value of the expression $k > c + d$ in node 7 to be *true*. Using the technique of finding the path traversal condition in Chap. 2, one gets the following condition for the traversal of the path $w = [1, 2, 3, 4, 5, 6, 7, 8]$

$$\mathtt{tr(w)} \iff \mathtt{1 > 3},$$

which clearly demonstrates the infeasibility of the path. Similarly, to execute instruction 16, the entry condition for a traversing path is $2 \leq 0$. Thus, neither instruction is executable and, consequently, nor are the branches (7 8) and (14 16). This, in turn, means that the statically identifiable Definition-Use Chains $8 \dashrightarrow 10$, $8 \dashrightarrow 15$ and $8 \dashrightarrow 16$, all involving the variable A defined in node 8, are infeasible. Now, since all the uncovered U_ Contexts contain definition-use chains involving the definition of A in node 8, it stands to reason that they are also infeasible. By the same token, all L_Contexts in Fig. 8.5 contain the definition of variable A in node 8 and, thus, *all* L_Contexts are infeasible. A clarification is needed, though: The idiosyncrasies of data flow notwithstanding, all required elements at instruction 16 are uncovered for the instruction itself is nonexecutable. Moreover, observe that the infeasibility of an instruction or a branch in an otherwise correct program suggests they can be removed without affecting the program's results. Indeed, it is easy to verify that when the following statements at 7 and 14

```
{7}    if k>c+d
          then a := c
          else b := d;
{14}   if d>0
          then a := s + a
          else b := k + a;
```

in the procedure Weird in Fig. 8.1 are replaced by, respectively, b := d and a := s + a, all instructions and branches in the procedure are covered by just the single test i = 1. To cover the data flow criteria, however, at least two more tests are needed; this is, of course, a coincidence rather than a general rule.

Figure 8.6 illustrates a fairly typical situation: Instruction and branch coverage are easiest to satisfy while Chains, U_Context, and L_Context coverage, in that order, *tend* to be the hardest to satisfy. In what follows we present some intimations that justify that ordering, albeit it is hard to establish it in general without making rather unrealistic assumptions about the program. However, the ordering seems to be quite consistent in reality. First, observe that the final 66.67% branch coverage in Fig. 8.7 is really artificially low. Clearly, branch coverage should be rather understood as *arc coverage*, requiring that every arc, rather than just branch, be exercised at least once. According to this, the actual arc coverage for procedure Weird is in fact 88%. This illustrates the fact that node and arc coverage are virtually equivalent in their demands for exercising the code.

Problem 8.2 *Which strategy is more demanding in terms of the number of tests required?*

Consider a Definition-Use Chain from node K to node M involving variable X. Assume that there are n variables including X that are used in M. Let each such variable have at most m definitions in the program. Now, to meet the node coverage at most two tests are needed to activate K and M, if the nodes do not lie on the same path through the program. However, to meet the Chain coverage, in the worst case one needs $n*m$ tests to activate all chains at M. That shows that more tests are needed to meet the Chain coverage than the instruction one and, by extension, the arc coverage. By the same token, to satisfy the U_Context coverage at node M one has to make sure that all feasible *n-tuples* of definitions of the variables used in M are exercised. That, of course, requires still more executions of the node. Following the same line of reasoning, the activation of L_Contexts becomes even more demanding. However, in that case, some clarifications are in place.

Let L be a nonempty set of live variables at node M, partitioned into the (disjoint) sets U and R, i.e., $L = U \cup R$, $U \cap R = \{\ \}$, where U is the set of variables used in M and R is the set of variables that are used on a path originating at M (excluding M itself), before being modified, if at all. Observe that if the set of U_Contexts at M is empty so is, of course, the set of L_Contexts at M. Moreover, in such a case there is a data flow anomaly at M: If M is reached on any execution at least one of the variables in U is undefined. Now, assume that the set of U_Contexts at M is not empty but the set of L_Contexts is. That means that on every path from the start S to M some variable in R is undefined when M is reached. However, in that case the existence of data flow anomaly at M is not necessarily guaranteed! To demonstrate this consider some variable, say X, in the set R such that no definition of X reaches M. Assume that X is used in some node K on a path from M to the exit E and X is not redefined on a path from M to K. In contrast to the "U_Context anomaly", which always causes an error whenever node M is executed, an "L_Context anomaly" at K exists only potentially. Clearly, the offending path from K to M may be unexecutable or, besides the path on which an undefined value of the variable X reaches K, there also may be a path from M to K along which a definition of X is supplied. This fact explains that in a perfectly correct program there may be many instructions for which no L_Contexts exist. In the extreme case there are no L_Contexts at all and, consequently, their "coverage" is always vacuously satisfied without any testing at all! On the other hand, however, the coverage of existing L_Contexts is hampered by the fact that the infeasibility of definitions that are part of U_Contexts and the corresponding L_Contexts leads to the infeasibility of L_contexts in a greater proportion than that of U_Contexts. This explains the fact that the coverage of L_Contexts is usually much harder than that of U_Contexts.

The above discussion shows that L_Contexts are not really well defined. However, their real weakness lies in their inability to propagate errors in the program, as illustrated in Sect. 8.5. Nevertheless, we have included L_Contexts here to illustrate one important didactic point: *Even most promising theories must be tested in practice!*

Problem 8.3 *Assuming that the program under test is correct (for its specification), is it possible that all Required Elements can be potentially exercised?*

Observe (regrettably, without a formal proof) that this is generally impossible since some Required Elements may be infeasible. However, there is a good news regarding Single-Entry Single-Exit (SESE) programs:

Instruction and Branch (Arc) testing should always reach 100% of coverage.

If some instructions or branches are infeasible, the program contains redundant statements and should be modified, as illustrated above in this section for statements 7 and 14 in the procedure Weird in Fig. 8.1. Unfortunately, no such claim can be made for data flow coverage criteria. However, for data flow testing, some Required Elements can be covered only by invalid "stress" tests, i.e., ones that violate the program precondition.

We have already observed that the choice of structural testing criteria is essentially arbitrary. That is, there is no sound theory on "What to test?"; the driving ideas here appear to be "Common Sense" and *"The More Tests the Better"* paradigm. That, of course is mitigated by the economics of testing: After all, as in the case of Black-Box testing, one cannot test indefinitely and has to stop at some point. In Sect. 8.6, we offer a modest attempt of redefining structural testing within the framework of program dependencies developed in Chap. 6.

We close this section with STAD-based observations on the relationships between Structural vs. Black-Box Testing. It has been demonstrated that although in contrast to Structural Testing, Black-Box Testing is nonsystematic, it is far easier to synthesize *some* BB-test than a well-defined structural test. Besides, experience shows that BB-testing is often the most powerful fault-detection technique. Thus, it is essential to establish the relationships between BB-testing and the attained structural coverage of the executable required elements. Our experiments with STAD have led to the following *typical* relationships between the structural strategies and a well thought out BB-test:

1. *Instruction coverage and branch coverage are easy to meet; in practice, for most procedures of "reasonable" size, a few test points are enough to assure their 100% (feasible) coverage.*
2. *Chain coverage is easier to satisfy than BB-induced coverage but more difficult to satisfy than branch testing.*
3. *A BB-test is practically equivalent to U_Context test. That is, the completeness of BB-testing can be measured indirectly through the completeness of U_context coverage. This is a very practical result, since U_Context can be used in lieu of Black-Box Testing, thus providing an objective measure of the programmer's creativity in the synthesis of a "judicious" BB-test.*

Observe that the questions referring to code coverage do not address the overall really important question, "*What is the fault detection power of structural testing techniques.*" As one may expect, in the current state of the art there is no positive answer to this fundamental question. Although this may be discouraging to some, we tend to view it rather as a challenge. Therefore, in Sect. 8.4 we discus the mechanism of error creation and propagation as an inspiration for program dependencies-based structural testing in Sect. 8.6.

8.4   Faults and Errors

One way to define a programming fault more precisely is to use the notion of the *Verification Schema* introduced in Chaps. 2 and 3. It was shown there that assuming *valid* assertions about the program's design, if the proof of its correctness fails then the program is incorrect. Now, this is another way of saying that there is a *fault* (bug) in the program. Naturally, one would like to fix the problem and, moreover, do it in the cheapest possible way. That means that one would like to identify the *smallest,* SESE code segment which, if corrected (*possibly in several places!*), renders the entire program correct. For example, if in the following statement D

$$D: \textbf{if } t \textbf{ then } A \textbf{ else } B \textbf{ end if;}$$

the statement A is faulty so is the entire D. Thus, the level of the fault abstraction corresponds to the level of design abstraction. Recall from Chaps. 2 and 3 that to prove correctness of program P one has to show the validity of a finite number of *verification conditions* at a certain level of program abstraction (decomposition). Each verification condition is of the following form

$$\{A\} \ S \ \{B\},$$

where S is a SESE program segment and A and B are, respectively, assertions at the at entry and exit of S. The verification condition is a proposition, "If for any state reaching S, assertion A is satisfied then S terminates and the final state at the exit of

S satisfies assertion *B*." If all verification conditions for *P* are valid then P is correct for its specification PRE and POST; otherwise, it is not.

Let *S* be a verification segment in *P* and *A* and *B*, respectively, the input and output assertions of *S*. There is a *fault* in *S* if and only if

1. *The verification condition for S, {A} S {B}, is invalid*
2. *All verification conditions other than the one for S are valid*
3. *The program is incorrect, i.e, {PRE} P {POST} is invalid.*
4. *There exists a correct version S* of S, such that if P* is P in which S has been replaced by S* then {A} S* {B} and {PRE} P* {POST} are both valid.*

Conditions (1) and (2) together constitute a *Single Fault Assumption* (SFA), according to which there is only one verification segment that is incorrect. In particular, condition (1) states that there exists a valid input to *S* that satisfies assertion *A* but the result produced by *S* does not satisfy assertion *B*. Recall from Chaps. 2 and 3 that per se that fact does not necessarily mean that the program is incorrect; indeed, the result of *S*, even if violating the assertion *B*, still may satisfy the weakest precondition at the exit of *S* of the correct output of the entire program. It is condition (3) that guarantees the incorrectness of the entire program. Condition (4) states that the program can be repaired by replacing *S* by its correct version *S**; this will be referred to as the *Fault Repairability Property* (FRP). Thus, the incorrectness of *P* is caused only by an *implementation fault* in *S* while the *design* of *P*, as specified by the set of assertions associated with the verification segments, is correct. Observe, however, the following two facts. First, for the same program *P* a segment other than *S* may alternatively be considered incorrect provided an alternative design assertions exist (cf. Introduction). Second, if the correct version *S** of *S* does not exist then the action specified by the design assertions *A* and *B* is simply "undoable." For example, for the following specification of *S*: $A(x) \Leftrightarrow x < 0$, $B(x, y) \Leftrightarrow y = \Leftrightarrow \sqrt{x}$, *B* can never be established and, consequently, any "implementation" of *S* either does not terminate or terminates with an undefined value of *y*.

The above notion of programming fault is general, capturing not only a class of simple "mutation faults" (e.g., $x := 0$ rather than $x := 1$) but also the case of "missing" statements and paths within *S*. Observe that if the FRP does not hold, the program cannot be repaired by modifying *S* *alone*; the repair must involve a higher level verification segment, of which *S* is a component. This is equivalent to treating multiple faults as a single fault by merging faulty segments into a larger unit that encapsulates those faults. Thus, as the verification schema itself, the concept of fault is *relative* with respect to the assumed level of abstraction (decomposition).

A fault in segment S is a *static* concept conveying the inability to prove the program correct. In contrast, the notion of program error is *dynamic*, defined with respect to a concrete execution of *S*. Let *X* be an input to program *P*. Assume that *X* causes execution of the faulty segment *S*. Let σ and σ' be, respectively, the states on entry and exit of *S* due to the processing of *X* by *P*. Assume first that *S* does not lie on a cycle and thus can be executed only once. If $A(X, \sigma')$[1] holds on entry to *S* and

---

[1] In general, the assertions *A* and *B* take as their arguments the current states and the values of the input vector *X*.

$B(X, \sigma')$ does *not* hold on exit from S, a *primary data error* has occurred at the exit of S. Thus, due to the action of S on *correct* input data to S (a component of the state σ), a primary error at the exit of S occurs when the values of some variables of the state σ' are incorrect. Usually those variables are defined in the faulty component S (fault of *commission*) but they may as well be variables that are not defined in S although they *should* have been (fault of *omission*). If S lies on a cycle, S can be executed more than once and a primary error can also occur more than once, perhaps affecting different variables and/or their components each time. Observe that for the first occurrence of a primary error $A(X, \sigma)$ holds on entry to S by definition while it does not necessarily hold for the subsequent iterations since the state has already been affected by the first primary error. Conversely, a primary error at the exit of S may "self-correct" on subsequent iterations owing to the fact that other, error-free state components are modified in such a way that the new state satisfies the assertion A (see test t3 in the Example 8.1).

A primary error *may* cause incorrectness of other variables and/or of control decisions on the execution. A *secondary error* is an effect of the propagation of a primary error due to either (1) the processing of *incorrect* inputs by a correct *and* correctly selected program statement (data errors) or (2) an incorrect selection of a statement for execution (control errors). If the error propagates to one of the exported parameters, say Y, and the final result Y violates the postcondition of the program, X is *revealing*. We adopt the convention that X is also revealing when the program does not terminate for X, when the postcondition[2] is undefined; clearly, we assume that nontermination is a constructively identifiable event. However, a primary error might not propagate to any variable in the program or to any exported parameter; in such a case, the fault is *masked*. Alternatively, a primary error may be generated and propagated to some local (or global) variables without, however, affecting the exported parameters. In such a case the fault is *internally revealed* but *externally masked*.

Example 8.1 *Consider again the function monotone in Fig. 1 of the Introduction, partially repeated in Fig. 8.10 for an easy reference. Recall from the Introduction that, for the current value of the variable i in the main loop, the code segment 10–16 in the procedure is supposed to find the length of a compatible sequence for A[i], i.e., the longest monotonically increasing sequence in A[1] through A[i−1] such that elements in the sequence are strictly less than A[i]. Also recall we found the procedure incorrect and identified more than one way to correct it. Consider the following two corrections, each corresponding to a fault (bug) in the code:*

Fault F: *Statement* **10**: `maxj:=1` *should read* `maxj:=0`.

Fault F′: Instruction **10**: `maxj:=1` is correct, but instructions 14, 15, and 17 are not. The correct code should be the following:

---

[2] The post condition should involve ALL exported parameters. Otherwise, some exported parameters may be unrestricted.

```
        begin
{ 1}    { <STAD> PARAMETER INITIALIZATION OF PARMETER A  }
{ 2}    { <STAD> PARAMETER INITIALIZATION OF PARAMETER n }
{ 3}    length[1] := 1;
{ 4}    pmax := 1;
{ 5}    maxl := 1;
{ 6}    i := 2;
{ 7}    while i <= n do
           begin
{ 8}         curr := A[i];
{ 9}          if curr < A[pmax] then
                begin
{10}              maxj := 1;
{11}              j := 1;
{12}              while j <= i-1 do
                    begin
{13}                  if A[j] < curr then
                        begin
{14}                      if maxj < length[j] then
{15}                        maxj := length[j];
                        end;
{16}                  j := j+1;
                    end;
{17}              length[i] := maxj+1;
{18}              if length[i] > maxl then
                    begin
{19}                  maxl := maxl+1;
{20}                  pmax := i;
                    end;
                end
              else
                begin
{21}              maxl := maxl+1;
{22}              length[i] := maxl;
{23}              pmax := i;
                end;
{24}         i := i+1;
           end;
{25}    monotone := maxl;
{26}    { <STAD> EXIT USE OF monotone (FUNCTION RESULT) }
{27} end;
```

Fig. 8.10 The body of procedure Monotone from Fig. 1 of the Introduction

```
14: if maxj<length[j]+1 then
15: maxj:=length[j]+1;
17: length[i]:=maxj;
```

In contrast to fault F, the underlying design assumption of fault F' is that maxj, computed by the loop 12–16, holds the length of a compatible subsequence for $A[i]$ *plus* one. Consequently, under fault hypothesis F, maxj=1 on entry to statement 11 is the first *data error* caused by F. Note that this primary error occurs on *every* iteration of the main loop. In contrast, under F', maxj=1 on entry to 11 *is* correct and the first *data error* caused by F' is in maxj on entry to statement 17; however, that error does not necessarily occur on every iteration of the main loop.

To illustrate the process of error creation and propagation consider the following tests (a VDM sequence notation is used throughout to specify array values, see Chap. 1):

```
t1: n=4, A=[1, 2, 3, 4]       -- correct result 4; faulty
                              -- segment not traversed
t2: n=4, A=[3, 1, 5, 7]       -- incorrect result 4, rather
                              -- than 3; fault revealed
t4: n= 4, A = [6, 10, 5, 12}  -- correct result 3, test
                              -- internally revealing,
                              -- externally masking.
t5: n=5, A = [6, 5, 4, 3, 2] -- incorrect result 2;
                              -- fault revealed
```

When run on test t1, the function produces a correct result. This is obvious, since the inner loop is never executed. In contrast, when run on test t2, the value of the result variable maxl is 4, rather than 3. The following is the *trace*, i.e, the sequence of instructions executed for the test (the notation $K–L$ stands for all the instructions between K and L):

```
T: 1-13, 16, 12, 17-20, 24, 7-9, 21-24, 7-9, 21-24, 7, 25.
```

Now, if the function is corrected according to the fault F hypothesis, i.e., statement 10 reads maxj:=0 rather than maxj:=1, the trace produced differs from T only in that the sequence *17–20* is replaced by the sequence *17–18*. Obviously, T is incorrect. Let us then analyze the creation and propagation of errors on T. The faulty statement 10 is executed only once, when length[2] is to be computed.

Thus, an incorrect value 1 assigned to maxj is the only occurrence of a primary error at instruction 11, *after* the faulty statement 10 has been executed. The incorrect value of maxj is then used in instruction 17 to compute length[2], which is assigned an incorrect value of 2, instead of 1. This is a *secondary data error*, caused by the propagation of the primary error. Observe, however, that the error in length[2] is the *first* occurrence of a primary error due to the F' fault hypothesis! Since on the *correct* trace the test length[2]>maxl in instruction 18 is *false*, maxl remains unchanged. In contrast, on the incorrect trace the above test is true due to the incorrectness of length[2], which leads to an erroneous execution of instructions 19 and 20. Consequently, the variables max1 and pmax are assigned incorrect values and thus are affected by secondary data errors. For the remaining two iterations of the main loop (for $i = 3, 4$), the inner loop is never entered but the corresponding values of the array length are incremented by 1 and pmax and max1 are also updated. Consequently, the final value of the output variable max1 is incorrect and the fault is *revealed*. Also note that incorrect contents of array length are [1, 2, 3, 4] rather than [1, 1, 2, 3]. Thus, the exported value and the internal state of the function are both incorrect.

Now, consider test t3. This time the statement 10:maxj:=1 is executed twice, on the third and fourth iteration of the outer loop, for $i = 3, 4$ respectively. However, despite the primary error being generated twice, *the returned final value of* max1 *is still correct!* Indeed, for $A[3]=5$ and $A[4] = 7$ the incorrect value 1 of maxj is correct since there does exist a compatible subsequence for $A[3]$ and $A[4]$, namely [3], and its length is correctly recorded in length[1]. Consequently, all the final values of the variables in the function and the returned result are computed correctly. Such a case, when the faulty statement is executed, primary error is generated but the final state of the program is correct will be referred to as *fault masking*. It happens when the initial state to the faulty segment, while violating the entry design assertion A, still satisfies the weakest precondition $\mathbf{wp}(S, B)$ of the exit design assertion B under S (see Chaps. 2 and 3).

Test t4 also produces the correct result 3 but, in contrast to t3, it corrupts the array length, which is (1, 2, 2, 3) rather than the correct value (1, 2, 1, 3). Such a test is *internally revealing* but *externally masking*. The name suggests that although the final result is correct, there is corrupt data in the code. Thus, the fault can potentially be detected if the correctness of variables *other* than the output one(s) were checked during testing.

Problem 8.4 *Define the weakest properties of tests revealing fault F in the function* monotone.

The key to a successful fault detection is a "sufficient" corruption of the array length. Toward that goal, observe the following two facts. First, the entry length[1]=1 is always correct. Second, for every A[k], k>1, such that A[k] is smaller than *all* the preceding entries, the corresponding entry length[k] is incorrectly set to 2, rather than to the correct value of 1. Now, consider some length[k] affected by such an error. The error propagates to every entry length[p], such that $A[p] > A[k]$ and the sequence $A[k], A[k+1], ..., A[p]$ is a longest one that ends at p (observe that there can be more than one longest sequences ending at p). Thus, the length of such a sequence will be incorrectly increased by 1. This will be a *secondary error* (in length[p]). That error *may* propagate to other secondary errors in the variables pmax and max1. That happens if length[p] is greater than the current longest sequence that ends at A[pmax]. Consequently, the fault is revealed if there exists a longest increasing monotone sequence in A that starts at position *other than 1* (tests t2, t5). Otherwise the fault is masked or externally masked (tests t1, t3, t4). Lessons learned in this section are used in the following section to analyze the fault detection power of structural testing.

8.5 Fault Detection Power of Code Coverage Testing

The discussion in Sect. 8.4 illustrates the fundamental difficulties of structural testing: Even if the suspected faulty component in the program is executed, there is no simple way to guarantee the generation of a primary error and its propagation toward the exit of the program. This is further aggravated by the difficulty to identify the fault itself. Consequently, in general, no specific fault is assumed in code coverage testing. Rather, the *"Everything-Can-Go-Wrong"* premise is adopted, without explicitly addressing either the creation or the propagation of errors. Having said that, it would not be fair to state that the coverage criteria discussed in Sects. 8.2 and 8.3 are entirely arbitrary. Even if lacking solid theoretical foundations, they are based on common sense and intuition. Moreover, one may argue that those strategies do test some implicit hypotheses about faults in the program. Thus, it is instructive to review typical structural testing methods in the light of the discussion in Sect. 8.4 to see what *implicit* assumptions about the possible faults and error propagation can be attributed to them.

Statement Coverage is met when every statement in the program is executed at least once. Thus, assuming that, at some level of decomposition of the program, a component, say C, is faulty, every statement in C will be covered at least once and the *necessary* conditions for the primary error origination are met. However, since statement coverage is the least demanding the likelihood that a primary error at the exit of C is generated is not high. The propagation of the primary error is totally ignored by the strategy, since any path continuing through the exit of C to the program exit is acceptable. Also acceptable is any path leading to the entry of C.

The implicit objective of *Branch Coverage* is the detection of *control errors*, i.e, wrong selection of a branch for execution. There are two possible faults that may cause such an error. First, the predicate $p(X)$ in **if** $p(X)$ ... (or **while** $p(X)$...) may be incorrect (*control fault*), causing a *primary control error*. Second, the variable X in $p(X)$ may be affected by a (primary or secondary) data error, thus potentially causing a *secondary control error*. Branch testing directly addresses only the primary control error, since no specific assignments to X are required. Again, propagation of the control error is not addressed.

Let M: $V:=f(X)$ be assignment statement to the variable V in node M. Recall that the *Definition-Use Chains* strategy requires the value of V be used in every potential reference of V that can be reached from M without V being redefined along the way. Apparently, Chain coverage is superior to statement coverage in both the creation of primary errors and their propagation. Clearly, a fault in the expression f may cause a primary error in the variable V. Since every possible use of V must be executed, in general the assignment has to be executed more than once, unless all the uses lie on a single path from the assignment, a rather unrealistic assumption. Moreover, since the values of X have to come from *all* possible definitions of X that reach M, that requires even more executions of M. Thus, the chances of the creation of a primary error at the exit of M are higher for Chain coverage than for node and branch coverage.

Observe that the variable X may be affected by a primary error generated before M is reached; thus, X at the exit of M can be also affected by a *secondary error*. Now, since all potential uses of the definition of X in M have to be activated, either kind of error has a greater chance to propagate. Thus, the necessary (albeit not sufficient) conditions for *one-step propagation* of the error in V are met, providing an improvement over statement and branch coverage. This also includes the case when data testing is combined with branch testing (*p-use*, [11]), i.e., when V is used in a predicate, and meets the necessary conditions to generate a secondary control error.

The *Required k-Tuples* [10] strategy involves the execution of sequences $[S_1, S_2, ..., S_k]$, for some k, $k > 1$, of statements in the program, such that there is data dependency of every statement in the sequence on its immediate predecessor. In principle, this approach meets the *necessary* (albeit not sufficient) conditions for the propagation of *data* (albeit not control!) errors. In other words, what is tested is the kth power of the Data Dependency relation DD (see Chap. 6) thus guaranteeing the necessary requirements for k-step *data error* propagation. Of course, in practice a constant value of k is not likely to be feasible. This restriction can be alleviated, however. For acyclic DD, k can be taken as the highest nonempty power of DD, while for cyclic DD the length of a simple cycle can offer a reasonable approach.

Similarly to Chain coverage, the implicit rationale of *U_Context* testing is the creation and propagation of primary errors due to a possible fault in the expression f in the statement $M:V := f(X, Y, Z)$ and propagation of secondary errors in V due to errors in the variables used in M. It appears that U_Context coverage is superior to Chain coverage in the primary error generation while its error propagation potential remains an open question.

To illustrate this, consider the assignment statement $M:V := f(X, Y, Z)$ and a definition $D(Y)$ of the variable Y. This definition has to be used in M with the presence of all possible definitions of X and Z and, consequently, usually more executions of $D(Y)$ are needed than for Chain testing. Thus, if one believes that "the more testing the better," the chances of a primary error creation, due to the implicitly assumed fault in the expression f, do increase.

It is an open question, however, whether U_Context testing enhances propagation of the presumed error in V when compared with Chain coverage. On one hand, the propagation seems to be enhanced by the fact that each execution of a use of V involves different "context," i.e, different sources of values of the remaining variables. That naturally requires more activations of the uses of V and, consequently, increases the chances of propagation of the error in V. On the other hand, as illustrated in Sect. 8.4, since an error is a violation of an assertion at the point of interest, propagation of errors depends, in general, on the values of all the free variables that appear in the assertion, rather than only some variables. Thus, for an error to propagate the state as a *whole* must violate the assertion involved. It is not yet clear whether this phenomenon works in favor of error masking or propagation. Certainly, this is an important research problem.

Finally, since L_Contexts when compared to U_Context involve more variables at the corresponding nodes, *L_Contexts* Coverage is more demanding in
terms of the number of tests needed. That, in general, *may* increase the chances
of the generation of a primary error compared to U_Context testing. However, the
error propagation is not necessarily improved by L_Context testing. To see this
consider some node, say *p*, in the flowgraph. Variables that are live at *p* but are
not used in it must be used in nodes other than *p*. However, those uses although
potentially reachable from *p* (otherwise the variables would not have been live at *p*)
are not necessarily reachable on *every* path from *p* to the exit *E* (see Chap. 7).
Consequently, the potential benefit of using more variables to propagate errors
may be lost.

8.6   Program Dependencies in Software Testing

It is intuitively obvious that dependencies between program entities (see Chap. 7)
are *the* vehicle for the structural analysis of error creation *and* propagation. To
illustrate this consider component *C* in the program. Assuming that *C* is faulty, the
necessary (albeit not sufficient) conditions for the origination of a primary error, is
the traversal of *C*. The necessary (but again, not sufficient) condition for the error
to propagate is the use of the incorrect value(s) at the exit of *C* in the computation
of the output variables of the program. Thus errors can propagate only to program
entities that depend in one way or another on the output variables of *C*. This also
includes the case when the affected variable is an exported parameter and can reach
the exit without being modified. As illustrated in Sect. 8.4, this is by far the best
situation for error propagation for *the shorter a path to the exit the lesser the chance
of error masking*.

Although there are no guaranteed rules how to enhance the chances of the creation and propagation of errors, some common sense heuristics can be offered. First,
it seems reasonable to expect that the chances of creating a primary error at the exit
of *C* increase if *C itself* is traversed in a fairly complicated way. Second, one may
expect that errors propagate more often if more program variables are affected by
the primary error. Consequently, the way *C* is reached, the way it is traversed and
the way the rest of the program is executed, are all subject to possible restrictions
to increase the likelihood of primary error creation and propagation. Thus, a
method is needed to identify the most promising program paths along which errors
are most likely to be created and propagated; testing effort should be directed at
traversing those paths. To illustrate the issues involved here consider the program
in Fig. 8.11.

Assume that the first **if** statement is the faulty (or suspected) segment. Recall
from Sect. 8.4 that this means the statement cannot be proved formally. To illustrate
this consider the following *verification schema* for the statement:

VC1: $\text{pre}(A, B, C, X, Y) \wedge c(A, B) \wedge X = \text{e1}(A\sim, B) \wedge A = \text{e2}(Y)$
$\Rightarrow$ $\text{post}(A\sim, B, C, X\sim, Y, A, B, C, X, Y)$

```
1:   get(A,B,C,X,Y);
2:   if c(A,B)
        3: then [ X := e1(A,B);  A := e2(Y) ]
        4: else [ Y := e3(A,B);  B := e4(X) ];

5:   if p(A,B)
        6: then [ X := f(A);    U := g(Y); T := r(A,Y) ]
        7: else [ Y := h(B);    W := z(X); Q := s(B,X) ];
8:   write(X,Y);
```

Fig. 8.11 A program segment

VC2: $pre(A, B, C, X, Y) \wedge \neg C(A, B) \wedge Y = e3(A, B\sim) \wedge B = e4(X)$
$\Rightarrow$ $post(A, B\sim, C, X, Y\sim, A, B, C, X, Y)$

where the general form **post**$(A\sim, B\sim, C\sim, X\sim, Y\sim, A, B, C, X, Y)$ of the postcondition has been assumed (recall that the tilde ~ stands for the initial value of the variable involved). Now, the entire statement is faulty if either VC1, VC2 or both are false. Observe that if, say, only VC1 (VC2) is faulty and can be corrected by modifying only the body of the **then** **(else)** clause then the fault is at the level the offending clause, while the fault at the entire **if** statement level is due to the encapsulation of that clause by the statement. In contrast, if VC1 and VC2 are *both* invalid then the correction involves either the bodies of both clauses and/or the predicate $c(A, B)$. The best we can do in this case is to formulate some fault hypotheses about the nature of the incorrectness of C and identify variables that are potentially affected by primary errors due the hypothesized faults. The detection of a fault can be facilitated by identifying *error-sensitive paths* along which the primary errors are likely to propagate toward the exit of the program.

Figure 8.12 shows *some* (of many possible) fault hypotheses *within* the faulty component (the first **if**) and the sets of variables affected by the faults; each hypothesized fault is viewed, of course, as a single fault *outside* the component. The results are self-explanatory although a comment is in place regarding fault F7. Clearly, if the fault "fires," i.e., an incorrect branch at 2 has been taken, *two* sets of variables are potentially affected by primary errors: Those that are defined in the correct branch, which has *not* been taken and those in the incorrect branch, which *has* been taken. Observe that the sets of potential primary errors can be identified statically. Moreover, a degree of likelihood (belief) can be assigned to each hypothesis, e.g., one may believe that single faults are more likely than multiple faults. Thus, F1, F2, and F7 would be more likely than F3 and F4, while F5 and F6 would be the least likely.

Now let us have a look at the structural mechanism of the propagation of the primary errors originating at the exit of the first **if** statement. They *may* propagate through the second **if** provided certain necessary (albeit usually not sufficient)

FAULT	PRIMARY ERRORS	PATH TAKEN
F1: e1 incorrect	{X}	then branch
F2: e3 incorrect	{Y}	else branch
F3: e1,e2 incorrect	{A,X}	then branch
F4: e3,e4 incorrect	{B,Y}	else branch
F5: e1,e2 incorrect, missing assignments to B,Y	{A,B,X,Y}	then branch
F6: e3,e4 incorrect, missing assignments to A,X	{A,B,X,Y}	else branch
F7: c(A,B) incorrect (control fault)	{A,B,X,Y}	either branch

Fig. 8.12 Fault hypotheses for the first if in the program in Fig. 8.11 and variables affected by primary errors at the exit of the statement

Error Propagation Hypotheses are assumed. In what follows we illustrate the process using the faults in Fig. 8.12 for the code in Fig. 8.11.

Fault F1 (primary error in X). A primary error in X may lead to the incorrectness of X itself at the exit 8, but only when the **else** branch is taken through the second **if**; otherwise X is redefined in the **then** clause. We refer to such situation, when an error-affected variable is not modified on a path to the exit of the statement that follows the faulty one, as the *inheritance* of the error (by the second **if** in our case). Observe, however, that even if the above conditions are met it does not necessarily mean that the incorrect value of X at the exit of the first **if** will remain incorrect. Indeed, as shown in Sect. 8.4, the corrupt value of X may satisfy the assertion at 8.

Fault F2. Similar to the previous case, left to the reader as an exercise.

Fault F3 (primary errors in A and X). To properly handle the case one needs to consider hypotheses about possible control errors through the second **if** statement. If the **then** branch is taken correctly, error in A propagates to a secondary error in X (the assignment $X:=f(A)$), overriding the original primary error in X, while the original primary error in A is inherited by the second **if**. If the else branch is chosen correctly, the error in X propagates to W and Q, while the original error in A is again inherited. Otherwise, if there is a decision error in $p(A, B)$, the variables defined in both branches are affected by error, while error in A is inherited, i.e., A, X, U, T, Y, W, and Q are all potentially incorrect.

Fault F4 (primary errors in B, Y). Similar to the previous case, left to the reader as an exercise.

Faults F5, F6, and F7 (primary errors in A, B, X, Y). If the **then** branch is taken correctly, variables X, U, and T are affected by secondary errors, while A, B, and Y are affected by the inherited primary errors. When the **else** branch is taken correctly variables Y, W, and Q are affected by secondary errors while A, B, and X retain their inherited primary errors.

Observe that the above analysis establishes only *potential* propagation of errors, rather than an absolute one; clearly, the qualifier "may" has been dropped to avoid an unnecessary cluttering of the text. However, the analysis may be useful in program debugging when the program's incorrectness has already been established and one wants to identify the most likely responsible "culprit." Assume, for instance, that the **then** branch in the second **if** has been traversed (a fact established by run-time monitoring) and both X and Y are incorrect at the exit 8 of the segment in Fig. 8.11. Apparently, the F5, F6, and F7 faults and the relevant error propagation hypotheses provide a possible explanation and a degree of *localization* of the errors. Now, the hypotheses can be analyzed and, if intermediate assertions are available, either rejected or accepted. Otherwise, if assertions are not available, the most likely hypothesis can be accepted.

To put the above ideas to practice, a suitable structural formal model of faults, primary error creation, and error propagation is needed. In the rest of this section, we outline the most general properties of such a model. A first step toward that goal could be the derivation of the direct Error Propagation relation ε on the Cartesian product of the sets of nodes and variables in the program, defined informally as follows. Assuming X and Y are (not necessarily distinct) variables and p and q are two nodes in the flowgraph such that $(p\ q)$ is an arc in it, the *error propagation relation ε* can be defined as follows:

$$(p, X)\ \varepsilon\ (q, Y)$$

if and only if an error in variable X at node p *may* propagate to an error in the variable Y at node q in a *single* step (it is assumed that X is at the bottom of p, *after* its execution while Y is at the top of q, *before* its execution). As the foregoing discussion demonstrates, an error can propagate due to the data dependencies or control dependencies in the program. Since that can be relevant to the error analysis, the Error Propagation Hypotheses (EPHs) involved should be suitably recorded. One way of doing that would be to label correspondingly the arcs of the relation ε, turning it virtually into a ternary (involving three elements) relation. Care has to be taken to properly record the propagation of *control errors*, whose effects on contaminated variables can only be evaluated at the *Immediate Attractor* IA(d) of the decision node d involved (see Chap. 6). Moreover, it may also be useful to refine the notion of secondary errors to identify the actual sequence of propagation steps. One way of achieving that is to compute and record the *powers ε^k* of the relation ε, $k = 1, 2, ...,$ Max. Recall from Chap. 6 that if ε is acyclic, Max is less than the number of distinct pairs (node, variable) in the flowgraph. In contrast, when ε is cyclic M is the minimal number such that every power ε^k, where k is equal to or greater than $M+1$, is identical to some smaller power(s) of the relation. In terms of error propagation

ε^1 captures the one-step propagation, ε^2 two-step propagation and so forth. Naturally, the positive *closure* ε^+ of ε captures the possibility of propagation in an arbitrary number of steps.

Assuming that the above model of incorrect program has been developed, how can one use it as a basis for structural testing? To arrive at a practical solution to the problem one would have to consider several issues. A quite "natural" temptation would be to require that for a postulated error in variable, say X at node p, all pairs $((p, X), (q, Y))$ such that $(p, X)\ \varepsilon^k (q, Y)$, for $k=1,\ldots$, Max, should be activated during testing. For all intents and purposes such a criterion is a generalization of the *required k-tuple* coverage proposed in [10] and discussed in Sect. 8.5. Surely, such a requirement might be computationally too demanding in practice. However, for better or worse this is irrelevant in the light of the discussion in the preceding sections of this chapter. We demonstrated there that (1) structural program coverage in and of itself is out of the question and can only be measured as a side effect of Black-Box testing and (2) the synthesis of tests for purely structural testing is realistic only for a very limited number of required elements missed during black-box testing. This observation offers a radically new perspective on structural testing: Rather than statically formulate a coverage criterion that may lead to a large number of infeasible required elements,

analyze the set of traces on the completion of Black-Box testing in order to asses the likelihood of fault masking and possibly suggest further testing to localize the fault.

This is based on the assumption that *all traces yield correct results*, i.e., they fail to detect the fault; otherwise a fault has been detected and the subsequent task is that of debugging, rather than testing. In what follows, we discuss some heuristics that may be used to assess the likelihood of hidden faults in the program and suggest new, promising structural tests geared toward testing for the existence of those faults.

Assume that for two nodes p and q, and the variables X and Y there is $(p, X)\ \varepsilon^k (q, Y)$, for some k, $k > 0$. Now, not every (q, Y) is necessarily relevant to testing and that is for several reasons, to name only few. First, the value of Y at q has to potentially propagate to some exported parameter O; thus, there must exist some n such that $(q, Y)\ \varepsilon^n$ (Exit, O). As shown in Chap. 7 that may not necessarily be guaranteed if there exist data flow anomalies in the code; in such a case the propagation of error in Y at q is irrelevant. Second, the discussion in Sect. 8.4 suggests that *the longer the chain of error propagation the greater the chance of masking the error.* Consequently, traces that yield correct results on a *shortest* route from the postulated primary error to the exit are less "suspect" of fault masking than traces traversing longer propagation paths. Thus, effort should be made to activate the shortest chains of error propagation. Observe that the length of the propagation chain, i.e., the value of k in ε^k, is not necessarily determined by the length of the trace. Third, it is intuitively obvious that *the likelihood of error propagation increases with the number of variables to which the error in question potentially propagates.* Thus if X at p is suspected incorrect one should try to activate all propagation chains starting at (p, X). In particular, as shown in Sect. 8.4, efforts should be made to generate control errors as they potentially corrupt all variables defined in the corresponding branches of decision statements. Fourth, one should try to pay more attention to parts of the code with low frequency of execution. If static analysis of the problem is unsatisfactory one can employ the statistical method of Dynamic Mutation Testing, a Monte Carlo technique, to statistically assess the likelihood of a postulated fault by a passing test suite [7].

Finally, it is important to keep in mind that the error propagation relation is in reality only a *template* for error propagation, rather than an accurate model for the real events. Indeed, in the case of structured variables like arrays, it is the individual entries of the data that is affected by errors, rather than the entire structure. Those entries cannot be identified by static analysis. Therefore, *dynamic* or *execution trace-based* analysis, introduced in Chap. 9, has to be used toward that goal. A general idea of applying such analysis is presented below. Toward that goal, observe that every program execution can be viewed as an *indirect* testing of some *implicit* fault and error creation and propagation hypotheses. To illustrate that fact suppose that for some input the execution trace $[S_1, S_2, ..., S_p]$, i.e., a sequence of (not necessarily distinct) statements S_i, $i = 1, 2, ..., p$, for some p, $p > 1$, has been executed, see Chap. 9 for a full definition. Assume that the state established by the trace at the exit of S_p has been found correct. On that basis one can formulate a series of hypotheses about the *presumed* fault, primary error creation and its propagation, and/or masking. For example, one can postulate that all statements in the sequence are either correct or, even if there is a faulty statement in the trace, no primary error has been created. Or one can hypothesize that there is some fault say, in S_k, $1 < k < p$, and a primary error was generated during execution of S_k, has propagated to some places along the trace but has been masked by the subsequent statements. A similar hypothesis sans masking can be formulated if the state at the exit of S_p is incorrect. Observe that in either case, if the hypotheses can be verified they offer a degree of *fault localization*, an immeasurable help in debugging.

Now, if intermediate assertions are available the veracity of these hypotheses can be established by evaluating the assertions on the states in question; otherwise, other methods are needed to estimate their likelihood. Toward that goal one can consider a *collection* of traces, rather than a single trace. In general, such a set partitions into a *passing* subset (containing traces that yield correct results) and *failing* subset (containing traces that yield incorrect results, i.e., *succeeding* in the detection of a bug). Various hypotheses can be formulated using the set-theoretic properties of those sets, i.e., their intersection, union, and difference. Those hypotheses must of course "**fit**" or "explain" all traces in the set.

8.7 Conclusions

The discussion in this chapter illustrates the fact that software testing is the most ambiguous and immature software verification technique around. Clearly, even debugging seems to be better defined – at least in that case one knows what one is looking for – an explanation of a concrete finding of incorrectness. And this is in spite of (or is it *because* of?) its long and prevailing use in practice and scores of papers, conferences, workshops, and symposia. Why is that? We believe that the root cause of that situation is the fact that testing suffers from *the virtual lack of theoretical foundations*. Indeed, in contrast to program testing, formal verification (program proving) and static analysis are both based on solid mathematical foundations. However, on closer inspection, the rather dismal status of testing appears quite normal. After all, program proving aims toward analyzing objects that are supposed to be correct or close to be so; static analysis deals with code that is syntactically correct. In contrast, testing deals with chaos. Therefore, real progress in the art of testing hinges heavily on the progress in its theory which, in turn, depends on the sound theory of *incorrect*, rather than correct, programs. Obviously, this is not going to be easy. In particular, since testing is essentially a real experiment, a sound theory of testing should address two issues: The underlying mathematical properties of incorrect programs and the pragmatic aspects of using those properties in practice. In what follows, we outline the most important problems that call for investigation.

The starting point here has to be the role of testing in the overall verification effort in which all three verification techniques – program proving, static analysis, and testing – are used in an *integrated* way. That is, although each technique should have its well-defined area of application, it is their interplay that is essential to the success of the verification process. It is natural for (proscriptive) static analysis to be carried out first. Indeed, only when the identified anomalies detected in the process are removed or explained away, does it make sense to move to other verification techniques. At this point it is safe to assume that for the foreseeable future program proving of entire programs is not a realistic proposition. A corollary to this proposition is that program proving should be reserved for *parts* of the program that are most likely to be incorrect and testing may be instrumental in the identification of those parts.

The above observations lead to the following threefold objectives of program testing. First, it is the *detection* of the fault as the ultimate success of testing. Second, for a *failing* (i.e., successfully detecting the fault) test suite, comprehensive testing scenario should also provide a measure of *fault-localization* information, by identifying possible faulty parts of the code. This is an intriguing possibility for it opens the door for an integrated testing/debugging scenario. Third, for a passing test suite, it is the *estimation* of the likelihood of a hidden fault that escaped detection. A "suspect" segment can be then analyzed and tested in more detail, including a possible attempt to prove it correct. If a testing scenario does support the three stated objectives, we say it meets the DEL *paradigm*, for (fault) Detection, (correctness) Estimation, and (fault) Localization.

The most popular (and quite natural) approach to initial testing is the "Everything-Can-Go-Wrong" paradigm, when no specific assumptions are made about classes of potential faults. However, in more advanced phases of testing and specifically during the Estimation phase a *fault-based* testing is more often adopted.

In that case, some classes of faults are hypothesized and tests are developed to test the hypotheses involved. This seems more realistic since in practice rarely every place in the program is suspected. Rather, one usually has strong confidence in some of parts of the code and suspects only a few of them. For example, the programmer may have doubts about the reasoning about the design and implementation of some component C; usually that is due to the inherent difficulty of the (sub) problem solved by C. Another way is to use some objective measures, to name only a few: A "rich" history of faults in C; the fact that C encapsulates modifications to a previously correct (or *thought* to be correct) program, cf. [8]; the fact that C has *not* been thoroughly exercised by the testing suite; the relative complexity of C, as measured by some metric.

For a *failing* test suite, the most likely fault that can be responsible for the observed error creation and propagation can be taken as the cause of the program incorrectness (fault localization). Recall that the accuracy of fault localization and the identification of the scope of errors caused by the fault can be significantly improved if, besides the correctness of the output variables, the correctness of other variables can also be verified. In an interactive scenario, the information about all variables potentially affected by a fault would prompt the programmer to check variables other than the exported ones; this might lead to the rejection of some hypotheses, thus helping in the fault localization process. This is also true for testing: Errors might not propagate to the output variables but might propagate to *other* variables, as shown in Sect. 8.4. Again, the lack of theoretical model makes this appealing approach difficult to apply. In the specific case of *mutation testing*, "mutants" of the original program are generated and tests sought to distinguish between them and the program being tested.

Finally, let us look at the estimation part of the DEL paradigm. For a *passing* test suite, if the most likely hypothesis is one for which *no* primary error is generated, the likelihood of that hypothesis can be taken as the likelihood that the program is indeed correct (correctness estimation); otherwise, if the most likely hypothesis is one for which a primary error has been generated but masked, a potentially "weak point" in the program that warrants further analysis has been identified. That can be done either in the deterministic or in the probabilistic fashion. In either case the objective is to provide a degree of belief, that there is no fault in the program, i.e, that *the program is indeed correct*. Most works on testing address the main goal, i.e, fault detection. The second goal, is an object of an ongoing research activity, most notably mutation testing [1], related to it the Propagation, Infection and Estimation (PIE) approach [9,12] and Dynamic Mutation Testing (DMT) [7,8]. In mutation testing fault hypotheses are formulated at the expression level, albeit in an arbitrary way. If an expression in the program is mutated and the mutant is "killed" during testing on the original test suite (i.e., it has led to an error), then the existence in the original program of the fault represented by the mutant is ruled out. If, on the other hand, the mutant is not killed then it becomes a candidate for a fault, deserving a further analysis. It indeed seems plausible that some "brutal" modifications of an expression, e.g., $X+Y$ in $V:=X+Y$ to $X*Y$, will increase the likelihood of a primary error generation in V. However, since that error will occur in the *modified* program, little is known about the chances for the primary error to occur in the *original* program. Moreover, no explicit mechanism is in place to enhance the propagation of errors. Even worse, since the propagation is tested on the *mutated* program, if the mutated (suspected to be faulty) expression lies on a cycle, an error that would have been propagated in the original program, might be masked by the incorrect statement in the mutated program.

The DMT is a Monte Carlo technique for the estimation of the probability of a fault in the program being masked on a passing test suite. Unlike mutation testing, DMT estimates the *sensitivity* of the program to the changes of variables potentially affected by primary errors at the exit of a suspected program component. In fact, the sensitivity is the relative size of the set defined by the weakest precondition of the predicate "the output is correct." When compared to mutation testing, DMT is much simpler to implement and it does address error propagation, although it does not address the creation of primary errors, an issue apparently better handled by mutation testing.

Exercise 8.1   *Assume that during testing a Definition-Use Chain say, from node n to m, has been activated; does that lead to the activation of an additional U_ Context? And, conversely, if a new U_context has been activated, does that lead to the activation of new Definition-Use Chains at n?*

Exercise 8.2   *Define a relation "error in variable X at point p may cause a control error at node q," i.e., q may be erroneously selected or deselected for execution due to an error in X at p.*

Exercise 8.3   *Define a relation δ from the set of decision nodes to the subsets of all nodes in the flowgraph such d δ T if and only if all nodes in the set T can be incorrectly selected or deselected for execution. HINT: Solve the problem first for the while (goto-less) programs.*

Exercise 8.4   *Defined formally the Error Propagation Relation ε introduced informally in Sect.8.6.*

References

1. R.A. DeMillo, A.J. Offutt, Constraint–based automatic test data generation, IEEE Transactions on. Engineering, 17(9), 909–910, 1991.
2. P.M. Herman, A data flow analysis approach to program testing. The Australian Computer Journal, 8(3), 347–354, 1976.
3. J. Laski, B. Korel, A data flow oriented program testing strategy, IEEE Transactions on. Engineering, SE–9(3), 347–354, 1983.
4. J. Laski, An algorithm for the derivation of codefinitions in computer programs, Information Processing Letters, 23, 1986, 85–90.
5. J. Laski, Path Expressions in Data Flow Program Testing, Proceedings of Compsaq 1990, The 14th International Computer Software and Applications Conference, Chicago, IL, Oct 29–Nov 2, 1990, pp.570–576.
6. J. Laski, Data flow testing in STAD, The Journal of Systems Software, 12(1), 1990, 3–14.

7. J, Laski, W, Szermer, P, Luczycki, Error masking in computer programs, Journal for Software Testing, Verification and Reliability, 5(2), 1995, 81–105.

8. J. Laski, W. Szermer, Identification of Program Modifications and its Applications in Software Maintenance, Proceedings of IEEE Conference on Software aintenance, Orlando, FL, Nov. 1992 , p. 2, IEEE Computer Society Press, Los Alamitos, CA.

9. K.W. Miller, et al., Estimating the probability of failure when testing reveals no failures, IEEE Transactions on. Engineering, 18(1), 33–43, 1992.

10. S.C. Ntafos, On required element testing, IEEE Transactions on. Eng., SE–10(6), 795–803, 1984.

11. S. Rapps, E. Weuyker, Selecting software test data using data flow information, IEEE Transactions on Software Engineering., SE–11(4), 367–375, 1985.

12. J. Voas, PIE: A dynamic failure–based technique, IEEE Transactions on. Engineering, 18(8), 717–727, 1992.

Chapter 9
Dynamic Program Analysis

Abstract A recorded history of program execution for a particular input is referred to as the trace for that input. *Trace analysis* or *dynamic analysis* offers help in dealing with undecidable problems in static analysis. This is due to the fact that, in contrast to the static case, the values of the variables on the trace are known. Thus, the ubiquitous in static analysis qualifier "may happen" can be replaced in dynamic analysis by "it did happen." In contrast to static analysis, where it is impossible in general to know the values of array indexes, in trace analysis, array entries are treated as separate variables. Also, access variables (Pointers) can be handled by replicating the dynamic process of creation and destruction of data on the trace. The notion of trace is defined first at the abstract level and then at the concrete, STAD level. Data and control dependencies on trace are defined as counterparts to the corresponding static concepts. Their application to the derivation of program slices demonstrates that dynamic analysis is a useful and necessary complement to static analysis.

9.1 Introduction

Static program analysis, formal proofs, and Black-Box testing can be, and frequently are, not only useful but also fun. That is, *fun!*, as a natural emotional reward for a job well done. However, programs are not written for reading and analysis; they are written to be executed. The object of *dynamic analysis* is the program's execution history, or *trace,* hence it will also be referred to as *trace analysis.* In an ideal scenario, if the program is correct there is no real need to monitor or otherwise analyze the executions. Certainly, users have no need to be interested in particular executions as along as their final results and the program efficiency are satisfactory. As we argued in Chap. 8 even structural testing does not call for the entire trace to be available; rather, it is concerned with only *some* properties of the trace, namely its traversal of the predefined class of Required Elements. Having said that, we argue the programmers do carry out some sort of dynamic analysis decisively more often than they do static analysis. Naturally, the main purpose of that analysis is *debugging.* As debugging tends to be the most painful stage in software development it can be fun only for a

J. Laski and W. Stanley, *Software Verification and Analysis,*
DOI: 10.1007/978-1-84882-240-5_10, © Springer Verlag London Limited 2009

chosen few. Essentially, debugging is the process of inspecting selected parts of the trace and formulating and testing fault hypotheses that may explain the program failure during testing.

Typically, programmers inspect the trace by suspending execution at certain breakpoints, reading the values of variables of interest and resuming the execution, only to repeat the procedure at other points on the trace. The process can be manual or *symbolic debuggers* can be used to assist the programmer. In either case, however, it is up to the programmer to formulate and test relevant fault hypotheses. At the time of this writing we know of no industrial tool supporting debugging in the above-mentioned sense. It is the objective of this Chapter to formulate the prerequisite foundations for trace analysis. The main tenet of this effort is the need for the integration of static and dynamic analysis around the same conceptual framework. More precisely, static analysis concepts provide only a *template* for things that may happen during execution. It is precisely for the execution that the ubiquitous in static analysis qualifier "*may happen*" can be replaced by "*it did happen.*"

In Sect. 9.2 we provide the background of trace analysis in abstract terms and illustrate it with the actual output produced by STAD. Then, in Sect. 9.3 we introduce the basic concepts of dynamic analysis as counterparts of the related concepts in static analysis. In particular, the notions of Dynamic Data and Control Dependencies on trace are defined. That is followed by two particular applications of dynamic analysis: The derivation of Dynamic Slices for program without access variables (Pointers) in Sect. 9.4 and the derivation of the slices for program with pointers in Sect. 9.5. It is shown that the dynamic approach may substantially reduce the size of the slice and allows one to analyze the execution in the presence of pointers, a problem intractable by static analysis. In Sect. 9.6 other potential applications are outlined.

9.2   Operational Semantics: States and Computations

The assertion-based notion of program correctness introduced earlier in the book involves all possible program executions. However, operationally the program's semantics is determined by its behavior on individual *paths* through the program. Recall that the following symbolic notation

$$\{PRE\}\ P\ \{POST\}$$

stands the following proposition:

$$PRE \Rightarrow \mathbf{wp}\ (P, POST)$$

where $\mathbf{wp}(P, POST)$ is the *weakest precondition* of POST for P, defined as follows: $\mathbf{wp}(P, POST)(x) \Leftrightarrow$ "for input x, the program terminates producing output y for which $POST(x, y)$ holds." In other words, if $\mathbf{wp}(P, POST)(x)$ holds, p terminates for x with a correct result. It is easy to show that

$$\mathbf{wp}\ (P, POST) \Leftrightarrow \exists p\colon Paths \cdot \mathbf{tr}(p) \wedge \mathbf{pwp}\ (p, POST),$$

where (1) *Paths* is a set of all paths through the program from the start *S* to the exit *E*, (2) **tr**(*p*) is the *path traversal condition* predicate which, if satisfied, guarantees the traversal of path *p*, and (3) **pwp**(*p*, POST) is the *partial weakest precondition* of POST for *p*, a predicate at the beginning of *p* which, if satisfied, guarantees POST at the end of *p*, *provided p* has been traversed in the first place. The *actual* (in contrast to the *postulated*) semantics of the program is determined by its behavior, i.e., the sum total of the properties of its executions. Consider program IntDiv in Fig. 9.1. If asked the question "What is the program doing?" even an experienced programmer, who has never seen a similar program, might have serious difficulties to answer if the specification of the program is not available. One way of gaining understanding of the program is to simulate its execution for some concrete input in hope to discover and generalize some patterns of relationships between program variables. Indeed, this is a time-honored practical method not only to discover the overall program's function but also to synthesize the assertions, typically the loop invariant. Simulation requires recording the sequence of values of all variables at the instructions executed. It is convenient to record the values of variables just *before* the instruction is to be executed, rather than *after* its execution. This allows one to properly record the targets of the decisions in **if** statements, if any. A pseudostep 0 is introduced to properly handle the initial situation. Fig. 9.2 shows the recorded execution for the program in Fig. 9.1; a question mark is used to denote undefined values.

The above example gives rise to several concepts. First, it is the notion of the state. Intuitively, a state is a collection of all pairs (variable, its value) in the program. Formally, a *state* is a function of the following signature:

$$s : \text{VARS} \rightarrow \bigcup \text{type}(v).$$

```
        program IntDiv;
        VAR x, y, r, q: integer;

        begin
{ 1}        readln(x,y);
{ 2}        q:=0;
{ 3}        r:=x;
{ 4}    while  y<=r do
            begin
{ 5}            q:=q+1;
{ 6}            r:=r-y
            end;
{ 7} end.
```

Fig. 9.1 A STAD-elaborated program computing the quotient (*q*) and remainder (*r*) of the integer division *x/y*

Fig. 9.2 Execution of the program in Fig. 9.1 for input $x = 10$, $y = 3$

STEP	INSTRUCTION	VALUES OF (x,y,r,q)
0	1 (S-start)	(?,?,?,?)
1	2	(10,3,?,?)
2	3	(10,3,?,0)
3	4	(10,3,10,0)
4	5	(10,3,10,0)
5	6	(10,3,10,1)
6	4	(10,3,7,1)
7	5	(10,3,7,1)
8	6	(10,3,7,2)
9	4	(10,3,4,2)
10	5	(10,3,4,2)
11	6	(10,3,4,2)
12	4	(10,3,1,3)
13	7 (E-End)	(10,3,1,3)
--	termination	---

where v ranges over the set VARS of variables. It is required that for every variable v in VARS, $s(v) \in$ **type**(v) i.e., an application of s to v returns a value from the set of values determined by the type of v. Assignments to program variables might change the state, e.g., after the assignment $v := 3$ is completed, $s(v) = 3$. The state is meaningful only *at some point of interest*, e.g., at some node n. A convention will be adopted that the state at node n is associated with the *top* of n, before n is executed. The alternative approach, i.e., associating states with the bottom of nodes, after their execution, would require recording the results of Boolean expressions in decision nodes. In general, the state is a *partial* function, defined only for some variables. This is because some variables may be undefined (not assigned any value) when the node of interest is reached. Although a print statement might return some value of an undefined variable, such a value cannot be predicted and the result of the application of the state function to that variable (at some point) is undefined. In such a case, a question mark "?" stands for an undefined result of the state function application. The IntDiv routine does not take any parameters and all objects appearing in it are state variables. However, in general, a subprogram may have parameters and those are then part of the state.

A *computation* in the program is an alternating sequence

$$s_0, n_0, s_1, n_1, \ldots, s_i, n_i, \ldots, s_f, n_f$$

of states and nodes that arises during an execution of the program, where n_0 is the start node S and n_f is the exit node E. Observe the convention that every s_i in the sequence is a state at the start of node n_i. The subsequence $n_0, n_1, \ldots, n_f, \ldots$ of nodes in the computation is, of course, a path in the flowgraph; such an actually executed path is the program *trace* for the *initial state* s_0 at the start node $S = n_0$. If the computation is finite and the last element n_f of the computation is the exit node E, the computation is said to *terminate* in the *final state* s_f. In what follows we use the term *trace* to stand for the trace proper (a sequence of nodes) and for a computation, the convolution of the trace proper and the sequence of states involved. The actual meaning will be clear from the context. An important fact is that, in general, the domain of the state function, i.e., the set VARS of program variables is not necessarily static. That is, VARS might contain not only explicitly declared variables but also locally introduced variables (e.g., the i in the **for** i := k **do** ...) as well as *anonymous (dynamic) variables,* i.e., objects created and destroyed during execution, such as pointer-based structures. Thus, during a computation not only the values of variables might change but so might the very structures of the state as dynamic variables are created or destroyed.

The set of all terminating computations can be used to define the *program function* $[P]$ that is computed by program P. Clearly, $[P]$ is the set of all pairs (s_0, s_f) such that s_f is the final state of a terminating computation for the initial state s_0. Thus, the notation $y=[P](x)$ means, "For the initial state x at entry S, program P terminates in the final state y at exit E." Remember, however, that x and y are both functions themselves, returning the values of variables in the program. Consequently, the signature of $[P]$ is State $\rightarrow$ States, where States is the set of all possible states, each state being a function on *all* program variables. To simplify the notation, for program P and the vectors X and Y of, respectively, input and output variables of P, we will write $Y = P(X)$, rather than $s_f(Y) = [P](s_0(X))$.

Several observations about $[P]$ are in place. First, in practice one is interested only in some subset of variables either at the start of the program, the exit or both, rather than in all variables. For example, the IntDiv program in Fig. 9.1 can be viewed as a transformation of x and y into q and r; thus neither the initial values of q and r nor the final values of x and y are of interest. It makes sense therefore to identify the (possibly overlapping) sets of the *input* and *output* (or *imported* and *exported*) variables of the program. Second, $[P]$ is, in general, a partial function, defined only for some states s_0. For example, the IntDiv program "works" only for $y > 0$, $x \geq 0$. A subset of the input space on which $[P]$ is defined is the *domain* of $[P]$ and is or, rather, should be specified by the program's precondition. Third, $[P]$ is a function only if the computations are *deterministic* or *quasideterministic*. In the former case, for every s_0 in the domain of $[P]$ there is exactly one unique computation; in the latter case, the computation itself may be nondeterministic (not necessarily unique) but the final state s_f is unique. Otherwise $[P]$ becomes a *relation,* since there can exist more than one final state for the same initial state. Most programs are deterministic. Nondeterminism can be introduced into the program intentionally or unintentionally. Monte Carlo methods, based upon random simulation of the problem at hand, are a typical example of intentional nondeterminism. Referencing an uninitialized variable is an example of an unintentional nondeterminism; in such a case there might be many program traces for the same input or one trace but with different final states for the same inputs. There exists languages that allow nondeterministic choice of statements for execution, e.g., the parallel execution operator $\|$ in VDM-SL.

9.3   Dynamic Analysis Concepts

Let T be a trace. The following data flow concepts are of dynamic nature because they are defined with respect to T, rather than with the program flowgraph. Consequently, they in general change from one trace to another. However, they have to be consistent with static concepts. In other words, static concepts serve as *templates* for the corresponding dynamic concepts. Conversely, dynamic concepts can be viewed as a *refinement* of their static counterparts [3], [4], [5]. To illustrate the discussion we call our loyal friend, the Monotone function in Fig. 1 of the Introduction, to duty again (mercifully, for the last time). In Fig. 9.3 we show the trace produced by STAD for the input array $A = [6, 3]$. The dynamic dependencies will be defined between the elements of the trace. Towards that goal, we have to provide a suitable model of those elements.

As T is an abstract sequence its elements are accessed by position, e.g., for T in Fig. 9.3 there is $T(21)= 7$. However, instructions can appear more than once in a trace; for instance, instruction 12 appears twice in T in Fig. 9.3. To handle multiple occurrences of the same instruction in the trace we take advantage of the fact that every instruction is characterized by its position in the sequence. Let N be the set of nodes in the flowgraph and N_T be the set of pairs (*instruction in T, its position in T*) defined as follows:

$$N_T = \{(Xp) \mid X \text{ in } N, T(p) = X\}.$$

The pair $(X\ p)$ will be written down as X^p and interpreted as "instruction X at the execution position p" and referred to as an *action*. Similarly to the static case, a *use* of variable v is an action X^p in which this variable is referenced and a *definition* of variable v is an action X^p which assigns a value to that variable. However, the very notion of variable is quite different in the dynamic case from that in the static case. Most importantly, in the framework of static program analysis an assignment to an array element is treated as a definition of the entire array. This does not seem a real obstacle in program optimization, the first area of application of data flow analysis. It does cause serious problems, however, in data flow testing and debugging, where it is highly desirable to identify the particular array entries manipulated by the program. For example, in the following sequence of assignments to array elements $A[3]: = x$; $A[5]:= y$, static analysis will identify the second assignment as one *killing* the first one. As a result, the first assignment will be identified as *ineffective* (redundant), although we deal here with an update of the array. It is precisely what the dynamic approach makes possible. In it, every array element is treated as a *separate variable* $X[i]$, for the current value of the index i.

Let $U(X^p)$ be a set of variables whose values are used in action X^p and $D(X^p)$ be a set of variables whose values are defined in X^p. It is essential to observe that, unlike their static counterparts, these sets are dynamic. Clearly, given two occurrences X^p and X^q of the same instruction X at positions p and q, $p \neq q$, these sets might be different in each case. Typically, this is due to the dynamic treatment of arrays. It is worth noting, however, that if a node in the flow graph corresponds to a procedure call the varying parts of the sets U and D might also involve scalar variables for not all parameters of the procedure have to be used or defined by the call. Treatment of

```
ENTER BLOCK   monotone        ********************
   A = ARRAY   VALUE PARAMETER
   n = 2         VALUE PARAMETER
----------------------------------------------------
Pos = 1     Node = MONOTONE:1
   write ... PROCEDURE CALL
   USED:    NO VARIABLES USED.
   DEFINED: PARAMETER INITIALIZATION ... A = ARRAY
----------------------------------------------------
Pos = 2     Node = MONOTONE:2
   write ... PROCEDURE CALL
   USED:    NO VARIABLES USED.
   DEFINED: PARAMETER INITIALIZATION ... n = 2
----------------------------------------------------
Pos = 3     Node = MONOTONE:3
   length[1] := 1 ... ASSIGNMENT
   USED:    NO VARIABLES USED.
   DEFINED: length[1] = 1
----------------------------------------------------
Pos = 4     Node = MONOTONE:4
   pmax := 1 ... ASSIGNMENT
   USED:    NO VARIABLES USED.
   DEFINED: pmax = 1
----------------------------------------------------
Pos = 5     Node = MONOTONE:5
   maxl := 1 ... ASSIGNMENT
   USED:    NO VARIABLES USED.
   DEFINED: maxl = 1
----------------------------------------------------
Pos = 6     Node = MONOTONE:6
   i := 2 ... ASSIGNMENT
   USED:    NO VARIABLES USED.
   DEFINED: i = 2
----------------------------------------------------
Pos = 7     Node = MONOTONE:7
   i <= n ... WHILE LOOP
   USED:    n = 2   i = 2
----------------------------------------------------
Pos = 8     Node = MONOTONE:8
   curr := A[i] ... ASSIGNMENT
   USED:    i = 2   A = ARRAY
   DEFINED: curr = 3
----------------------------------------------------
Pos = 9     Node = MONOTONE:9
   curr < A[pmax] ... IF STATEMENT
   USED:    pmax = 1   A = ARRAY   curr = 3
----------------------------------------------------
Pos = 10    Node = MONOTONE:10
   maxj := 1 ... ASSIGNMENT
   USED:    NO VARIABLES USED.
   DEFINED: maxj = 1
```

Fig. 9.3 The STAD 3.0-generated trace for the Monotone function of Fig. 1 from introduction for the input array A = [6,3]

```
Pos = 11      Node = MONOTONE:11
   j:=1 ... ASSIGNMENT
   USED:      NO VARIABLES USED.
   DEFINED:j = 1
------------------------------------------------------------
Pos = 12      Node = MONOTONE:12
   j<=i-1 ... WHILE LOOP
   USED:      i = 2   j = 1
------------------------------------------------------------
Pos = 13      Node = MONOTONE:13
   A[j]<curr ... IF STATEMENT
   USED:      curr = 3   A = ARRAY    j = 1
------------------------------------------------------------
Pos = 14      Node = MONOTONE:16
   j:=j+1 ... ASSIGNMENT
   USED:      j = 1
   DEFINED:j = 2
------------------------------------------------------------
Pos = 15      Node = MONOTONE:12
   j<=i-1 ... WHILE LOOP
   USED:      i = 2   j = 2
------------------------------------------------------------
Pos = 16      Node = MONOTONE:17
   length[i]:=maxj+1 ... ASSIGNMENT
   USED:      maxj = 1   i = 2
   DEFINED:length[i] = 2
------------------------------------------------------------
Pos = 17      Node = MONOTONE:18
   length[i]>maxl ... IF STATEMENT
   USED:      maxl = 1   length = ARRAY    i = 2
------------------------------------------------------------
Pos = 18      Node = MONOTONE:19
   maxl:=maxl+1 ... ASSIGNMENT
   USED:      maxl = 1
   DEFINED:maxl = 2
------------------------------------------------------------
Pos = 19      Node = MONOTONE:20
   pmax:=i ... ASSIGNMENT
   USED:      i = 2
   DEFINED:pmax = 2
------------------------------------------------------------
Pos = 21      Node = MONOTONE:7
   i<=n ... WHILE LOOP
   USED:      n = 2   i = 3
------------------------------------------------------------
Pos = 22      Node = MONOTONE:25
   monotone:=maxl ... ASSIGNMENT
   USED:      maxl = 2
   DEFINED:monotone = * Function result *
------------------------------------------------------------
EXIT BLOCK monotone.                  .....................
```

Fig. 9.3 (continued)

records (structures) is apparently easier. Although one can consider a change to any field in the record as a change to the entire record a more accurate approach is to treat every field in a record as a separate variable.

Similarly to the static case we define the notions of dynamic, trace-related dependency relations. Dynamic data dependency (DDD) models a situation where one action assigns a value to an item of data and the other action uses that value. For instance, in the execution trace of Fig. 9.3, action 8^8 assigns a value to variable `curr` and action 13^{13} uses that value. Dynamic control dependency (DCD) identifies the *last* decision (test) action responsible for the selection for execution of other actions. For example, action 13^{13} has been selected due to the evaluation of the expression in action 12^{12}. In contrast, no action on the trace is selected due to the expression in 13^{13} itself. Both dependencies are binary relations on the set N_T of actions on T; their formal definitions are given below.

Let T be a trace and X^p and Y^q, $1 \leq p < q \leq$ len(T), be two actions on T. Action Y^q is *Dynamic Data Dependent* on X^p, symbolically Y^q DDD X^p, iff there exists a variable v such that: (1) v is used in Y^q, (2) v is defined in X^p and (3) there is no other definition of v on T between position p and q. In other words, X^p is the *last* definition of the variable v reaching Y^q. Action Y^q is *Dynamic Control Dependent* on X^p, symbolically Y^q DCD X^p, iff there is no other decision action Z^r on T, $p < r < q$, such that Y is statically control dependent on Z. Clearly, X^p is the *last* decision action on T that might have resulted in the deselection of Y for execution. We suggest here without a proof (the Reader should appreciate our self-control in resisting the urge to prove a suitable theorem) that the dynamic dependencies between actions imply static dependencies between the involved instructions albeit not necessarily the other way round. For instance, if Y^q DDD X^p then Y DD X obviously follows but if Y DD X then, given arbitrary two actions Y^q and X^p, Y^q DDD X^p does not necessarily follow since there may exist position t on T, $p < t < q$, such that the variable defined in X^p and used in Y^q is redefined in $T(t)$. A similar argument can be advanced in the case of control dependencies. In the next sections, we illustrate the use of the dynamic dependencies. It should be obvious, however, that one may define more dynamic concepts as refinement of their static counterparts, such as trace-related live variables, reaching definitions, and others of [6].

9.4   An Application: Dynamic Program Slicing

As originally defined in [7], a slice of program P is an *executable* part of P that computes the same function as P does in a subset V of program variables at some point q of interest. Now, if the set V contains those variables in the program that have been found incorrect at q, the slice is then used to help locate the cause of the incorrectness. V might be, however, a set of variables that are correct at q, too; the slice might then support program comprehension. If one is only interested in the statements that are involved in the computations (rather than a syntactically valid code) one gets a "partial program" as in [2]. The original motivation behind the idea was to help in debugging: It might be reasonably expected the that the size of the slice is generally smaller than that of the entire program and thus narrowing the size of the suspected code.

A static slice involves all potential program executions, including those which are infeasible (that is why there are potential). In debugging practice, however, we typically

```
Data Dependencies for block Monotone

Node  1 is data dependent on nodes: {   }
Node  2 is data dependent on nodes: {   }
Node  3 is data dependent on nodes: {   }
Node  4 is data dependent on nodes: {   }
Node  5 is data dependent on nodes: {   }
Node  6 is data dependent on nodes: {   }
Node  7 is data dependent on nodes: { 2, 6, 24 }
Node  8 is data dependent on nodes: { 1, 6, 24 }
Node  9 is data dependent on nodes: { 1, 4, 8, 20, 23 }
Node 10 is data dependent on nodes: {   }
Node 11 is data dependent on nodes: {   }
Node 12 is data dependent on nodes: { 6, 11, 16, 24 }
Node 13 is data dependent on nodes: { 1, 8, 11, 16 }
Node 14 is data dependent on nodes: { 3, 10, 11, 15..17, 22 }
Node 15 is data dependent on nodes: { 3, 11, 16, 17, 22 }
Node 16 is data dependent on nodes: { 11, 16 }
Node 17 is data dependent on nodes: { 10, 15 }
Node 18 is data dependent on nodes: { 5, 6, 17, 19, 21, 24 }
Node 19 is data dependent on nodes: { 5, 19, 21 }
Node 20 is data dependent on nodes: { 6, 24 }
Node 21 is data dependent on nodes: { 5, 19, 21 }
Node 22 is data dependent on nodes: { 21 }
Node 23 is data dependent on nodes: { 6, 24 }
Node 24 is data dependent on nodes: { 6, 24 }
Node 25 is data dependent on nodes: { 5, 19, 21 }
Node 26 is data dependent on nodes: { 25 }
Node 27 is data dependent on nodes: {   }
```

Fig. 9.4 Static data dependencies for function monotone from Fig. 1

deal with a particular incorrect execution and, consequently, are interested in locating the cause of incorrectness (programming fault) of *that* execution. For this reason, we are interested in a slice that preserves the program's behavior for a specific input, rather than that for the set of all inputs for which the program terminates. This type of program slice, will be referred to as a *dynamic slice*. To illustrate dynamic slicing consider again (and, truly for the last time!) the function Monotone in Fig. 1 of the Introduction. By inspecting the static dependencies in Fig. 9.4 and 9.5 one can easily find out that the static slice derived for the exit statement of the function constitutes the entire function. Now, consider the input $A = [6, 3]$ on a call to the function and the corresponding trace in Fig. 9.3. The dynamic data and control dependencies for that trace are shown, respectively, in Fig. 9.6 and 9.7.

Now, to find out which actions on the trace affect action 25^{22} on the exit from the procedure, one could compute the positive transitive closure of the union (DDD $\cup$ DCD)$^+$ and identify actions X^p such that X^p (DDD $\cup$ DCD)$^+$ 25^{22} .

```
Node  7 is directly controlled by nodes: { 7 }
Node  8 is directly controlled by nodes: { 7 }
Node  9 is directly controlled by nodes: { 7 }
Node 10 is directly controlled by nodes: { 9 }
Node 11 is directly controlled by nodes: { 9 }
Node 12 is directly controlled by nodes: { 9, 12 }
Node 13 is directly controlled by nodes: { 12 }
Node 14 is directly controlled by nodes: { 13 }
Node 15 is directly controlled by nodes: { 14 }
Node 16 is directly controlled by nodes: { 12 }
Node 17 is directly controlled by nodes: { 9 }
Node 18 is directly controlled by nodes: { 9 }
Node 19 is directly controlled by nodes: { 18 }
Node 20 is directly controlled by nodes: { 18 }
Node 21 is directly controlled by nodes: { 9 }
Node 22 is directly controlled by nodes: { 9 }
Node 23 is directly controlled by nodes: { 9 }
Node 24 is directly controlled by nodes: { 7 }
```

Fig. 9.5 Static control dependencies for function monotone from Fig. 1 of the Introduction

Fig. 9.6 Dynamic Data Dependencies (DDD) for the trace in Fig. 9.3

$$DDD(\ 7^7)\ =\ \{\ 2^2,\ 6^6\}$$
$$DDD(\ 8^8)\ =\ \{\ 1^1,\ 6^6\}$$
$$DDD(\ 9^9)\ =\ \{\ 1^1,\ 4^4,\ 8^8\}$$
$$DDD(12^{12})\ =\ \{\ 6^6,\ 11^{11}\}$$
$$DDD(13^{13})\ =\ \{\ 1^1,\ 8^8,\ 11^{11}\}$$
$$DDD(16^{14})\ =\ \{11^{11}\}$$
$$DDD(12^{15})\ =\ \{\ 6^6,\ 16^{14}\}$$
$$DDD(17^{16})\ =\ \{10^{10}\}$$
$$DDD(18^{17})\ =\ \{\ 5^5,\ 6^6,\ 17^{16}\}$$
$$DDD(19^{18})\ =\ \{\ 5^5\}$$
$$DDD(20^{19})\ =\ \{\ 6^6\}$$
$$DDD(24^{20})\ =\ \{\ 6^6\}$$
$$DDD(\ 7^{21})\ =\ \{\ 2^2,\ 24^{20}\}$$
$$DDD(25^{22})\ =\ \{19^{18}\}$$

Notation: Y^q in $DDD(X^p)$ means that action Y^q dynamically data depends on action X^p

Problem 9.1 *Identify actions on the trace that affect the value of the variable* $max1$ *at action* 25^{22} *without computing the transitive closure of* $DDD \cup DCD$.

Owing to the positional ordering of actions on the trace one can identify the actions in question by starting at 25^{22} and moving backward on the trace along the data and control dependencies on the trace. For example, 25^{22} is data dependent on

Fig. 9.7 Dynamic control dependencies (DCD) for the trace in Fig. 9.3

$$DCD(8^8) = \{7^7\}$$
$$DCD(9^9) = \{7^7\}$$
$$DCD(10^{10}) = \{9^9\}$$
$$DCD(11^{11}) = \{9^9\}$$
$$DCD(12^{12}) = \{9^9\}$$
$$DCD(13^{13}) = \{12^{12}\}$$
$$DCD(16^{14}) = \{12^{12}\}$$
$$DCD(12^{15}) = \{12^{12}\}$$
$$DCD(17^{16}) = \{9^9\}$$
$$DCD(18^{17}) = \{9^9\}$$
$$DCD(19^{18}) = \{18^{17}\}$$
$$DCD(20^{19}) = \{18^{17}\}$$
$$DCD(24^{20}) = \{7^7\}$$
$$DCD(7^{21}) = \{7^7\}$$

Notation: Y^q in $DCD(X^p)$ means that action Y^q is dynamically control dependent on action X^p

19^{18} which, in turn, is data dependent on 5^5 and control dependent on 18^{17} and so on. Here are the actions that affect the returned value of monotone at action 25^{22}:

$$1^1, 2^2, 4^4, 5^5, 6^6, 7^7, 8^8, 9^9, 10^{10}, 17^{16}, 18^{17}, 19^{18}, 25^{22}$$

and the involved instructions (nodes) in the procedure:

$$1, 2, 4, 5, 6, 7, 8, 9, 10, 17, 18, 19, 25.$$

This set is the dynamic slice for the variable max1 at action 25^{22}. Observe that the corresponding static slice for max1 at node 25 is the entire function.

Problem 9.2 *We argued in Chap. 8 that using simpler input data for testing is recommended for shorter input may provide better localization information. Does the above discussion confirm that hypothesis?*

It certainly does! Clearly, if instead of the array [6, 3] we took a longer array, the dynamic slice would most certainly involve all statements in the program. On the other hand, however, more complex inputs (longer arrays in our case) may be more likely to reveal the fault.

9.5 An Application: Handling Dynamic Data Structures

A major problem in static software analysis is the treatment of pointers (access variables) that serve as indirect addresses of dynamically created and possibly later destroyed anonymous data structures. Pointers create unique problems since a pointer variable actually represents *two* variables: the pointer itself, with its value either undefined, or defined but unknown, with the exception of the nil value, and the object pointed at. There are many potential dangers that face the programmer using pointers. Besides the typical data flow anomalies discussed in Chap. 7, there are pointer-specific anomalies such as *dangling pointers* (pointing to nonexistence objects), and *inaccessible objects*, with no pointer to them available. Data flow anomalies may of course involve also the *objects* pointed to but, unfortunately, those objects cannot be statically identified. Consequently, not only static analysis of programs with anonymous objects is virtually impossible but also the reasoning about programs using them is very hard. It is thus no surprise that pointers are not allowed in many safety-critical missions, cf. [1]. Nevertheless, the dynamic approach advanced in [4] offers some help here.

The main idea underlying dynamic analysis of programs with pointers is to replicate the anonymous addressing scheme maintained by the language run-time heap housekeeping system. The objective is similar to what programmers do when trying to understand code with pointers: They painstakingly record the dynamic objects created and draw the links between the pointers and the objects pointed to by them. Our approach achieves that objective by treating every object created dynamically by the Pascal procedure new(p) as a separate and directly addressable variable. For this purpose, a list of dynamic objects must be created and manipulated during program execution. In this manner, it is possible to determine which dynamic objects are pointed to by pointer variables at every point of program execution. It is also possible to determine which fields in dynamic records are referenced or modified. We illustrate the approach using the programs in Fig. 9.8 and 9.10, modified versions of the examples in [4]. To distinguish between dynamically created objects, a unique name is assigned to

```
     procedure BuildList(
              L: OUT DataPointer);
     TYPE
        DataPointer= ^DataLocation;
        DataLocation = record
           data: integer ;
           link: DataPointer ;
           end ;
     VAR
        l, p: DataPointer ;
        x    : integer;

     begin
{ 1}    new(p) ;          { creates dynamic record OBJ_1 }
{ 2}    l := p ;
{ 3}    l^.data := 3 ;   { OBJ_1.data := 3 }
{ 4}    new(p) ;          { creates dynamic record OBJ_2 }
{ 5}    l^.link := p ;
{ 6}    p^.data := 5;    { OBJ_1.data := 5 }
{ 7}    p^.link := nil ;
{ 8} end;
```

Fig. 9.8 A procedure with pointers and the relevant type definition

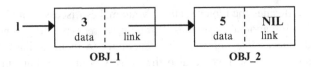

Fig. 9.9 A linked list created by the procedure in Fig. 9.8

```
     Procedure minmax(
             L   : DataPointer;
             min,
             max: OUT integer);
        VAR
          L, p: DataPointer ;

        begin
{ 1}     p := L^.link ;
{ 2}     max := L^.data ;
{ 3}     min := L^.data ;
{ 4}     while p <> nil do
           begin
{ 5}         if max < p^.data then
{ 6}           max := p^.data ;
{ 7}         if min > p^.data then
{ 8}           min := p^.data ;
{ 9}         p^.data := (max + min) ;
{10}         p := p^.link ;
         end ;
{11}  end.
```

Fig. 9.10 A procedure that computes the sum of the minimum and maximum of a linked list pointed to by L. Type DataPointer is defined in Fig. 9.8

each of them. A simple approach has been adopted here: Following the node splitting technique in Chap. 7, the very first execution of the procedure new assigns the name OBJ_1 to the dynamic object created. The next execution of new assigns the name OBJ_2 to the next object; every subsequent execution of new increases the object number by one. In this manner, a unique name for every dynamic object is guaranteed. At every position of the trace objects pointed to by pointers are explicitly recorded. For example, during execution of the procedure in Fig. 9.8 the linked list shown in Fig. 9.9 is created; its abstract, VDM –SL value is simply [3, 5].

During the first execution of the procedure new (line 1) the first dynamic record has been created with the name OBJ_1. During the second execution of new (line 4) the second dynamic record with the name OBJ_2 has been created. Consequently, one gets the following set of all variables in the program of Fig. 9.8:

```
{x,l,p,OBJ_1.data,OBJ_1.link,OBJ_2.data, OBJ_2.link}
```

```
1¹        p := L^.link                /* p := OBJ_1.link */
2²        max := L^.data              /* max := OBJ_1.data */
3³        min := L^.data              /* min := OBJ_1.data */
4⁴        p <> nil
5⁵        max < p.data
7⁶        min > p^.data               /* min > OBJ_2.data */
8⁷        min := p^.data              /* min := OBJ_2.data */
9⁸        p^.data := (min+max)        /* OBJ_2:data := (min+max) */
10⁹       p := p^.link                /* p := OBJ_2.link */
4¹⁰       p <> nil
11¹¹      EXIT
```

Fig. 9.11 A trace of the procedure minmax of Fig. 9.10 processing the list [3,5]

This example illustrates the fact that, in our approach, the set of variables in the program depends on a particular execution. To illustrate the derivation of dynamic slices for program with pointers, consider the procedure minmax of Fig. 9.10 executed on the linked list in Fig. 9.9, pointed to by L. Fig. 9.11 shows the trace of the execution.

Now, using the technique used in Sect. 9.4 the Reader can identify the dependencies on the trace and use them to find the dynamic slice at hand. For example, if one is interested in the slice responsible for the computation of the value of the variable max at position 11^{11} then one gets the set

$$\{2^2, 11^{11}\}$$

of actions involved and, consequently, the set instructions $\{2, 11\}$ as the slice. If, however, one is interested in the part of the program responsible for the computation of the variable min at 11^{11} the following is the set of actions involved

$$\{1^1, 3^3, 4^4, 7^6, 8^7, 10^9, 4^{10}, 11^{11}\}$$

and the corresponding slice is

$$\{1, 3, 4, 7, 8, 10, 11\}.$$

Again, in contrast to the above examples, static slices derived for the corresponding slicing criteria are the entire program itself.

9.6 Conclusions

It is hard to assess the efficacy of program slicing without a body of experimental data. On the one hand, program slicing, particularly in its dynamic variety, usually narrows the *possible* location of the fault to a subset of program actions that appear in the execution; that should make the debugging proper easier. On the other hand, faults in programs might be committed by *omission*, not only by *commission*. Consequently, if there are missing statements in the code, they are *not* included in either slice. There is certainly a possibility that their absence might be easier to detect due to the smaller search space. Now, even as the trace slice offers smaller search space than its static counterpart, the loss of information about the possible error propagation might be actually greater in the dynamic slice, since faulty or potentially affected by errors statements that are not executed do not appear in the slice. Consider, for example, the following statement

if p(X) **then**   V:=f(X) **else** Z:=f(X);

in which the assignment $V:=f(x)$ is either faulty or the variable X used in it is in error. Static slice that preserves the value of V at the exit is simply **if** $p(x)$ **then** $V:=f(x)$; which does contain the faulty statement. Now, suppose that during execution the **else** branch has been taken. Then the dynamic slice for V at the exit of the statement is empty since no action on the trace defines V.

The above discussion shows that the full potential of program slicing has yet to be investigated and its proper applications determined. It is likely that slicing may be a very useful tool for *reasoning* about the program, to infer the properties of the program from the properties of an execution, rather than for supporting debugging proper. Also, the original pragmatic objectives of program slicing warrant further scrutiny. Clearly, it is not clear whether, as postulated in [7], the static slice should be a stand-alone, syntactically correct executable program itself; perhaps debugging would be better served if carried out within the context of the entire original code. Similarly, the requirement in [4] that the dynamic slice preserve the same number of iterations of loops looks somewhat arbitrary.

We believe that dynamic analysis should be used as a complementary part of static analysis, servings as its refining tool. Obviously, this is an area for further exploration. Although it is hard to predict further developments in this area, we believe that problems like formulating fault hypotheses and error propagation hypotheses should be the main area of research in the foreseeable future. We did discuss some of the possibilities while discussing structural testing in Chap. 8. The ultimate objective here is to develop an integrated approach to testing and debugging using static analysis as a template and dynamic analysis as its execution-based refinement.

Exercise 9.1   *Let T be a trace. Write and abstract algorithm, preferably in VDM_SL notation which, given a position q on T, returns a set of variables that are undefined at q.*

Exercise 9.2   *Write an algorithm that given trace T derives the DDD relation for T.*

Exercise 9.3   *Write an algorithm that given trace T derives the DCD relation for T.*

Exercise 9.4   *Assume that some variable v at position p on T is incorrect.Identify all positions and variables that can be affected by the error.*

Exercise 9.5   *While modeling the dynamic data structures propose a numbering method that accounts for the deleted objects.*

References

1 J. Barnes, High Integrity Software, The SPARK Approach to Safety and Security, Addison-Wesley, Reading, MA, 2003.

2 J.F. Bergeretti, B.A. Carre, Information flow and data flow analysis of while-programs, ACM Transactions on Programming Languages and Systems, 7(1), 37–61, 1985.

3 B. Korel, J. Laski, Dynamic program slicing, Information Processing Letters, 29(3),155–163,1988.

4 B. Korel, J. Laski, Dynamic slicing of computer programs, Journal for Systems and Software, 13(3),187–195,1990.

5 B. Korel, J. Laski, Algorithmic software fault localization, Proceedings of 24th Annual Hawaii International Conference on System Science, Jan 1991, Vol II, pp. 246–252.

6 J. Laski, Programming faults and errors: Towards a theory of program incorrectness, Annals of Software Engineering, 4, 79–114, 1997.

7 M. Weiser, Program slicing, IEEE Transactions on Engineering, SE-10, 352–357, 1984.

Index